The Political Economy of Terrorism

The Political Economy of Terrorism presents a widely accessible approach to the study of terrorism that combines economic methods with political analysis and realities. It applies economic methodology – theoretical and empirical – along with political analysis to the study of domestic and transnational terrorism. In so doing, the book provides both a qualitative and a quantitative investigation of terrorism in a balanced, up-to-date presentation that informs students, policymakers, researchers, and the general reader of the current state of knowledge of the subject. Included in the treatment are historical aspects of the phenomenon, a discussion of watershed events, the rise of modern-day terrorism, examination of current trends, the dilemma of liberal democracies, evaluation of counterterrorism, and analysis of hostage incidents. Rational-actor models of terrorist and government behavior and game-theoretic analysis are presented for readers with no prior theoretical training. Where relevant, the authors display graphs using the data set *International Terrorism: Attributes of Terrorist Events* (ITERATE) and other data sets.

Walter Enders holds the Bidgood Chair of Economics and Finance at the University of Alabama. He has published numerous research articles in eminent journals such as the *Review of Economics and Statistics*, *Quarterly Journal of Economics*, *American Economic Review*, *Journal of Economic Literature*, *Journal of Business and Economic Statistics*, and the *American Political Science Review*. Professor Enders's *Applied Econometric Time-Series* is a leading book in the field. He is a current holder (along with Todd Sandler) of the National Academy of Sciences' Estes Award for Behavioral Research Relevant to the Prevention of Nuclear War for their pathbreaking work on understanding terrorism.

Todd Sandler holds the Robert R. and Katheryn A. Dockson Professorship of International Relations, Economics, and Law at the University of Southern California. He has written or edited nineteen books, including *Global Collective Action*, *Economic Concepts for the Social Sciences*, *The Political Economy of NATO* (with Keith Hartley), and *Global Challenges: An Approach to Economic, Political, and Environmental Problems*, all published by Cambridge University Press, as well as more than two hundred journal articles in economics and political science. Professor Sandler's work on terrorism dates back to 1983. In 2003, he was the corecipient (with Walter Enders) of the National Academy of Sciences' Estes Award for Behavioral Research Relevant to the Prevention of Nuclear War.

The Political Economy of Terrorism

WALTER ENDERS

University of Alabama

TODD SANDLER

University of Southern California

CAMBRIDGE
UNIVERSITY PRESS

CAMBRIDGE UNIVERSITY PRESS
Cambridge, New York, Melbourne, Madrid, Cape Town, Singapore, São Paulo

Cambridge University Press
40 West 20th Street, New York, NY 10011-4211, USA

www.cambridge.org
Information on this title: www.cambridge.org/9780521851008

First published 2006

Printed in the United States of America

A catalog record for this publication is available from the British Library.

Library of Congress Cataloging in Publication Data
Enders, Walter, 1948–
The political economy of terrorism / Walter Enders, Todd Sandler.
p.   cm.
Includes bibliographical references and index.
ISBN 0-521-85100-9 – ISBN 0-521-61650-6
1. Terrorism.   2. Terrorism – Economic aspects.   I. Sandler, Todd.   II. Title.
HV6431.E54   2006
303.6'25 – dc22   2005016251

ISBN-13   978-0-521-85100-8 hardback
ISBN-10   0-521-85100-9 hardback

ISBN-13   978-0-521-61650-8 paperback
ISBN-10   0-521-61650-6 paperback

To Linda Enders and to the memory of
Henry Sandler (1939–2005)

Contents

Tables and Figures

FIGURES

Preface

Prior to the four hijackings of 11 September 2001 (hereafter 9/11), the study of terrorism was an active field of research, with many new books appearing each year. Since 9/11, the study of terrorism is an even more active field of research, with even more books appearing each year. Hence, one must wonder why another book merits one's attention.

This book presents a widely accessible political economy approach that combines economic methods with political analysis and realities. In so doing, the book provides both a qualitative and a quantitative investigation of terrorism in a balanced, up-to-date presentation that informs students, practitioners, policymakers, researchers, and the general reader of the current state of knowledge. Most books on terrorism focus on historical, cultural, factual, and conceptual details and shy away from rational-choice-based analyses backed by statistical inference. Our book presents not only the historical and conceptual issues, but also the scientific-based analyses of the behavior of terrorists and government policymakers. Moreover, we are concerned with knowing how these adversaries make rational decisions in a strategic interactive framework. That is, how do the choices of the terrorists influence governments' counterterrorism policies, and how do these policies affect the choices of the terrorists? The strategic interactions among targeted governments are also investigated. To establish the relevancy of the theories presented, we display data and review statistical findings from a variety of studies.

Although we are particularly interested in rational-choice models and their empirical verification, we are no less interested in the history of terrorism, the causes of terrorism, and the dilemma faced by liberal democracies. Unlike other books, this book identifies rational explanations for observed behavior – for example, why terrorist groups cooperate and form networks with one another, while targeted governments are slow to cooperate. We address many questions, including the following: When confronted with a common terrorist threat, why do targeted governments rely on defensive measures that merely deflect attacks to soft targets, and often eschew proactive responses that would reduce the threat for all governments? Why do countries fail, at times, to adhere to a stated policy of not conceding to hostage takers' demands when it is in their long-run interests never to concede? Which counterterrorism policies work best?

By applying simple economic models and statistical analyses, our book provides a unique perspective on the study of terrorism. This perspective is increasingly being used at the Centers of Excellence, funded by the Department of Homeland Security. To better understand terrorism and to counter its threat, society must apply varied techniques and knowledge from many disciplines – for example, history, sociology, law, psychology, statistics, and economics. Our book draws insights from all of these disciplines. If one looks through a typical book on terrorism, especially those used in college courses, one will find few, if any, statistical displays of the incidence of terrorist events over time. More important, these books do not present any analysis or explanation of these patterns of events. Most books rely, instead, on some "watershed" events or case studies to draw some general principles. By contrast, we present data on terrorist events over time to bolster our investigation of numerous watershed incidents. Thus, our book is rich in detail about past terrorist events and the changing pattern of terrorism.

Our book is intended for use in college-level economics, political science, and public policy classes on terrorism. The book will also be appropriate for classes at military colleges. Our approach will particularly appeal to teachers who want to emphasize a rational-choice basis for understanding terrorism and policies to ameliorate its threat. The book assumes no pre-knowledge of the techniques used. Thus, the game-theoretic methods are explained in detail for readers who have never seen a game matrix or game tree. The book is also useful for researchers who are new to the field and who may be driven to study terrorism because of their interest in the topic or the availability of funding from numerous sources since 9/11. Our book allows a researcher to gain the requisite background in the field, because we have incorporated a rich and diverse set of references and techniques. The interested reader can consult our references for further details about a particular approach or analysis. In addition, the book should interest people in the Department of Homeland Security, the intelligence community, the defense sector, law enforcement, and the insurance industry, all of whom have to address myriad issues concerning modern-day terrorism. Our book provides a different way of thinking about terrorism.

We have profited from perceptive comments on various drafts from two anonymous reviewers. We have received helpful support and counsel from Scott Parris, the economics editor at Cambridge University Press (CUP). We also appreciate the efforts of the production staff at CUP, who transformed the typescript into a book. Sara Fisher typed and retyped the many drafts of the book; we appreciate her care and cheerfulness. We acknowledge our debt to our coauthors of articles, where some of the concepts applied here were originally developed. Prominent on this list are Dan Arce, Jon Cauley, Harvey Lapan, Kevin Siqueira, and John Tschirhart. Others include Scott Atkinson, Dwight Lee, B. Peter Rosendorff, and John Scott. This project succeeded because of the support of our wives – Linda Enders and Jeannie Murdock – and our children. Todd Sandler acknowledges research funding from the Center for International Studies, University of Southern California.

Tuscaloosa and Los Angeles Walter Enders
April 2005 *Bidgood Chair of Economics and Finance*
  University of Alabama

  Todd Sandler
  Robert R. and Katheryn A. Dockson
  Professor of International Relations,
  Economics, and Law
  University of Southern California

ONE

Terrorism

An Introduction

The events on 11 September 2001 (henceforth 9/11) served as a wake-up call to the world that transnational terrorism poses grave risks. The four simultaneous hijackings on 9/11 represent watershed terrorist incidents for a number of reasons. First, the deaths associated with 9/11 were unprecedented: the human toll was equal to the number of deaths from transnational terrorism from the start of 1988 through the end of 2000 (Sandler, 2003). Second, the losses associated with 9/11 topped $80 billion and caused insurance companies to end automatic coverage of terrorist-induced losses.[1] Since 9/11, many companies have been unable to afford terrorism insurance. Third, 9/11 showed that ordinary objects can be turned into deadly weapons with catastrophic consequences. Despite the huge carnage of 9/11, the death toll could have been much higher had the planes struck the towers at a lower floor. Fourth, 9/11 underscored the objectives of today's fundamentalist terrorists to seek maximum casualties and to induce widespread fear, unlike the predominantly left-wing terrorist campaigns of the 1970s and 1980s that sought to win over a constituency.[2] Fifth, 9/11 mobilized a huge reallocation of resources to

---

[1] On the implications of 9/11 for the insurance industry, see Kunreuther and Michel-Kerjan (2004a) and Kunreuther, Michel-Kerjan, and Porter (2003). Approximately half of the losses from 9/11 were covered by the insurance companies, including $11 billion in lost business, $2 billion of workers' compensation, $3.5 billion in property losses at the World Trade Center, and $3.5 billion of aviation liability. To address insurers' unwillingness to provide terrorism insurance following 9/11, the US Congress passed the Terrorism Risk Insurance Act (TRIA) of 2002 to cover up to $100 billion of terrorism insurance until the end of 2005.

[2] On the changing nature of terrorists, see Enders and Sandler (2000, 2005a, 2005b), Hoffman (1998), White (2003), and Wilkinson (2001).

1

homeland security – since 2002, the US Department of Homeland Security (DHS) budget has grown by over 60% to $36.2 billion for the fiscal year 2004 (DHS, 2003). In fiscal year 2005, the DHS budget grew another 10% to $40.2 billion (DHS, 2004). A little over 60% of DHS's budget goes to defending against terrorism on US soil. This expenditure is small compared to proactive measures taken in fighting the "war on terror," including the invasion against the Taliban and al-Qaida in Afghanistan on 7 October 2001. Still other proactive spending involves improving intelligence, tracking terrorist assets, and fostering cooperative linkages with other countries. Sixth, protective actions taken by rich developed countries have transferred some attacks against these countries' interests to poorer countries – for example, post-9/11 attacks in Egypt, Indonesia, Morocco, Kenya, Saudi Arabia, and Turkey.

The events of 9/11 heightened anxiety worldwide and resulted in trade-offs in terms of trading reduced freedom for greater security; society had not been willing to surrender as much freedom prior to 9/11. Society lost innocence on that fateful day that it will never regain. The threat of catastrophic terrorist events – though their probability is low – is etched indelibly in everyone's mind. The Madrid train bombings on 11 March 2004 have made Europe more aware that large-scale terrorist events can occur on European soil. The anxiety that terrorists seek to create is amplified by people's proclivity to overreact to low-probability but ghastly events.

The study of terrorism has been an active field of research in international relations since the early 1970s and the start of the modern era of transnational terrorism (that is, terrorism with international implications or genesis). Of course, the interest in the study of terrorism grew greatly after 9/11, with many new courses being taught at the undergraduate level worldwide. Subscriptions to the two field journals – *Terrorism and Political Violence* and *Studies in Conflict & Terrorism* (formerly *Terrorism*) – that publish scholarly articles increased following 9/11. General journals in the social sciences are now more willing to publish articles on terrorism. Grant opportunities to study terrorism have also increased greatly through DHS, government agencies, and private foundations. These opportunities can now be found not only in the United States but worldwide. Scholarly conferences on terrorism have also grown in number in the last few years.

The purpose of this book is to present a widely accessible political economy approach that combines economic methods and political analysis. Where possible, we apply theoretical and statistical tools so that the reader can understand why governments and terrorists take certain actions even when, on occasion, these actions may be against their interests. Often, we are able to explain behavior that appears counterintuitive once the underlying *strategic* interactions among agents (for example, among targeted governments) are taken into account. Throughout the book, we provide insights that run counter to conventional wisdom but that are supported by the data. Our reliance on statistical analysis means that we do *not* eyeball the data in order to draw conclusions that may not hold up to statistical scrutiny. Our approach relies on statistical inference, which is less apt to change tomorrow as new terrorist groups with new objectives and modes of action come on the scene. Our intention is to offer a fresh approach that can inform not only students but also researchers, practitioners (for example, insurers), policymakers, and others interested in an up-to-date treatment of the political economy of terrorism.

DEFINITIONS OF TERRORISM

Terrorism is the premeditated use or threat to use violence by individuals or subnational groups in order to obtain a political or social objective through the intimidation of a large audience beyond that of the immediate victims. Two essential ingredients characterize any modern definition of terrorism: the presence or threat of violence and a political/social motive. Without violence or its threat, terrorists cannot make a political decision maker respond to their demands. Moreover, in the absence of a political/social motive, a violent act is a crime rather than an act of terrorism. Terrorists broaden their audience beyond their immediate victims by making their actions appear to be random, so that everyone feels anxiety. In contrast to a drive-by shooting on a city street, terrorist acts are not random but well-planned and often well-executed attacks where the terrorists account for risks and associated costs as well as possible gains.

In addition to violence and a political motive, a minimalist definition hinges on three additional factors: the victim, the perpetrator, and the audience. Of these three, the most controversial is the identity of the *victim*. Is an attack against a passive military target or a peacekeeper a terrorist act? The Israelis include an assault against a passive military target as a terrorist attack, whereas other countries may not if the military person is part of an occupying force. Virtually all definitions consider terrorist attacks against civilians as terrorism. The data set *International Terrorism: Attributes of Terrorist Events* (ITERATE) includes terrorist actions against peacekeepers, but not against an occupying army, as acts of terrorism.[3] While not as contentious as the victim, the *perpetrator* also presents some controversy. If a state or government uses terror tactics

---

[3] On ITERATE, see Mickolus (1980, 1982) and Mickolus, Sandler, and Murdock (1989).

against its own citizens (for example, Stalin's reign of terror), is this terrorism? We apply the convention to call such actions *state terror* but not terrorism. In our definition, the perpetrators are individuals or subnational groups but not the state itself. States can, however, support these subnational terrorist groups through safe havens, funding, weapons, intelligence, training, or other means. When a state assists a terrorist group, the resulting terrorist act is known as *state-sponsored terrorism*. Libya is accused of state sponsoring the downing of Pan Am flight 103 over Lockerbie, Scotland, on 21 December 1988, and agreed in 2003 to compensate the victims' families. The US Department of State brands a number of nations – Cuba, Iran, Libya, North Korea, Sudan, and Syria – as state sponsors of terrorism.[4] Finally, the *audience* refers to the group that the terrorist act is intended to intimidate. For example, a terrorist bomb aboard a commuter train is meant to cause anxiety in the public at large, because such bombs can be placed in any train or public place. The audience thus extends beyond the immediate victims of the attack. On 9/11, al-Qaida's audience was everyone on the planet, not just the unfortunate victims associated with the four hijackings and their aftermath.

Why do terrorists seek such a wide audience? Terrorists want to circumvent the normal political channels/procedures and create political change through threats and violence. By intimidating a target population, terrorists intend that this population will apply pressure on political decision makers to concede to their demands. From a rational calculus viewpoint, political decision makers must weigh the expected costs of conceding, including possible countergrievances from other groups,[5] against the anticipated costs of future attacks. If the latter costs exceed those of conceding, then a besieged government should rationally give in to the demands of the terrorists. Suicide attacks have gained prominence since 1983, because they raise the target audience's anxiety and, in so doing, greatly increase the government's anticipated costs from future attacks. This follows because a suicide attack kills on average thirteen people, while a typical terrorist incident kills less than one person (Pape, 2003). Thus, governments have more readily given in to *modest* demands following suicide campaigns – for example, Hezbollah's car bombing of the US Marine barracks in Lebanon on 23 October 1983 resulted in the US withdrawal from Lebanon, whereas the October 1994–August 1995

---

[4] In the April 2003 issue of *Patterns of Global Terrorism 2002*, the US Department of State (2003) also included Iraq on this list.

[5] Such other groups may view government concessions as an invitation to engage in their own terror campaigns.

Hamas suicide campaign against Israel led to the partial Israeli withdrawal from the West Bank (Pape, 2003, Table 1). Concessions also encourage more terrorism as the government loses its reputation for toughness – these reputational costs must also be weighed against the gains of giving in (e.g., released hostages or an end to attacks). Terrorist tactics are more effective in liberal democracies, where governments are expected to protect lives and property. Understandably, suicide campaigns have been almost exclusively associated with liberal democracies.

Some Alternative Definitions

To show how definitions may vary, we investigate a few official ones, starting with that of the US Department of State, for which "terrorism means premeditated, politically motivated violence perpetrated against noncombatant targets by subnational groups or clandestine agents, usually intended to influence an audience" (US Department of State, 2003, p. xiii). An interesting feature of this definition is the characterization of the victims as "noncombatants," meaning civilians and unarmed or off-duty military personnel. Accordingly, a bomb planted under a US soldier's private vehicle in Germany is an act of terrorism. This nicely illustrates how the designation of a victim can be quite controversial. The State Department's definition is silent about whether a threat is a terrorist act.

The US Department of Defense (DoD) defines terrorism as "the unlawful use or threatened use of force or violence against individuals or property to coerce or intimidate governments or societies, often to achieve political, religious, or ideological objectives" (White, 2003, p. 12). Three contrasts between the DoD's and the State Department's definition are worth highlighting. First, the *threat* of violence is now included. Second, the noncombatant distinction is dropped, so that the roadside bombing of a US convoy in Iraq would be terrorism. Third, religious and ideological motives are explicitly identified. Even two departments of the same government cannot fully agree on the definition. Nevertheless, these definitions identify the same five minimalist ingredients – violence, political motivation, perpetrator, victim, and audience. The definitional problem lies in precisely identifying these ingredients. Slightly different definitions of terrorism also characterize those of the Federal Bureau of Investigation (FBI), the Defense Intelligence Agency, and the Vice President's Task Force on Terrorism of 1986 (White, 2003, p. 12).

The political nature of defining terrorism comes into focus when the official UN definition is examined: "terrorism is the act of destroying or injuring civilian lives or the act of destroying or damaging civilian or government property *without the expressly chartered permission of a specific government*, this by individuals or groups acting independently... in the attempt to effect some political goal" (emphasis added) (White, 2003, p. 12). A difficulty with this definition is that it may not brand a state-sponsored skyjacking or bombing as an act of terrorism if it is sanctioned by a specific government – for example, Iran's action to maintain the takeover of the US embassy in Tehran on 4 November 1979 for 444 days. Loopholes such as this arise when so many nations have to agree on a definition and governments do not want to tie their own hands in the future. Since 9/11, the United Nations has ignored its official definition and taken a more pragmatic approach, branding violent acts perpetrated by subnational groups for political purposes as terrorism (United Nations, 2002b, p. 6). This new pragmatic definition agrees closely with our definition.

Another definitional issue concerns distinguishing terrorism from warfare. In its classic sense, war targets combatants with weapons that are highly discriminating in order to limit collateral damage on civilians. Unlike war, terrorism targets noncombatants in a relatively indiscriminate manner, as 9/11 or the downing of Pan Am flight 103 illustrates. Unfortunately, the firebombings of Dresden and Tokyo during World War II blur the wartime distinction about noncombatants and discriminating attack. For our purposes, we distinguish warfare and terrorism in this standard way despite some issues of this kind. The Dresden and Tokyo bombings were not terrorist attacks, because they were perpetrated by governments, not subnational groups, during a declared war.

Definitions are essential when putting together data to examine propositions, trends, and other aspects of terrorism. A well-defined notion is needed so that events can be classified as terrorism for empirical purposes. To this end, we rely on our definition, which takes a middle ground with respect to other definitions and comes close to the US Department of State's definition and the pragmatic UN definition following 9/11.

Transnational Terrorism

Another essential distinction is between domestic and transnational terrorism. *Domestic terrorism* is homegrown and has consequences for just the host country, its institutions, citizens, property, and policies. In a domestic incident, the perpetrators, victims, and audience are all from the host country. In addressing domestic terrorism, a country can be self-reliant if it possesses sufficient resources. Antiterrorist policies need not involve other countries insofar as neither the terrorist acts nor the government's responses need impose costs or confer benefits on foreign interests. Domestic terrorist campaigns result in a country taking antiterrorist measures to limit the threat.

Most terrorist events directed against the United States do not occur on its soil. The kidnapping in January 2002 and subsequent murder of reporter Daniel Pearl in Pakistan; the destruction of the Al Khubar Towers housing US airmen in June 1996 near Dhahran, Saudi Arabia; and the bombing of the US embassies in Kenya and Tanzania in August 1998 are but three gruesome examples of *transnational terrorism*. Terrorism is transnational when an incident in one country involves perpetrators, victims, institutions, governments, or citizens of another country. If an incident begins in one country but terminates in another, then it is a transnational terrorist event, as is the case for a hijacking of a plane in country *A* that is made to fly to country *B*. An attack against a multilateral organization is a transnational incident owing to its multicountry impact, as in the case of the suicide car bombing of the UN headquarters in Baghdad on 19 August 2003. The toppling of the World Trade Center towers was a transnational incident because victims were from ninety different countries, the mission had been planned abroad, the terrorists were foreigners, and the implications of the event (for example, financial repercussions) were global.

With transnational terrorism, countries' policies are interdependent. Efforts by the European countries to secure their borders and ports of entry may merely shift attacks aimed at their people and property abroad, where borders are more porous (Enders and Sandler, 1993, 1995; also see Chapter 5). US actions that deny al-Qaida safe havens or that destroy its training camps limit the network's effectiveness against all potential targets, thereby conferring a benefit on other countries. Intelligence on a common transnational terrorist threat that is gathered by one nation can benefit other potential target countries. As such, transnational terrorism raises the need for countries to coordinate antiterrorist policies, a need that countries had resisted until 9/11. Even now, this coordination can be much improved (see Chapters 6 and 7).

OTHER ASPECTS OF TERRORISM

The motives of terrorists may vary among groups. Traditionally, many terrorists are motivated by ethno-nationalistic goals to establish a homeland for an oppressed ethnic group. The Tamils in Sri Lanka fall into this

Table 1.1. *Some Terrorist Tactics*

Terrorist Operations
• Hostage missions (e.g., skyjacking, kidnapping, and barricade and hostage taking)
• Bombings
• Assassinations
• Threats and hoaxes
• Suicide attacks
• Armed attacks
• Sabotage
• Nuclear-related weapon attacks
• Chemical or biological attacks
Other Actions
• Bank robberies
• Propaganda
• Legitimate efforts to gain political recognition

category, as did the Sudanese People Liberation Army's (SPLA's) struggle against the Muslim majority in the north of Sudan.[6] The Palestinians are also applying terrorism as a way to gain a state. Terrorism may also be motivated by nihilism, left-wing ideology, religious suppression, intolerance, social injustice, or issue-specific goals. In recent years, some groups have resorted to terrorism to establish a fundamentalist-based regime (Hoffman, 1998). For example, Harakat ul-Jihad-I-Islami/Bangladesh wants to establish Islamic rule in Bangladesh; Al-Jihad (also known as the Egyptian Islamic Jihad) wishes to set up an Islamic state in Egypt; and Jemaah Islamiyah intends to create a pan-Islamic state out of Indonesia, Malaysia, Singapore, the southern Philippines, and southern Thailand (US Department of State, 2003). Many other rationales – for example, publicizing an alleged genocide, a millennium movement, and animal protection – have motivated terrorists' violence against innocent victims.

Terrorists employ varied modes of attack to create an atmosphere of fear and vulnerability. Some common tactics are displayed in Table 1.1. Hostage missions are logistically complex and risky, and include kidnappings, barricade and hostage taking (that is, the takeover of a building and the securing of hostages), skyjackings, and the takeover of nonaerial

---

[6] The SPLA and the Sudanese government signed an accord in January 2005 that ended hostilities. This long-term struggle between the SPLA and the Muslim majority must not be confused with the state terror of the Sudanese government directed against the inhabitants of Darfur in 2004 and 2005.

means of transportation. Ransoms from kidnappings have been used by some terrorist groups as a revenue source to support operations. This is especially true of some Latin American terrorists who have kidnapped business executives for ransom. Bombings can take many forms, including explosive, letter, and incendiary bombs. Bombings are by far the favorite tactic of terrorists, accounting for about half of all terrorist incidents (Sandler and Enders, 2004). Assassinations are politically motivated murders. Threats are promises of future action, while hoaxes are false claims of past actions (for example, falsely claiming that a bomb is aboard a plane). Suicide attacks can involve a car, a lone terrorist carrying explosives, or some other delivery device (for example, a donkey cart). Other terrorist modes of attack involve armed attacks (including sniping and shootouts with authorities) or sabotage.

Since the 20 March 1995 sarin attack on the Tokyo subway by Aum Shinrikyo, the growing worry has been that terrorists will resort to weapons of mass destruction (WMD) in the form of a nuclear weapon, a radiological ("dirty") bomb, a chemical weapon, or a biological weapon (see Chapter 11). The dirty bomb consists of a conventional bomb that disperses radioactive material, which contaminates an area for years to come and causes delayed deaths. Other terrorist actions involve bank robberies or criminal acts to finance operations. In some cases, terrorists also spread propaganda and use legitimate political actions to induce change. For example, Hamas, Hezbollah, the Irish Republican Army, and Euskadi ta Askatasuna (ETA) have political wings that promote the group's viewpoint.

Terrorists must allocate resources between terrorist attacks and legitimate means for achieving political goals. Ironically, actions by the authorities to limit protest may close off legitimate avenues of dissent and push terrorists into engaging in more attacks. Even among attack modes, terrorists must weigh expected costs and expected benefits from different actions in order to pick the best combination for their campaigns.

POLITICAL APPROACH TO THE STUDY OF TERRORISM

The primary contributors to the study of terrorism during the last thirty-five years have been the political scientists, who have enlightened us on terrorist campaigns, groups, tactics, motives, finances, state support, and trends. Much of their analysis has been comparative – for example, when researchers distinguish among terrorist groups or countries harboring terrorists. The comparative approach has taught us much about what is common and what is different among terrorist groups. For instance, political scientists have characterized many of the European terrorist organizations coming out of the antiwar protests of the late 1960s as "fighting communist organizations" with a Marxist-Leninist ideology, an anticapitalist orientation, a desire to limit casualties, and a need for an external constituency (Alexander and Pluchinsky, 1992). Over the last few decades, political scientists have identified the changing nature of terrorism – for example, the rise of state sponsorship in the early 1980s and the more recent increase in fundamentalist-based terrorism. Political scientists have also analyzed the effectiveness of antiterrorist policies, but typically without applying statistical inference – Brophy-Baermann and Conybeare (1994) is an important early exception. Since 9/11, political scientists have been more interested in empirical analyses of terrorism. Until recently, political scientists rarely relied on rational-actor models of terrorist behavior – for example, Bueno de Mesquita (2005) applied such models.

An advantage of the political science approach has been its eclectic, multidisciplinary viewpoint encompassing historical, sociological, and psychological studies. Historical studies identify common features among terrorist campaigns and indicate how the nature of terrorist tactics and campaigns has evolved over time. Sociological analyses examine norms and social structure within terrorist organizations. In recent psychological studies, researchers have identified internal and external variables associated with the escalation of violence in terrorist events.[7] Factors that induce an individual to become a suicide bomber include both sociological – the approval of a group – and psychological considerations. Other psychological studies indicate the personality traits of different types of terrorists, including those who use the internet to coordinate attacks.

ECONOMIC APPROACH TO THE STUDY OF TERRORISM

Economic methodology has much to offer to the study of terrorism because it adds theoretical models and empirical analyses that have not been prominent. The application of economic methods to the study of terrorism started with Landes (1978), who applied the economics of crime and punishment to the study of hijackings in the United States. His study

---

[7] Major contributors to psychological studies in terrorism include Jerrold M. Post and Eric D. Shaw – see Post, Ruby, and Shaw (2000, 2002). See also the excellent recent survey by Victoroff (2005) on the mind of the terrorist.

derived an "offense function," which relates the number of hijackings to policy variables – for example, probability of apprehension, presence of sky marshals, probability of conviction, and average length of sentence – that can be controlled by the authorities. Landes then estimated this offense function using data from past US hijackings to ascertain the marginal impact that each variable had on the number of hijackings. For example, Landes quantified the immediate and large influence that the installation of metal detectors at US airports in January 1973 had on the number of hijackings. In a scientific tradition, Landes first built a theoretical behavioral model of terrorists that he later tested using the data. Over the next twenty-five years, other economists and political scientists have followed his methodology.[8] After 9/11, many economists have turned their attention to examining terrorism insurance, antiterrorism policy evaluation (see Chapter 4), terrorist-imposed risks, and economic impacts of terrorism (see Chapter 9).[9]

Economists have applied rational-actor models in which terrorists are portrayed as calculating individuals who optimize some goal subject to constraints. If the parameters of these constraints change, then a rational actor is expected to respond in a predictable fashion. Thus, actions taken by a government to harden a target should induce the terrorists to shift their attacks to relatively less-guarded venues (so-called softer targets). While this insight is now commonplace, we received a good deal of initial resistance to this notion when we first introduced it in a series of articles over twenty years ago.[10] People resisted characterizing terrorists as rational, because their goals and methods are not only repugnant but also differ from those of most people. In economics, rationality is not judged by objectives or norms of acceptable behavior but by the manner in which an agent responds to environmental and other constraints. *By responding in a sensible and predictable fashion to changing risks, terrorists are judged to be rational.* Although weak compared to the governments that they confront, terrorists have waged some long-lived campaigns with few resources against formidable odds. They have also achieved numerous successful operations in the process. Terrorist groups order the operations in their campaigns according to risks: the least risky operations are

---

[8] See, for example, Brophy-Baermann and Conybeare (1994), Enders, Sandler, and Cauley (1990a, 1990b), and Li (2005).

[9] Recent examples include Drakos and Kutan (2003), Heal and Kunreuther (2003), Kunreuther and Heal (2003), and Viscusi and Zeckhauser (2003).

[10] Articles in this series include Enders and Sandler (1993), Im, Cauley, and Sandler (1987), Sandler, Tschirhart, and Cauley (1983), and Sandler and Lapan (1988).

used the most often and the most risky operations the least. Terrorist logistical success rates are very high. These stylized facts bode well for the rational-actor characterization of terrorists; this characterization is also applied to governments that oppose the terrorists.

In keeping with a rational-actor depiction, economists and later political scientists have applied game theory to the study of terrorism.[11] Game theory is an appropriate methodology for examining terrorism for a number of reasons. First, game theory captures the strategic interactions between terrorists and targeted governments, where actions are interdependent and, thus, cannot be analyzed as though one side were passive. Second, strategic interactions among rational beings, who are trying to act according to how they think their counterparts will act and react, characterize the interface among terrorists (for example, between hardliners and moderates) or among alternative targets (for example, governments that are taking defensive measures). Third, game theory permits adversaries to issue threats and promises for strategic advantage – for example, a no-negotiation declaration intended to keep terrorists from taking hostages, or a terrorist group's pledge to engage in suicide bombings in order to gain concessions. Fourth, game-theoretic notions of bargaining are applicable to hostage negotiations and terrorist campaign–induced negotiations over demands (see Chapter 7).[12] Fifth, uncertainty and learning in a strategic environment are relevant to all aspects of terrorism in which the terrorists or the government or both are *not* completely informed. Game theory concerns the knowledge possessed by the players and allows earlier actions to inform players over time.

The economic approach also provides for the testing of theories with advanced statistical methods. For example, consider the potential impact of terrorism on tourism. When deciding on an appropriate vacation spot, tourists consider not only the exchange rate, costs, scenery, temperature, and other amenities, but also the risk of terrorism. After Greece experienced a spate of terrorist attacks in the mid-1980s, the Greek tourist industry suffered significant economic losses as tourists vacationed elsewhere. Enders, Sandler, and Parise (1992) formulated a consumer choice model to indicate the form of the tourist trade-off and then tested this trade-off with data from Greece and other countries. Their method put a

---

[11] Early game-theoretic papers include Lapan and Sandler (1988, 1993), Overgaard (1994), and Selten (1988).

[12] Bargaining papers include Atkinson, Sandler, and Tschirhart (1987), Lapan and Sandler (1988), and Sandler, Tschirhart, and Cauley (1983).

price tag on Greek losses. A recent study applied their method to Greece, Israel, and Turkey for 1991–2000 (Drakos and Kutan, 2003).[13] The subsequent testing of theories provides many policy insights in the study of terrorism. For example, once the price tag for tourist losses is identified, a country can make a more informed decision on the potential gains from securing airports and other tourist venues. Knowing the losses allows a government to better allocate resources to curbing terrorism.

POLITICAL ECONOMY APPROACH

We combine economic methods and political analysis to provide a political economy orientation. At times, each approach stands by itself; at other times, they must be joined to help us understand terrorism issues. Economists often lose track of the roots of their discipline as a highly policy-relevant political economy put forward by Adam Smith, David Ricardo, and Thomas Robert Malthus. To accomplish our study of terrorism, we return to these roots and include the implications of political factors. Why, for example, are liberal democracies more prone to terrorist campaigns than autocracies? The answer to this question requires a political economy orientation (see Chapter 2). In addition, both political and economic factors are important when ascertaining whether governments will cooperate sufficiently when addressing common terrorist threats. We must account not only for the potential gains derived from such cooperation, but also for the proclivity of nations to maintain autonomy over security concerns. Another essential factor in evaluating collective action against terrorism is the tendency for governments to rely on the efforts of other governments when the terrorist threat is truly common. The possibility of international organizations and agreements to circumvent this tendency is a political issue that can be better understood using economic methods – for example, analysis of public goods. Our focus on policy questions also gives our study a political economy orientation.

Political factors are particularly relevant when distinguishing between domestic and transnational terrorism. In the case of domestic terrorism, a central government is empowered to act and direct resources through income, value-added, and other taxes to finance security and other measures against terrorism. After 9/11, the US government moved swiftly to create the DHS, thereby bringing twenty-two agencies together in the

---

[13] Another relevant paper is Enders and Sandler (1991), which examines the impact of terrorism on the Spanish tourist industry. See Chapter 9 for a fuller discussion.

same department to improve coordination. To address the weaknesses in airport security, the federal government trained and deployed professional screeners countrywide to shore up any weak links that existed. At the international level, there is no supranational government that can direct efforts to eliminate weakest links in a globalized world where a vulnerable airport poses potential risks to all passengers passing through that airport. Even baggage originating at such an airport can jeopardize passengers 10,000 miles away when transferred unscreened to the cargo hold of their plane.[14] Solving such interdependent security concerns internationally presents a much different political dilemma than fixing the problem domestically (see Chapters 4 and 6).

HISTORY OF TERRORISM

Terrorism is an activity that has probably characterized modern civilization from its inception. One of the earliest recorded examples is the *sicarii*, a highly organized religious sect consisting of "men of lower orders" in the Zealot struggle in Palestine during 66–73 A.D. (Laqueur, 1978, p. 7). Our brief historical survey of terrorism starts at the Age of Enlightenment in the eighteenth century, at a time when commoners were no longer the property of the state but persons whose lives and property were to be protected by the state. Thus, the notion of liberal democracy was born out of the American (1775–1783) and French (1789–1795) Revolutions. Ironically, the term *terrorism* was first used with the advent of state terror as the post-revolutionary government of France massacred the French nobility and associates (White, 2003).

The Russian Anarchists and Revolutionaries

The more common use of the term *terrorism* arose a half century later with the appearance of the socialist radicals in Europe during the 1840s. These radicals resorted to bombings and assassinations – modern-day terrorist tactics – to terrorize the established order in a failed attempt to bring about a revolution.[15] Following the philosophy and teachings of Pierre Joseph Proudhon, anarchists later adopted the same terrorist tactics in the 1850s and thereafter, with the aim of creating a government-less

---

[14] See the careful analysis of such airline security risks and what can be done about them in Heal and Kunreuther (2005).

[15] The material in this section draws from Combs (2003), Hoffman (1998), White (2003), and other sources.

state. Based on the writings of Mikhail Bakunin and Sergey Nechaev, the Russian anarchists formed Narodnaya Volya (henceforth People's Will) and engaged in a terrorist campaign involving the assassination of government officials. People's Will operated between 1878 and 1881; its most noteworthy assassination victim was Czar Alexander II, whose murder resulted in Alexander III ending reforms and repressing those who sought political change in Russia. Though its campaign was unsuccessful, People's Will was a major factor in shaping modern-day terrorism. First, People's Will had a clear transnational influence by exporting its tactics, adherents, and philosophy abroad, most notably to the labor movement in the United States. Second, the terrorist tactics of People's Will were copied by anarchist and nationalist movements throughout Europe in the late 1800s and early 1900s. Third, People's Will was the forerunner to the Russian Revolutions of 1905 and 1917. In 1917, the world saw that a well-planned terrorist campaign with a large constituency could overthrow a ruling government – this was a shocking revelation that influenced nationalist/separatist struggles thereafter. Fourth, the Irish Republican Army (IRA) under the leadership of Michael Collins applied and honed the terrorist tactics of People's Will during Ireland's 1919–1921 fight for independence from Britain. Once again, terrorist tactics were applied successfully in a nationalist movement.

After the Japanese defeat of the Russians, the 1905 Russian Revolution began with two events: a demonstration by unemployed workers in St. Petersburg and a mutiny by the Russian navy. The revolution was repressed by the Russian government, whose brutality forced the movement underground and sowed the seeds for a future revolution. This second revolution began in February 1917 with a general strike in St. Petersburg that resulted in a countrywide revolt, with the Russian army joining the workers. A new Russian government headed by the Mensheviks gained power but was unpopular because of Russian participation in World War I. Aided by the Germans, Lenin returned to Russia and took over the leadership of the Bolsheviks with the intention of engineering a revolt to topple the Menshevik government. During this second revolution of October 1917, Lenin and Trotsky used terrorist tactics – bombings and assassinations – against the government and its middle-class constituency. Once in power, Lenin and Trotsky applied state terror to silence opponents. While in exile in Mexico, Trotsky was later assassinated to silence him. To ensure that there was no going back to czarist Russia, the Bolsheviks executed Czar Nicholas II and his family in 1918. An important innovation was Lenin's threat to export terrorism (White, 2003) – not unlike the Islamic revolutionaries' threat over sixty years later, following the establishment of an Islamic government in Iran under Khomeini – as a means to keep other governments out of the new communist government's affairs.

Terrorism and the State of Israel

Next, we turn to the Middle East and the Zionists' struggle for a homeland during 1947–1948. Two terrorist groups – Irgun Zvai Leumi and the Stern Gang – applied and refined the methods of Michael Collins as a way to make British rule in Palestine costly. These groups relied on bombings and assassinations directed at British targets to raise the cost of not conceding to Jewish demands for statehood. To raise British stakes further, the Jewish terrorists escalated their campaigns into urban guerrilla warfare so as to keep British troops occupied. The terrorists hoped that the British public would tire of the casualties from hit-and-run attacks and grant Israel independence – the strategy eventually worked. In so doing, they demonstrated the effectiveness of urban terrorism worldwide. Ironically, the Jewish terrorists initially applied the Irish methods of Collins, which they perfected and then "exported" back to the Irish to be used in their confrontations with British troops after 1969.

Algeria and Cyprus

We next turn to the anticolonial revolutions as represented by those in Algeria (1954–1962) and Cyprus (1956–1959). The Algerian revolt against French rule was led by the Front de Libération Nationale (FLN), which took its tactics from those of the Jewish terrorists, as laid out in Begin's book *The Revolt*. The movie *The Battle of Algiers* illustrated the urban guerilla warfare waged by the FLN, whose primary targets were the police, the French military, and symbols of authority. Because attacks on these targets were having little influence on French or Algerian public opinion, the FLN raised the stakes and bombed the milk bars. Women were used to plant the bombs in these bars, where victims included ordinary French citizens. These brutal attacks resulted in the French military being brought in. From the movie, one learns that the subsequent repressive and brutal measures – the tortures and executions – by the French military backfired, hardening the terrorists' resolve and giving the FLN the high moral ground and more recruits. The Muslim majority in Algeria started to turn against French rule because of its repressive response.

By staging its attacks in Algiers, where there were many foreign journalists and residents, the FLN succeeded in capturing world attention. The FLN *internationalized* its struggle further by having terrorist campaigns coincide with propitious events – for example, the opening session of the UN General Assembly (Hoffman, 1998, p. 57). Although the FLN knew that it could never defeat the French forces, it reasoned correctly that a terrorist-based war of attrition would eventually raise the cost to the French sufficiently that independence would be granted. A similar tactic was used by the Cypriot insurgents, who also borrowed their tactics from the Jewish terrorists of the 1940s and also tried to internationalize their campaign.

Irish Troubles after Independence

Irish independence in 1921 did not end the trouble in Ireland, because Northern Ireland remained under British rule. As the civil rights and economic prospects of the Catholic minority waned in Northern Ireland, Catholic discontent grew. From 1930 until the end of the century, the fight for Irish unification was orchestrated by the IRA and the more militant Provisional IRA. The bloodshed increased greatly when the British army was deployed to Northern Ireland in 1969 to maintain order. With the arrival of British troops, the Provisional IRA's urban guerrilla warfare tactics evolved, making attacks against police and soldiers appear random and relentless in Belfast, Londonderry, and other urban centers in Northern Ireland. The Provisional IRA borrowed methods used in the late 1940s by Jewish terrorists in Palestine and in the 1950s by Algerian terrorists. The cities provided cover for the terrorists, who could tie down the British troops and make British rule difficult and costly. To place additional costs on the British public, the Provisional IRA exported its bombing campaign to British cities in the hope that a besieged and fearful British public would pressure its government to support Irish unification. Once again, we see the importance of the audience in a terrorist campaign.

The Tupamaros

In Uruguay (1968–1972) and elsewhere in Latin America, similar tactics were applied in other nationalist and separatist struggles. The Tupamaros in Uruguay added kidnappings and bank robberies to its urban guerrilla warfare tactics as a means to finance its activities. Like the Jewish and Algerian terrorists, the Tupamaros practiced urban terrorism. Clearly, these terrorists were influenced by both the Irgun Zvai Leumi and the FLN when they designed their 1968 urban terror campaign for Montevideo. Like their predecessors, the Tupamaros refined the technique of urban terrorism and managed to tie up the authorities. Unlike their predecessors, they failed to win over a constituency; people viewed the Tupamaros as needlessly brutal. Moreover, the working class never identified with these privileged students, who claimed to be leading a Marxist-Leninist revolution of redistribution. The group is important because its urban terrorist method influenced the fighting communist organizations in Europe during the modern era of terrorism (see Chapter 2).

Terrorism and a Palestinian State

A final noteworthy historical terrorist campaign is the ongoing Palestinian struggle against Israel for a Palestinian state, a struggle that began after the 1967 Arab-Israeli War. The Palestinian Liberation Organization (PLO) and its splinter groups studied IRA, Jewish, and Algerian terrorist tactics in designing their own campaign against Israel. The PLO saw the importance of internationalizing their fight, a tactic made even more important because Israel refused to recognize them. If the world came to recognize the PLO and its grievances, then the PLO believed that Israel would also have to address its concerns. The PLO's new tactics signaled the rise of modern transnational terrorism; terrorists began to stage their acts abroad in order to attract the world's attention. The advent of satellite broadcasts meant that terrorist acts half a globe away could be viewed live as dramatic events unfolded. We will return to the PLO in Chapter 3.

Summing Up

We summarize our brief history in Table 1.2, where the first column indicates the cause of the terrorist campaign, the second lists the terrorists, and the third denotes their tactics. A number of important lessons can be drawn from this select historical record. Throughout history, terrorists have borrowed from their predecessors and, in so doing, have improved their methods. Terrorists pay attention to other terrorists' operations even when they are on opposing sides – for example, the Palestinian terrorists copied the Zionist terrorist methods. To attract media exposure, the terrorists tend to stage their campaigns in urban centers where the media can report their attacks.[16] Over time, terrorist campaigns have been

---

[16] Sendero Luminoso (Shining Path) in Peru is something of an exception to this general rule, since most of their attacks were in rural settings.

Table 1.2. *Historical Terrorist Campaigns*

Cause of Terrorist Campaign	Terrorists	Tactics
French Revolution	The new government's treatment of those once in power	Applied state terror.
Socialist revolution in Europe, 1840s and beyond	Subversive radical democrats; anarchists (e.g., Pierre Joseph Proudhon)	Bombings and assassinations.
Russian anarchists, 1878–1881	Narodnaya Volya (People's Will); leaders included Mikhail Bakunin and Sergey Nechaev	Assassinations of government officials.
Russian Revolutions, 1905, 1917	Anarchists and Bolsheviks	Assassinations, bombings, and other tactics. A threat to export terrorism abroad to governments meddling in communist affairs.
Irish independence and unification, 1919–1921	Irish Republican Army led by Michael Collins	Studied tactics of Narodnaya Volya and applied their methods.
Irish unification, 1930 on	Irish Republican Army	Changing methods over time, including adopting urban guerrilla tactics.
Israel's struggle for a homeland, 1947–1948	Irgun Zvai Leumi, Stern Gang	Studied methods of Collins from the IRA. Bombings and assassinations, urban guerrilla warfare.
Anticolonial revolutions – e.g., Algeria (1954–1962), Cyprus (1956–1959)	Various groups – e.g., Front de Libération Nationale	Bombings and assassinations. Urban guerrilla warfare.
Latin American revolutions – e.g., Uruguay (1968–1972), Cuba (1950s)	Tupamaros in Uruguay, Ernesto (Che) Guevara in Cuba, and Carlos Marighella in Brazil	Urban guerrilla warfare. Kidnappings, bombings, assassinations, propaganda, and bank robberies.
Palestinian struggle against Israel for a Palestinian state, 1967 on	Palestine Liberation Organization (PLO) and splinter groups (e.g., Black September)	Studied IRA's and Israel's methods. Used transnational attacks.

Source: Hoffman (1998), White (2003).

increasingly internationalized in order to capture world attention. Some nationalist/separatist campaigns have succeeded, becoming too costly for the authorities through a war of attrition waged by the terrorists. If the terrorists manage to maintain a constituency, they have a greater likelihood of success. Brutal countermeasures by the authorities increase this constituency and *do not* work in the authorities' favor. Similarly, terrorists' brutality may lose them support.

SOME KEY CONCEPTS

To set the stage for our political economy approach, we must define a few terms that appear at various points throughout the book. An *externality* arises when the action of one agent imposes consequences – costs or benefits – on another agent, and when these consequences are not accounted for by the transaction or its associated price. In its simplest terms, an externality means that a market price may not result in resources being directed to their most valued use, because important costs and/or benefits are not reflected in the price. In the case of a negative externality or external cost, an externality results in too much of the activity, as the provider is not made to compensate for harm done to others. In the case of a positive externality or external benefit, an externality results in too little of the activity, as the provider is not compensated for the benefits conferred on others. When an externality-generating activity provides benefits or costs to agents in another country, a *transnational externality* occurs.

If defensive measures taken by one country divert a terrorist attack to another country, a transnational externality results. Ironically, actions by a country to secure its own airports may merely transfer the attack to a less-secure foreign airport, where the diverter's own citizens are murdered (Arce and Sandler, 2005; Sandler and Lapan, 1988; Sandler and Siqueira, 2005). This example constitutes a negative externality, where countries engage in too much security in an arms-race-like attempt to deflect attacks. If countries become aware that their citizens may still be at risk, then this may curb somewhat their overprovision of defensive measures. As a second example, intelligence on a common terrorist threat provided by one country to authorities in another country represents a positive externality. Here, underprovision is the concern. As terrorists redefined their tactics in the case of the IRA, the Zionist terrorists, and the Tupamaros, these terrorists generated a positive externality for other terrorists. Actions taken by the world press to report successful terrorist tactics speed the dissemination of these external benefits.

Another essential concept is that of a *pure public good*. Publicness here does not necessarily refer to government provision; rather, it means that the good's benefits possess two properties that distinguish these goods from those that can be readily traded in markets. First, a pure public good's benefits are *nonexcludable*, with payers and nonpayers gaining from the good once it is provided. If a targeted country preempts a terrorist group by capturing its members and destroying its infrastructure, then this action protects all potential target countries from attacks. In so doing, preemptive action against a common terrorist threat confers nonexcludable benefits. Since the provider cannot keep others from benefiting from the public good, consumers have a natural incentive to take advantage of the public good without paying for it, which leads to a *free-rider* problem and an anticipated underprovision of the public good.

Second, the benefits of a pure public good are *nonrival* in the sense that one user's consumption of these benefits does not detract, in the least, from the consumption opportunities still in store for others. Like magic, a pure public good keeps giving benefits as more consumers show up. Again consider the preemption of a common terrorist threat. The safety stemming from the action does not diminish in the slightest if there are six, seven, or fifty potential target nations. Each at-risk target receives the same enhanced safety, but may value it differently. Once taken, the preemption protects all potential target nations. Next, suppose that the provider of the pure public good has the means to exclude someone from benefiting from the good. Is it socially desirable to do so? The nonrivalry property of a pure public good makes it inefficient to deny access to anyone who gains, because extending consumption to another user creates benefits while costing society nothing. That is, there is zero additional cost to society from extending consumption, so the extra benefit to the new consumer makes for a net gain to society, thereby justifying making consumption as inclusive as possible. If, however, congestion or other costs result from extending consumption, then there is a rationale for excluding someone unless she compensates for the costs that her consumption causes.

An important class of public goods, where exclusion should be practiced, is the *club good*, whose benefits are easily excluded and only partially nonrival owing to congestion considerations. Congestion costs mean that another consumer diminishes the benefits to the existing consumers. If, for example, the same security force that guards ten airports is made to guard an eleventh, then the safety provided to the original ten airports is diluted as the force is thinned. When the new airport must compensate for this thinning or be denied protection, the hiring of new guards can be financed from the compensation in order to maintain the same level of vigilance. Clubs finance club goods by charging members for the crowding that they cause.

PURPOSE OF THE BOOK

The purpose of this book is to present an up-to-date survey of the study of terrorism, while incorporating contributions from political science, related disciplines, and economics. To our knowledge, our book is the first to highlight theoretical and statistical contributions. In so doing, we demonstrate the novel insights that follow from applying such methods, including game theory. For example, empirical methods can identify cycles, trend (if any), and abrupt changes in terrorists' behavior. Such methods can also be used to generate forecasts, evaluate policies, and to gauge the economic consequences of events (for example, the effects of a series of hijackings on airline revenues). Theoretical analysis can address such questions as: should governments share information if they do not coordinate defensive operations? When theoretical methods are applied, conclusions may initially be surprising owing to perverse incentives among adversaries or targets. Thus, nations may work at cross purposes as they put more weight on their own benefits and ignore how their actions impact others. There are many collective action problems associated with the ways in which governments decide upon their counterterrorism measures. As a consequence, many measures are inefficiently supplied.

Our study investigates both domestic and transnational terrorism. The policy implications of addressing terrorism often differ between the two forms of terrorism owing to institutional concerns. Nevertheless, some insights with respect to domestic terrorism extend with little alteration to transnational terrorism. Our empirical investigation focuses on the latter, because we do not have data on domestic terrorism, which constitutes the greater number of incidents worldwide by a factor of nine.

PLAN OF THE BOOK

The body of the book contains ten chapters. The dilemma posed by terrorism for liberal democracies is discussed in Chapter 2. Liberal democracies walk a tightrope: too small a response makes them look unable to protect lives and property, while too large a response makes them look tyrannical.

Either an underreponse or an overresponse will lose the government support. Many factors in liberal democracies (for example, freedom of movement and freedom of association) provide a supportive environment for terrorism. In Chapter 3, a statistical overview is presented that examines past patterns of transnational terrorism. Additionally, we demonstrate how statistical analysis can inform policy evaluation and forecasting.

Chapter 4 investigates counterterrorism policies with the use of elementary game theory and related tools. These policies are divided into two classes: proactive and defensive policies. Strategic implications are shown in general to differ between these two policy classes. Proactive or offensive policies are more difficult to put in place, while defensive policies are easier to implement but may generate negative impacts on other countries. At the transnational level, greater coordination of antiterrorism policies is needed but has been slow to materialize. Chapter 5 further investigates these negative implications by focusing on the *transference* of attacks caused by the policy choices of targeted governments. Transference results when actions to secure borders deflect the attack to a country with less-secure borders. In Chapter 6, we contrast terrorist cooperation with government noncooperation. We are especially interested in elucidating the collective action implications associated with government cooperation. Means for fostering greater government coordination are indicated.

Chapter 7 concerns hostage-taking incidents, where a game-theoretic analysis is sketched. The efficacy of a policy of never negotiating and never conceding to hostage-taking terrorists is evaluated. In Chapter 8, we apply some statistical analysis to investigate how things are different after 9/11. Chapter 9 displays how statistical tools can be applied to study the economic impact of terrorism – for example, its impact on tourism and/or foreign direct investment. An evaluation of US homeland security is presented in Chapter 10, followed by an evaluation of the future of terrorism and concluding remarks in Chapter 11.

TWO

The Dilemma of Liberal Democracies

A liberal democracy rules by the mandate and wishes of its citizens. Periodic elections place candidates into legislative and executive offices based on some voting rule, such as a simple majority or plurality of votes cast. The political system may be two-party majoritarian, proportional representation, or some similar system. The "liberal" adjective underscores that the system preserves the civil and political rights of citizens and foreign residents (see Doyle, 1997). In a well-functioning liberal democracy, the political and civil rights of the minority are protected by the ruling government. The press is allowed to report the news, and everyone has the right to express his or her views. As a result, people can criticize the government and its policies without fear of reprisals. Suspected criminals have civil rights – for example, to be charged with a crime, to obtain counsel, and to have a fair trial. Election results are tallied in an open and accurate fashion. When a government loses an election, it relinquishes office and allows for a peaceful and orderly transition of power.

An essential requirement of a liberal democracy is the protection of its people's lives and property. A government that fails to provide this security will lose support and be voted out of office. If, for example, a liberal democracy is unable to control a terrorist campaign that murders innocent individuals on city streets or on public transit, then the government will appear inept and lose popularity. Ironically, a liberal democracy protects not only its citizens and residents but also the terrorists who engage in attacks on its soil. The political and civil freedoms that define a liberal democracy provide a favorable environment for terrorists to wage their terror campaigns. To date, evidence indicates that liberal democracies are more plagued by terrorism than their autocratic counterparts, even though grievances may be greater in autocracies (Eubank and Weinberg, 2001; Li, 2005; Li and Schaub, 2004; Weinberg and Eubank, 1998).

The primary purpose of this chapter is to examine the dilemma for liberal democracies posed by terrorism, first noted by Wilkinson (1986), and to indicate their likely response. This dilemma involves engineering a reaction to the terrorist threat in which the government is viewed as providing security without compromising the principles upon which a liberal democracy rests. A secondary purpose is to depict the changing nature of terrorism since 1968 and its implications for liberal democracies. As terrorists seek to surpass past atrocious attacks in order to capture headlines, the carnage associated with terrorism has escalated. This progression has crucial implications for the way in which liberal democracies respond, because citizens may be willing to sacrifice civil freedoms for greater security as terrorists' innovative attacks demonstrate heightened risks. A tertiary purpose is to examine the role of the media in the fight against terrorism. Often simple solutions – for example, not reporting terrorist attacks in order to starve terrorists of the publicity that they crave – have consequences that may be worse than the alternative of not restricting the press. A nonreporting policy may allow other kinds of censorship that a government deems to be in "our" security interest. An important message of the chapter is our call for further research to quantify the relationship between liberal democracies and terrorism.

WHY ARE LIBERAL DEMOCRACIES PRONE TO TERRORISM?

The simple answer is that many of the protections provided by a liberal democracy to a country's citizens serve to aid and abet terrorists in their campaigns of violence (Schmid, 1992). Factors conducive to terrorism include freedom of association, which allows terrorists to form groups and networks with other groups. There is also freedom of speech, which permits terrorists to spread dissent through political wings. Many terrorist groups – for example, Hamas, the Palestine Liberation Organization (PLO), the Irish Republican Army, Euzkadi ta Askatasuna (ETA), and Hezbollah – have political wings that disseminate their messages through legitimate means that might be quashed in less liberal societies. These political activities can reinforce recruitment to the military wing. Terrorists rely on free speech to propagate their propaganda, but the same is true of targeted governments. In liberal democracies, people have freedom of movement and greater rights to cross international borders than in autocracies. Liberal democracies present terrorists with a target-rich environment. Efforts in recent years to put barriers outside of federal buildings in the United States after the 19 April 1995 Oklahoma City bombing will merely deflect future attacks to high-profile business and public buildings with lesser defenses. The right to privacy makes it more difficult for governments to spy on suspected terrorist groups without showing just cause. Liberal democracies also provide greater opportunities to obtain weapons, paramilitary training, and bomb-making information and materials than autocracies. There are greater funding possibilities through both legal and illegal channels.

Perhaps the greatest facilitators of terrorism in liberal democracies are the built-in *restraints* that protect people's civil liberties and inhibit taking actions against suspected terrorists. Restraints on government – for example, unwarranted search and seizure – allow terrorists the freedom to acquire vast arsenals, provided that their actions do not arouse the suspicions of authorities. At the time of the sarin attack on the Tokyo subway on the morning of 20 March 1995, Aum Shinrikyo had $1.4 million in financial assets, a stockpile of 4.2 million lethal doses of sarin, a biological weapons program, and AK-47 production facilities (Campbell, 1997). The group had even acquired a Russian MI-17 helicopter with a spray attachment to disperse sarin or other chemical agents into the air over Tokyo. Aum Shinrikyo had 10,000 members in Japan and upwards of 30,000 followers in Russia. Obviously, Japanese liberalism had allowed this organization to become quite formidable before any action was taken. Only luck and incompetence limited the death toll from the subway attack to just twelve people. Liberal democratic restraints not only permit a terrorist group to become a significant threat, they also limit actions against suspected and known terrorists. Differences in punishment practices among countries can inhibit extradition – for example, countries without a death penalty will not extradite captured terrorist suspects to a country with a death penalty. Once captured, suspected terrorists are guaranteed rights to a fair trial and appeals if convicted. After 9/11, the Bush administration, however, limited many of these legal rights; suspected terrorists apprehended in Afghanistan and elsewhere have been held at Guantánamo Bay, Cuba, in indefinite detention as enemy combatants.

A related issue concerning the relationship between liberal democracy and terrorism has to do with the form of democracy. Which kind of democratic system – proportional representation or majoritarian rule – is more conducive to terrorism? Because proportional representation (PR) gives more viewpoints, even extreme ones, a presence in government, terrorism *may* be less prevalent under PR than under a majoritarian system.

In an *ideal* PR system, seats in parliament are allocated in proportion to the percentage of votes that a party wins. An *indirect* test of this hypothesis is provided by Eubank and Weinberg (1994, pp. 429–30), who related the number of parties in a country to the presence of terrorist groups. Contrary to expectations, they found that "the more parties, the more likely that a nation will have terrorist groups" (Eubank and Weinberg, 1994, p. 430). This finding is consistent with a reverse causality – the presence of more parties implies more extreme views, whose proponents may resort to terrorism. A more direct test by Li (2005), discussed in the next section, gives evidence that PR *is* associated with less terrorism than other democratic systems, as conventionally hypothesized.

There is another consideration that encourages an association between liberal democracy and terrorism. Terrorists are after political concessions that stem from a besieged and threatened public pressuring a government to restore security. In some instances, this pressure may induce the government to concede to some of the terrorists' demands, as was the case when Hezbollah executed the suicide attack against the US Marine barracks in Lebanon on 23 October 1983. Following the attack, which killed 241, the United States withdrew its peacekeepers from Beirut as demanded by Hezbollah. A suicide campaign waged by Hezbollah against Israel in the early 1980s resulted in the Israelis withdrawing their military from southern Lebanon (Pape, 2003). An autocracy is less likely to accede to terrorists' demands, because an autocratic government is less responsive to public pressure and can apply draconian measures against the terrorists or their families. Furthermore, some terrorist attacks may not be reported, thereby limiting public awareness.

BASIC DILEMMA OF LIBERAL DEMOCRACIES

Terrorism poses a real dilemma for a liberal democracy. If it responds too passively and appears unable to protect life and property, then the government loses its legitimacy and may be voted from office. If, however, the government reacts too harshly, then it also sacrifices popular support and may even increase popular support for the terrorists. President Carter's inability to end the Iranian takeover of the US embassy in Tehran probably cost him the 1980 election. The failed rescue mission on 24 April 1980, where a US helicopter crashed into one of the transport planes, killing eight soldiers, in the desert near Tabas, Iran (Mickolus, 1980, p. 884), also made the Carter administration appear inept. The Italian government of Bettino Craxi collapsed on 17 October 1985, just five days after it released

Abu Abbas, the mastermind of the hijacking of the *Achille Lauro* cruise ship (Mickolus, Sandler, and Murdock, 1989, vol. 2, p. 285). Following the 11 March 2004 Madrid train bombings, the Spanish government lost the general election after it tried to pin responsibility for the bombings on Euzkadi ta Askatasuna when the evidence pointed to Islamic fundamentalists. Ineptitude in handling terrorism clearly has consequences for liberal democracies.

Too strong a response can also have severe and harmful consequences. This was the case when French troops tried to crush the Front de Libération Nationale (FLN) terrorists in Algeria in the late 1950s and early 1960s; French brutality turned the native Algerian Muslim community against the French and in favor of the terrorists (Hoffman, 1998). In some instances, world opinion may turn against a government when its antiterrorist measures are too harsh – for example, world reaction to the US handling of detainees at Guantánamo Bay, Cuba, or to Israel's assassination of Hamas leaders in 2004. Recent theoretical analysis shows how direct action against terrorists – known as proactive measures (see Chapter 4) – can increase terrorist recruitment, which harms all potential targets at home and abroad (Frey, 2004; Frey and Luechinger, 2003; Rosendorff and Sandler, 2004; Siqueira, 2005). Thus, such offensive measures may have a downside.

IS THERE MORE TERRORISM IN LIBERAL DEMOCRACIES?

Given the supportive environment that liberal democracies offer to terrorists, we would expect to find more terrorism in liberal democracies compared to their autocratic counterparts. The first analysis of this correlation is by Eubank and Weinberg (1994); their study ascertained whether terrorist groups tended to be more prevalent in liberal democracies than in nondemocracies for the 1954–1987 period based on an odds-ratio test. In Table 2.1, countries are pigeonholed into four categories: democracies with and without terrorist groups, and nondemocracies with and without terrorist groups. In the third row of Table 2.1, the odds that terrorists are present are computed for each type of political system by taking the ratio of groups being present to their being absent – that is, these odds are $44/27 = 1.6296$ for democracies and $27/58 = 0.4655$ for nondemocracies. A ratio greater than one indicates a positive association between the political system and the presence of terrorist groups, while a ratio less than one denotes a negative association between the political system and the presence of terrorist groups. The statistical significance of the odds in Table 2.1 is computed by finding the *odds ratio*, which equals

Table 2.1. *Odds Ratio for Presence of Terrorist Group*

	Democracies	Nondemocracies
Terrorist group presence	44	27
Terrorist group absence	27	58
Odds of terrorists' presence	1.6296	0.4655

Odds ratio = 3.50; chi-square = 14.24; $N = 156$.
$p < .001$; variance = 1.39.
Source: Eubank and Weinberg (1994).

3.5 (= 1.6296/0.4655). Thus, terrorist groups are 3.5 times more likely to be found in democracies than in autocracies. This odds ratio has a chi-square (goodness-of-fit) statistic of 14.24, which gives a one-in-a-thousand chance that it occurred randomly. Thus, democracies are associated with terrorist groups operating on their soil. When the authors compared other categories of democracies – for example, interrupted and partial democracies – the results were similar.

Although this analysis is very innovative, it suffers from some problems. There is a tendency in authoritarian regimes to underreport terrorism; this tendency biases the results in favor of the authors' hypothesized association. The tendency for underreporting is greater for the presence of terrorist groups than for the occurrence of terrorist incidents. Although an authoritarian regime would have difficulty in hiding the fact that a bomb had exploded in a major city or that a commercial aircraft had been hijacked, it could easily keep quiet the name of a group claiming responsibility unless the claim were made directly to the media. Even then, the government could bring pressure on the domestic media not to disclose the group's identity. The government has an interest in hiding such information so that people do not believe that the government faces significant challenges to its rule.

Terrorism may be present in repressive regimes but carried out at the individual level, owing to the risks involved in forming groups that might attract government attention or be infiltrated. Thus, we should see more acts by individuals in authoritarian regimes, but this does not mean that such regimes are free from terrorism. Timothy McVeigh had an accomplice but was not part of an established group; thus the group measure may miss the presence of terrorism even in liberal democracies. Nevertheless, this underreporting bias is anticipated to be higher in autocracies.

In the Eubank and Weinberg (1994) analysis, the hosting of one or more terrorist groups characterized the country as confronting terrorism. This measure is particularly poor at measuring spillover terrorism, where groups stage their terrorist activities in one country while being based elsewhere. Throughout the 1970s and 1980s, Middle East terrorism spilled over to Europe; for example, forty-three incidents in Europe were of Middle Eastern origin in 1987 (US Department of State, 1988). A country such as Austria experienced a lot of spillover transnational terrorism – forty-one incidents from 1980 to 1987, including the 27 December 1985 armed attack on Vienna's Schwechat Airport (Mickolus, Sandler, and Murdock, 1989) – but hosted no groups during the sample period considered by Eubank and Weinberg. Thus, the presence or absence of terrorist groups can give a very misleading view of terrorist activities.

State sponsorship also presents a problem for Eubank and Weinberg's group-based analysis. During the Cold War, it is believed that the communist bloc was responsible for sponsoring terrorist events in the West. State-sponsored groups had home bases (for example, Syria, Libya, Algeria, and Tunisia) outside the countries where the acts were staged. For example, the North Korean agents responsible for blowing up Korean Air Lines flight 858 on 30 November 1987 are thought to have acquired the bomb from another North Korean operative in Belgrade (US Department of State, 1988). Eubank and Weinberg (1994) list North Korea, a repressive regime, as having no terrorist groups; the implication, then, is that North Korea is not involved in terrorism.

A more accurate way to test for the presence or absence of terrorism in liberal democracies is to use terrorist event data, which indicate the level of terrorism in a host country. In a follow-up study, Weinberg and Eubank (1998) took this recommendation (see Sandler, 1995) and analyzed the correlation between regime type and the presence of terrorist *events* for 1994–1995. They indeed found that terrorism was more prevalent in democracies. Moreover, they discovered that democracies are more prone to terrorism during a regime transition period.

Although their study is an improvement over their earlier work, it raises further issues that must be addressed. First, only two years of data were examined; these years might not be representative of other years. Data are available for the entire 1968–2003 period. Has the relationship between political system and terrorism changed over time? Only a more complete study can answer this question. Second, the authors have not investigated a crucial issue raised, but not really answered, in their first study – that is, to what extent has terrorism been exported from autocratic to democratic regimes.[1] This migration may be motivated, in part, by the

---

[1] A proper answer requires an examination of the nationality of the perpetrator, the home base of the terrorists, and the location of the terrorist incident (Sandler, 1995).

greater anticipated media coverage in democracies. The migration question can be addressed if event venues and the perpetrators' home countries are related to one another. Third, Weinberg and Eubank (1998) used only transnational terrorism that includes no domestic terrorist incidents. Surely, domestic incidents must be included in order to determine whether terrorism is related to a country's political regime. Fourth, these authors only reported correlations and did not examine which factors, including regime type, explained the prevalence of terrorism. In this regard, one needs to quantify what *level* of terrorism, in terms of the number of incidents, is related to regime type and other determinants. Researchers have begun to address this concern by reporting some statistical findings that indicate the factors that influence the level of terrorism in countries (Blomberg, Hess, and Weerapana, 2004; Li and Schaub, 2004). Such quantitative measures can assist governments in allocating resources to counterterrorism activities.

In a recent study, Li (2005) provided the most careful analysis to date on the relationship between democracy and transnational terrorism. His study distinguished essential characteristics of democracies – for example, press freedoms, political constraints on the executive, and political participation among potential voters. Among other results, Li found that press freedoms and political constraints are positively associated, as hypothesized, with greater transnational terrorism. Proportional representation systems experience significantly less transnational terrorism than other democratic alternatives. Greater regime durability reduces transnational terrorism at home.

To date, all of the evidence points to liberal democracies as being associated with terrorism. While this relationship appears robust and unequivocal, there is still much to learn about it. For example, is the relationship sensitive to sample period and sample countries? Is the terrorism home-grown or exported from abroad?

CIVIL LIBERTIES VERSUS PROTECTION TRADE-OFF

To explain how civil liberties are traded off against greater security in a liberal democracy, we present a microeconomic-based indifference curve analysis of this trade-off.[2] In Figure 2.1, expected damage from terrorist attacks is measured on the vertical axis, while the level of civil liberties is measured on the horizontal axis. Curve AB represents the constraint that

---

[2] This analysis modifies and expands on the presentation in Viscusi and Zeckhauser (2003). Their presentation is a standard analysis of the trade-off between a risk and a return.

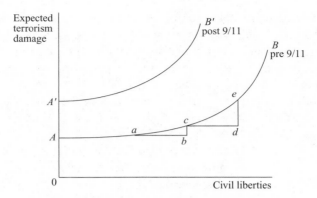

Figure 2.1. Terrorism–civil liberties constraint.

a society faces in a liberal democracy confronted with a terrorist threat. At a given point in time, all choices on or above AB are feasible, but trade-offs below AB are infeasible. The "cost" of increased civil liberties is greater exposure to terrorism and its expected damage for the reasons discussed earlier in the chapter – for example, freer media make the country a more attractive venue for terrorist attacks. With enhanced liberties, terrorists can engage in larger organizations and larger-scale attacks. Along AB, each increase in civil liberties comes at the expense of larger expected terrorism-induced losses, so that the constraint is positively sloped. In moving from a to c and then from c to e along AB, civil liberties increase by ab and cd, respectively, where $ab = cd$, but the change in anticipated terrorism losses escalates from cb to ed, where $ed > cb$. As a consequence, AB rises at an increasing rate. This implies that a very free society can achieve the largest reduction in terrorist risks as some freedoms are first removed – say, in moving from e to c. Each additional sacrifice of freedom gains less additional security from terrorist attacks. In Figure 2.1, curve AB represents the perceived terrorism-liberties constraint before 9/11. The events of 9/11 made people aware that for each level of civil liberties, the expected terrorism damage is higher. Thus, the perceived post-9/11 constraint, $A'B'$, is above and steeper than AB.

The taste side depends on society's indifference map, which indicates how society is willing to trade off terrorism risks for civil liberties.[3]

---

[3] Indifference maps are discussed in any intermediate microeconomics textbook. Most introductory textbooks of economics have a discussion of indifference curves in the consumer theory chapter. For more about indifference curves, the reader should consult one of these books. Also, see Chapter 5.

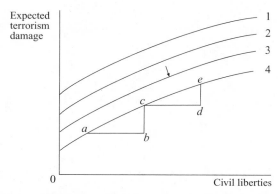

Figure 2.2. Indifference map for terrorism–civil liberties trade-off.

Consider indifference curve 4 in Figure 2.2, which depicts all combinations of expected terrorism damage and civil liberties – for example, bundles *a*, *c*, and *e* – that provide equal levels of satisfaction to society. Because expected terrorism losses represent a "bad" and civil freedoms denote a "good," the indifference curves are upward-sloping, indicating that society is willing to accept greater anticipated losses only if compensated with more civil liberties.[4] Similarly, society is *willing to sacrifice* some of its liberties in return for greater security – that is, fewer and less severe terrorist attacks. The shape of an indifference curve shows that for each increase in civil liberties, society is less willing to accept further risks in terms of terrorism. In moving from *a* to *c* and then from *c* to *e* on indifference curve 4, each equal increment in civil liberties (*ab* = *cd*) results in smaller tolerated increases in risk as *ed* < *cb*. We have chosen this trade-off because it agrees with the notion that societies are less risk-accepting as freedoms expand; thus, a very free society is more willing to *sacrifice* freedoms for security (in moving from *e* to *a*) than a less free society.

In Figure 2.2., the well-being of society *increases* when moving from indifference curve 1 to lower indifference curves (in the direction of the arrow), so that indifference curve 4 represents the highest satisfaction level of the four curves displayed. This follows because lower indifference curves have *reduced risks for each level of civil liberties* and, thus, are improvements in social welfare. Only four indifference curves are drawn

---

[4] On the vertical axis, we could have put reduced terrorism risk instead of expected terrorism losses so as to show the trade-off of two goods. With reduced terrorism risk on the vertical axis, the indifference curves would have the normal shape – that is, convex-to-the-origin, downward-sloping curves. Moreover, the constraint would be a concave-to-the-origin, downward-sloping curve.

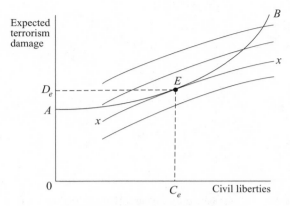

Figure 2.3. Social equilibrium.

in Figure 2.2., but through any point there is an indifference curve. If a society or group within the society is more accepting of risks or less willing to give up freedoms, then its indifference curve would be steeper, indicating that it would tolerate greater risk for every gain in freedom.

In Figure 2.3, the constraint and tastes are put together to find the social equilibrium, where the greatest feasible level of social welfare is attained on constraint AB. Part of the indifference map – four of the multitude of indifference curves – is displayed. Because social welfare increases with lower indifference curves, the social optimum is reached at tangency E between AB and indifference curve xx. Lower indifference curves, while desirable, are unobtainable given the constraint. At E, society experiences C_e civil liberties and D_e in expected terrorism damage. If society is less accepting of risks, then its entire indifference map will be flatter, with an optimum to the left of E along AB. When, however, society is less willing to accept restraints on its civil liberties, its indifference curves (not shown) will be steeper, and the equilibrium will be to the right of E along AB, where liberties are expanded at the expense of greater risks. At point E, society's optimal trade-off of risks and liberties equals the feasible trade-off along AB. Technological innovations and/or international cooperation may shift the AB constraint downward, thus lowering potential terrorism losses for each level of civil liberties.

Authoritarian regimes are less accepting of challenges to their rule for fear that tolerance may encourage further challenges. Moreover, such regimes have little or no interest in civil liberties. The ruler's indifference curves are effectively horizontal, and the ruler's optimum is at point A, where measures are taken to limit terrorism to the minimal feasible level

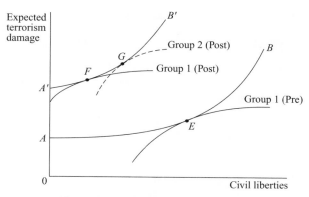

Figure 2.4. Alternative equilibriums.

of damage. This would then explain why Eubank, Weinberg, and others have found so little evidence of terrorism in authoritarian regimes.

The potential effect of 9/11 is displayed in Figure 2.4. Ignore the dashed indifference curve and consider citizen Group 1 both before and after 9/11. Prior to 9/11, Group 1 is in equilibrium at E, with a relatively high level of civil liberties and a low level of expected terrorism damage. After 9/11, AB shifts to $A'B'$ as terrorists' innovations demonstrate greater risks for every level of civil liberties. Also, 9/11 sets in motion a drive for terrorists to find new, more devastating attacks in the escalation process. $A'B'$ is also steeper than AB. In Figure 2.4, Group 1's indifference curves become flatter as people become less risk-accepting, so that all indifference curves in this group's preference map become flatter. Only one representative indifference curve is displayed in the two scenarios to avoid clutter. The post-9/11 equilibrium for Group 1 is at F, with higher risks and reduced civil liberties compared to E. In the United States, this explains why the public was generally accepting of the Patriot Act, which curtailed many civil liberties (for example, restrictions on habeas corpus, reduced immigration rights, and greater electronic surveillance) in the name of security against terrorism. In West Germany, the population basically supported the issuing of identity cards during the height of left-wing terrorism in the 1970s and 1980s.

Next, consider the presence of a second group in society – Group 2 – with a reduced willingness to trade away civil liberties for lower terrorism risks. This may be due to a worry that they may be singled out owing to past experiences – for example, police profiling of African Americans in traffic stops. In Figure 2.4, Group 2's representative (dashed) indifference curve favors a higher level of civil liberties at the cost of greater terrorism risks compared to Group 1. Its equilibrium is at point G along $A'B'$. Using surveys, Davis and Silver (2004) showed that this is indeed true after 9/11 – "African Americans are much less willing to trade civil liberties for security than whites or Latinos" (p. 28). In an experimental situation, Viscusi and Zeckhauser (2003) reported analogous results, finding that people whose rights have been infringed upon in the past are less willing to sacrifice civil freedoms after 9/11 than those whose rights have never been compromised.

THE ROLE OF THE MEDIA

The media involve all means and channels of information and entertainment (Wilkinson, 1997). As such, the media include television, movies, documentaries, theater, music, newspapers, magazines, books, photography, and other visual arts. The influence of the media in every facet of our lives has grown with technological innovations that have effectively shrunk the globe.

Periods of globalization have been associated with increased international terrorism. The first wave of globalization in the 1880s and beyond coincided with the emergence of the anarchists, who emigrated from Russia to Europe and then to North America (see Chapter 1; Rapoport, 2004). The anarchists assassinated political leaders, planted bombs, and engaged in sabotage in order to foment revolution. Their terrorist acts coincided with advances in global communications (for example, the telegraph and daily newspapers) and transportation (for example, faster and larger ocean liners). The second wave of globalization in the latter third of the twentieth century also coincided with an era of increased terrorism. Innovations in communication and transportation – communication satellites, the internet, high-speed commercial air travel, and the digital revolution – were associated with the new era. Over the last two decades, the internet has been increasingly used by terrorists to disseminate propaganda, spread terror (for example, the beheading of Nicholas Berg was posted on the internet on 12 May 2004), coordinate activities, make demands, and send warnings.[5] Terrorists have also relied on the internet to gather intelligence – for example, an al-Qaida computer found in a cave in

---

[5] On information terrorism and the use of the internet, see Post, Ruby, and Shaw (2000). Also, consult Bunker (2000) on weapons of mass disruption that rely on networks for replication purposes. Computer viruses are examples of weapons of mass disruption that may be used by terrorists to create large economic losses in a targeted economy.

Afghanistan contained a downloaded copy of a US General Accounting Office report on US infrastructure vulnerabilities.

Terrorists and the media represent a symbiotic relationship. To create an atmosphere of fear, terrorists need the media and their ability to reach every corner of the globe almost instantaneously. The events of the Munich Olympics on 5 September 1972 and the toppling of the World Trade Center on 9/11 were transmitted live worldwide. The terrorists exploit all forms of media to gain wider support and recruit new members. During the 1970s and 1980s, left-wing terrorists relied on the media to confirm their claims of responsibility through coded communications, passwords, and other tell-tale signs that allowed groups to get credit for terrorist acts that could be claimed by others (Alexander and Pluchinsky, 1992; Mickolus, Sandler, and Murdock, 1989). In essence, the media made a terrorist act a private good that could not be shared among groups. Coverage of grisly terrorist acts – for example, the massacres at Vienna's Schwechat Airport and Rome's Fiumicino Airport on 27 December 1985, masterminded by Abu Nidal – traumatizes the global community. These attacks changed the flying public's concept of airport risks for many years to come. Such publicity augments the economic consequences of terrorist acts; for example, media coverage of 9/11 added to the huge losses suffered by the airline industry (Chapter 9; Drakos, 2004).

Terrorists may use the media to spread their propaganda. A case in point involves the hijacking of Trans World Airlines (TWA) flight 847 en route from Athens to Rome on 14 June 1985. Prior to the release of the remaining thirty-nine hostages on 30 June 1985, the hooded terrorists held a news conference during which they discussed their views and grievances (Mickolus, Sandler, and Murdock, 1989, vol. 2, p. 224). In many hostage-taking incidents, terrorists issue statements about their cause during negotiations. The publication of a political statement is often a condition for the release of the hostage(s) (Mickolus, 1980; Mickolus, Sandler, and Murdock, 1989). Terrorists will frequently send propaganda statements to the media when claiming responsibility for a terrorist act. The *New York Times* and *Washington Post* published a rambling 35,000-word manifesto by the Unabomber that condemned technology and modern civilization. On 3 April 1996, the arrest of Theodore Kaczynski, the Unabomber, came after David Kaczynski recognized his brother's writings from the published manifesto and alerted the authorities to his brother's whereabouts in Montana.

Terrorists also rely on the media to portray government responses as brutal in the hopes of winning popular support. This tactic was particularly true of the left-wing terrorists of the 1970s and 1980s. This motive is less applicable to fundamentalist terrorists, who are less interested in winning over a constituency. However, this motive may apply to Hamas, which wants to show Israeli reactions as excessive so that world opinion will turn against Israel.

By reporting logistical innovations, the media inadvertently assist terrorists to adopt new methods that prove effective. On 24 November 1971, D. B. Cooper hijacked Northwest Airlines flight 305, a Boeing 727 en route from Washington, DC, to Seattle. Cooper demanded $200,000 in twenty-dollar bills and four parachutes, which he was given on the tarmac in Seattle in exchange for the passengers and two of the stewardesses (Mickolus, 1980, pp. 287–8). He then demanded to be flown to Mexico via Reno, Nevada. While en route to Reno, he parachuted from the rear door of the plane and was never seen again.[6] His method was then copied unsuccessfully by seventeen hijackers, leading the airlines to redesign the Boeing 727, DC-8, and DC-9 so that their rear doors could not be opened in flight (Landes, 1978, p. 4). Unintentionally, the media can lead to a wave of copycat events. This was also true in the 1980s after the media reported that a hijacker had commandeered a plane to Cuba by claiming to have a flammable liquid in a bottle. Many subsequent hijackers used this method (Enders, Sandler, and Cauley, 1990a, 1990b). Such *demonstration effects* can lead to cycles in terrorist attacks as successful methods disseminate rapidly and failures quickly lead to curtailing planned attacks.

Like the terrorists, the media are interested in the size of their audience. A larger audience means higher viewer ratings and advertisers' demand for television and larger profits for the print media. Thus, the goals of the media and terrorists are, at times, aligned so that grisly terrorist acts or the tense drama of a hijacking that can end any moment in bloodshed can serve the interests of both. Over time, the terrorists see a need to escalate the shock value and the death toll of their attacks in order to capture and maintain the media's attention. Driven by the need for viewers and readers, the media focus on the more spectacular events, thereby increasing the terrorists' demand for such events.

The media can also serve useful purposes. First, the media can inform the public about heightened terrorism alerts. In so doing, they can pass

---

[6] He jumped somewhere over Oregon or Washington when the plane was cruising at 200 miles per hour at an altitude of 10,000 feet. When he left the plane in his blue business suit, the wind chill was −69° F. Apparently, the parachutes had been sewn shut, so there is little chance that he survived the jump (Mickolus, 1980, p. 287).

along vital information about what to watch for. Second, the media can assist in the capture of terrorists, as was the case with the Unabomber. The media published sketches of the parachuting terrorist D. B. Cooper, in the hope that someone might see him and turn him in; but this never happened. Third, the media can provide a forum for discussion so that the public can better assess the risks and learn the measures taken to curtail them. Such forums can educate the public about how to respond if they ever become the target of a terrorist attack. Fourth, the media can expose the hypocrisy of the terrorists, if appropriate, thereby costing them support. When the brutality of the Tupamaros was reported to the people of Uruguay in the 1960s, it alienated many of their supporters (White, 2003, pp. 119–29). Once a terrorist group loses its constituency, the authorities can show less restraint and the terrorists risk being turned in by reward seekers. The media may facilitate this process by exposing terrorists' excesses. Fifth, the media may provide the government with a means to take its case to the public to counter charges made by the terrorists.

The net impact of the media can be evaluated only if both the beneficial and not-so-beneficial aspects are compared. To date, there has been very little empirical work to assess the net impact of the media on terrorism. In an innovative paper, Nelson and Scott (1992) applied statistical techniques to determine whether media coverage encouraged additional terrorist events.[7] In particular, these authors tested whether media attention, as measured by the number of column inches devoted to terrorism in the *New York Times*, influenced terrorism events during the ensuing period. For 1968–1984, these authors showed that media coverage of high-profile terrorist incidents did *not* induce additional terrorist acts. In addition, terrorist events during the previous period did not explain media coverage during the next period; only current terrorist incidents determined contemporaneous media coverage. Finally, these authors identified incidents' characteristics that attracted the most media coverage. US and Israeli attacks gained attention in the *New York Times*, especially when Americans were killed. The number of hostages, the sequential release of hostages, and the passing of terrorists' deadlines (for example, a deadline for killing a hostage) had an important influence on the amount of media attention afforded to hostage incidents. Their study should be extended to include additional newspapers in order to circumvent the *New York Times*

---

[7] These authors used a vector-autoregression (VAR) technique – see Chapter 3 on time-series methods and Chapter 5 on their application to other terrorism scenarios.

bias toward US and Israeli events, which clearly showed up in the results. Such extensions require a lot of effort to record the data in terms of news media coverage of terrorist incidents. Such research, like the Nelson and Scott (1992) study, is essential to gauge the impact of media coverage on terrorism.

A standard policy recommendation to curb any negative impact of media coverage of terrorism is to rely on the media to exercise voluntary self-restraint (Wilkinson, 1997). Forced restraint on the media is censorship, which constitutes a loss of civil liberties. There are times when the media must decide whether showing a grisly act is in poor taste, or whether reporting terrorists' innovative methods may encourage further terrorist acts. The media may also need to restrain themselves from reporting a rescue operation while in progress, because it could alert the terrorists and jeopardize the mission – for example, the dispatch of Delta Force was reported by the media during the *Achille Lauro* hijacking (Mickolus, Sandler, and Murdock, 1989, vol. 2, p. 283). A similar news tip-off occurred during the hijacking of Pan Am flight 73 on 5 September 1986 at the Karachi airport. The *New York Times* reported that a Delta Force commando unit had been dispatched to the scene. Prior to its arrival, the hijackers began killing the passengers – 22 died, and 100 were injured (Mickolus, Sandler, and Murdock, 1989, vol. 2, pp. 454–5). There was, however, no evidence that the hijackers knew of the *New York Times* report. The bloodshed ensued when the airplane's lights dimmed as the plane's generators ran out of power. The hijackers mistakenly thought that the Pakistani officials had deliberately lowered the lights to allow for a rescue operation.

TERRORISM IN THE AGE OF GLOBALIZATION

The modern era of terrorism is often characterized as starting in 1968, after the 1967 Arab-Israeli War. In contrast to earlier epochs of terrorism, the modern era is said to be marked by the "internationalization of terrorism" (Hoffman, 1998, pp. 67–75). In a seminal study, Rapoport (1984) indicated that early terrorists – the Thugs in the thirteenth century and the Assassins in the eleventh, twelfth, and thirteenth centuries – moved across state borders and relied on safe havens from which to strike, so that the internationalization of terrorism began well before the "modern epoch" of terrorism. What is different after 1968 is the manner in which terrorists take advantage of innovations in transportation and communication that

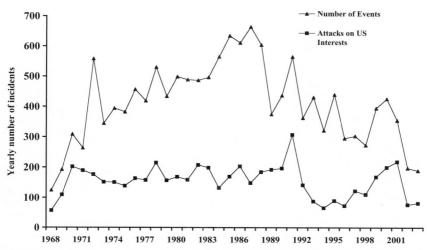

Figure 2.5. Transnational terrorist incidents: 1968–2003. *Source:* US Department of State (1988–2004) and Sandler and Enders (2004).

allow them and the news of their deeds to spread globally in relatively little time. The internet, satellite phones, and other advances in communication permit attacks to be coordinated at widely dispersed places. In addition, modern-day terrorist groups can exist in multiple countries at the same time – for example, al-Qaida operates in Yemen, the United States, Saudi Arabia, Afghanistan, and elsewhere.

Another distinguishing characteristic of the modern epoch, compared to the anarchists of the 1880s, or the anticolonists of the 1950s and 1960s, is the extent of transnational attacks. Figure 2.5 illustrates the rapid rise of transnational terrorist incidents, from 125 events in 1968 to 558 attacks in 1972. For the entire period displayed, transnational terrorist attacks averaged 412 incidents each year, with the largest number of incidents occurring during the period 1985–1988. Another striking feature is the comparatively large number of incidents directed at US interests. As shown in Figure 2.5, the plot of US attacks generally matches the plot of all attacks, with many matching peaks and troughs. In Figure 2.6, the proportion of transnational attacks against US interests is displayed. For 1968–2003, 40% of all transnational terrorist attacks were against US citizens or property. This focus on US interests also distinguishes the modern era of terrorism, in which the United States is a prime target, from earlier eras in which the United States was not the prime target.

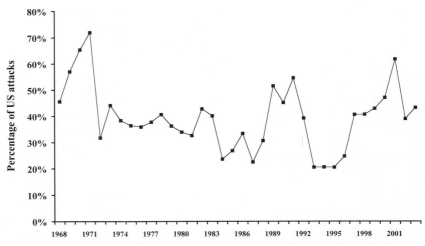

Figure 2.6. Proportion of US transnational terrorist incidents: 1968–2003. *Source:* US Department of State (1988–2004) and Sandler and Enders (2004).

Significant Events

Like Hoffman (1998), we consider the 22 July 1968 hijacking of an El Al flight en route from Rome to Tel Aviv by three Popular Front for the Liberation of Palestine (PFLP) terrorists as a watershed event in the modern epoch of transnational terrorism. The PFLP terrorists commandeered the Boeing 707 with its ten-member crew and thirty-eight passengers (including the hijackers) approximately twenty minutes into the flight by threatening to explode grenades.[8] The terrorists were also armed with a pistol. This event is noteworthy for a number of reasons. First, there was clear evidence of state sponsorship *after* the plane landed in Algiers, as Algerian authorities secured the hostages and held some until 1 September 1968, when a deal was finally struck. Once the plane was in Algiers, the Algerian government freed the twenty-three non-Israeli passengers. Five days later, they released the Israeli women and children, but held onto the Israeli men. Second, the incident forced the Israelis to negotiate directly with the Palestinian terrorists – the one thing the Israelis had said they would never do (Hoffman, 1998, p. 68). Third, the media coverage showed other terrorists that such incidents could gain worldwide attention. The length of the incident – approximately forty days – meant that this single event was

---

[8] For a description of this event, see Mickolus (1980, pp. 93–4). The facts given in this paragraph come from Mickolus's account of the incident.

a major news story for weeks. Fourth, one of the terrorists helped land the hijacked plane in Algiers, marking the first time that a terrorist had flown a hijacked plane. Fifth, a $7.5 million ransom was paid by the French government to the hijackers, who were flown to a safe haven at the incident's conclusion. In addition, sixteen Arab prisoners from the 1967 Arab-Israeli War were released by Israel. The incident thus demonstrated to other would-be hijackers that this mode of attack could be financially and politically lucrative. Not surprisingly, many similar hijackings followed. Sixth, the hijacking represented a transnational externality (that is, an uncompensated interdependency among two or more countries), a common feature of modern-day terrorism. A grievance in the Middle East spilled over to Europe; ransoms paid by the French government encouraged subsequent hijackings in other countries. The presence of a transnational externality indicates the need for countries to coordinate their antiterrorism policies. Seventh, the terrorists attracted so much attention by creating a crisis situation, where a false move could result in the loss of the plane and its passengers. The incident demonstrated the need for high drama from the outset to encourage the media to allocate reporters and other assets to cover the incident. In future incidents, the terrorists would kill a passenger or two at the incident's outset to create the necessary drama.

Such hijackings not only made the world aware of a cause, but also fostered recruitment of terrorists to the cause. The July 1968 El Al hijacking appeared to change the mindset of the terrorists by encouraging international incidents. Another important terrorist event took place on 26 December 1968 at the Athens airport, when two PFLP terrorists threw incendiary grenades and fired a machine gun at an El Al plane boarding for a flight to New York via Tel Aviv (Mickolus, 1980, p. 105). One passenger was killed, and a stewardess was wounded. Unlike the earlier El Al hijacking, this attack went awry. The event is significant because it demonstrated to the terrorists that hijackings and attacks on aircraft carry grave risks for the perpetrators.

During the late 1960s and early 1970s, there were countless hijackings from the United States to Cuba (Landes, 1978). Most of these hijackings were peaceful, with the plane landing in Cuba, the hijacker(s) being led away by Cuban authorities, and the plane and passengers returning to the United States with Cuban souvenirs. The epidemic of hijackings, inspired by the 22 July 1968 hijacking, became so severe that metal detectors were eventually installed in US airports on 5 January 1973, thereby ending the epidemic in the United States for eight years, until ways to circumvent these detectors were devised.

Another significant terrorist event, defining the modern epoch, involved the hijacking of TWA flight 840, a Boeing 707 en route from Rome to Athens, on 29 August 1969 (Mickolus, 1980, p. 131). Two PFLP terrorists – Leila Ali Khaled and Salim K. Essawi – were involved in the hijacking of the plane, which carried eighty-five passengers and twelve crew members. This incident followed the "script" of the July 1968 hijacking, with the plane landing in a country – Syria – that helped secure the hostages and protect the hijackers. Once in Damascus, Leila Khaled had the passengers and crew leave the plane before she blew up the cockpit, causing $4 million in damage to the $8 million plane (Mickolus, 1980). Syria released most of the passengers and crew but held onto two Israeli hostages until 5 December 1969, when Israel released seventy-one prisoners to Egypt and Syria. Israel also received two military pilots, captured in Egypt, in the prisoner exchange. Syria allowed the two terrorists to go free on 13 October 1969. Leila Khaled later took part in a failed hijacking on 7 September 1970 in the Netherlands (Mickolus, 1980). With flight 840, the terrorists once again captured the world's attention in a tense drama, made even more poignant by blowing up the cockpit. Thus, the terrorists raised the stakes in order to keep the media watching. Countries again made concessions to end the crisis, thereby demonstrating that terrorism could pay. Moreover, the terrorists went free.

Many other dramatic hijackings followed – for example, the hijacking of a Japan Air Lines flight on 31 March 1970 by the Japanese Red Army Faction – until metal detectors significantly decreased, but did not eliminate, hijackings (see Chapter 5). Until protective measures were taken and the public's interest seemed to wane, the start of the modern epoch of terrorism relied on hijackings. Earlier epochs of terrorism that involved transnational events had not relied on hijacking planes. Terrorist attacks after 1968 also included bombings against both official (for example, the 25 February 1969 PFLP bombing of the British consulate in East Jerusalem) and civilian targets (for example, the 18 July 1969 PFLP firebombing of Marks and Spencer on Oxford Street, London). The modern epoch of terrorism involved terrorists diversifying their attacks. As skyjackings became more difficult after 1973, terrorists shifted to kidnapping and barricade-and-hostage-taking missions (Enders, Sandler, and Cauley, 1990a).

Primary Terrorist Influences, 1968–1990

Terrorists were primarily secular during the first portion of the modern epoch of terrorism. There were two primary terrorist influences:

the ethno-nationalist groups and the left-wing terrorists. The Palestinian, Latin American, Irish, and Basque terrorists epitomized the former, while the "fighting communist organizations" of Europe (for example, the Red Army Faction in West Germany, Combatant Communist Cells in Belgium, Dev Sol in Turkey, Direct Action in France, the Red Brigades in Italy, the Popular Forces of 25 April in Portugal, and 17 November in Greece) represented the latter. By far, the Palestinian terrorists were the most important influence and actually formed linkages with the Provisional Irish Republican Army (PIRA) and the leftist groups (Alexander and Pluchinsky, 1992, pp. 8–11). These linkages allowed for joint training, the sharing of operatives, and logistical support. Thus, the operation of loose terrorist networks dates back to the start of modern-day terrorism.

Many terrorist groups split off from the PLO because it was too conservative in its terror campaign for some of its members. Breakaway groups included PFLP, PFLP-General Command, the Palestine Liberation Front (the hijackers of the *Achille Lauro*), Black September (infamous from the Munich Olympics), and the Abu Nidal Organization (ANO). ANO was headed by Sabri al-Banna, who began forming his own clandestine group while in Iraq in 1972 (Nasr, 1997). During the late 1970s, ANO engaged in numerous assassinations, especially of PLO members[9] – for example, Said Hammami in London on 4 January 1978, and Ali Yassin in Kuwait on 15 June 1978 (Mickolus, 1980). Arguably, ANO was the most significant transnational terrorist threat from 1976 until 1991, when it was responsible for assassinating Abu Iyad, the second in command to Arafat in the PLO, on 14 January 1991 in Tunis.

Noteworthy ANO attacks include:[10]

- the 4 June 1982 attempted assassination of Shlomo Argov, the Israeli ambassador to the United Kingdom, at the Dorchester Hotel in London;
- the 6 August 1982 machine pistol and grenade attack on Jo Goldenberg's restaurant in Paris;
- the 16 September 1982 assassination of a Kuwaiti diplomat in Madrid, Spain;
- the 19 September 1982 armed attack on a synagogue in Brussels, Belgium;

---

[9] The information on ANO comes from Nasr (1997) and Seale (1992).

[10] All incidents are described in detail in Mickolus, Sandler, and Murdock (1989) under the dates listed. Also see Seale (1992) on ANO and its operations.

- the 25 October 1983 assassination of the Jordanian ambassador in New Delhi, India;
- the 23 November 1985 hijacking of Egyptair flight 648 en route from Athens to Cairo;
- the 27 December 1985 near-simultaneous armed attacks on the Rome and Vienna airports;
- the 5 September 1986 attempted hijacking of Pan Am flight 73 in Karachi, Pakistan; and
- the 6 September 1986 armed attack on the Neve Shalom synagogue in Istanbul.

These are but a tiny fraction of ANO's attacks. These attacks have been singled out for a number of reasons. The 4 June 1982 attempted assassination of Ambassador Argov led to Israel's invasion of southern Lebanon. The 6 August 1982 restaurant attack illustrates the spillover of Middle Eastern terrorism to Europe, as do the September 1982 incidents in Madrid and Brussels. The 25 October 1983 incident is representative of ANO's assassination campaign against diplomats from Jordan, Israel, Kuwait, the United Kingdom, and the United Arab Emigrates (UAE). The EgyptAir hijacking left sixty-one dead, including eight children, when a rescue mission in Malta gave the hijackers sufficient time to hurl three grenades at the passengers. The Karachi hijacking of Pan Am flight 73 also ended in bloodshed when the hijackers opened fire on the passengers (Mickolus, Sandler, and Murdock, 1989, vol. 2, pp. 452–7). At the trial, the five captured terrorists disclosed their intention to blow up the plane over an Israeli city – thus, this incident is a forerunner of 9/11. The attacks on the Rome and Vienna airports illustrate the brutality of ANO, as does the massacre of twenty-two worshipers at Istanbul's Neve Shalom synagogue.

Although secular, ANO was the predecessor to al-Qaida. ANO engineered the simultaneous attacks that later became the hallmark of al-Qaida. When not assassinating diplomats or PLO members, ANO engaged in "spectaculars" in order to produce grisly images that would stay in society's collective consciousness – for example, the victims lying beside an airport snack bar in the December 1985 attacks. ANO was not concerned about collateral damage and went for maximal casualties. Like al-Qaida, ANO was organized into different committees involving military operations, political doctrine, financing, and intelligence (Seale, 1992). ANO also engaged in attacks over a geographically dispersed region.

A distinguishing characteristic of ANO was that it was state-sponsored during the era of state sponsorship in the 1980s. Sponsors of ANO included Iraq (1974–1983), Syria (1981–1987), and Libya (1987–1992). ANO ended its operations about the time that al-Qaida began its operations.

Fundamentalist Terrorists – the "Fourth Wave"

The character of modern-day terrorism started to change as left-wing and secular terrorists began to be replaced by religious, fundamentalist terrorists. Since 1980, the number of religious-based groups has increased as a proportion of active terrorist groups: two of sixty-four groups in 1980; eleven of forty-eight groups in 1992; sixteen of forty-nine groups in 1994; and twenty-five of fifty-eight groups in 1995 (Hoffman, 1997, p. 3). The Palestinian terrorists were secular until the rise of Hamas and Hezbollah in the 1980s. The fighting communist organizations and the ethno-nationalist terrorists wanted to win the hearts and minds of a constituency, so they generally avoided casualties except those of individuals viewed as the establishment or the "enemy." The same was generally true of the PLO and PIRA. When mistakes occurred and collateral damage resulted, the secular terrorists often apologized.

Today, fundamentalist terrorist groups purposely seek out mass casualties, viewing anyone not with them as a legitimate target, as 9/11 sadly demonstrated. Rapoport (2004) referred to religious-based terrorism as the "fourth wave" and found Islam to be at the center of this terrorist trend. In fact, today's fundamentalist terrorists are members of all of the major religions (Hoffman, 1998; White, 2003); however, the primary force is Islam. The rise of fundamentalist terrorism is said to begin the fourth quarter of 1979, with two significant events: the takeover of the US embassy in Tehran by Islamic fundamentalist students on 4 November 1979, and the Soviet invasion of Afghanistan on 25 December 1979. Since the rise of fundamentalist terrorism, the proportion of incidents with deaths or injuries has increased greatly (Sandler and Enders, 2005). Enders and Sandler (2000) established that a significant rise in casualties from transnational terrorism can be traced to the fourth quarter of 1979. Quarters on either side of this quarter did not display such large increases in casualties. In recent years, an incident is almost 17 percentage points more likely to result in death or injury compared to the earlier era of leftist and ethno-nationalist terrorism.

Table 2.2. *Features Distinguishing Left-Wing from Fundamentalist Terrorists*

Left-wing Terrorists	Fundamentalists
• Maintain constituency	• Uninterested in constituency
• Symbolic target, minimal collateral damage	• General target, maximal collateral damage
• Speak for group	• Speak for God
• Influence a wider audience	• Not audience-oriented
• Pursue a political goal	• Act is a goal in itself
• Degrade enemy	• Demonize, dehumanize enemy
• Secular	• Religious
• Claim responsibility	• Often do not claim responsibility
• Nonsuicide missions	• Suicide missions as a mode of attack

There are many basic differences between the left-wing terrorists who dominated terrorism in the 1970s and early 1980s and the fundamentalist terrorists who have dominated terrorism in the 1990s and beyond. Table 2.2 indicates nine essential contrasts. Because they believe that they speak for God and view all nonbelievers as legitimate targets, the fundamentalists are not worried about alienating the public. For these terrorists, the deaths visited on their victims are sufficient payoff of their attacks. Thus, the fundamentalists do not issue advance warnings of their attacks so as to maximize the carnage. For the fundamentalists, the terrorist act is a sufficient end, particularly if it kills the nonbelievers, including women and children. Fundamentalist terrorists do not feel a need to claim responsibility for their terrorist acts, performed in the name of God. In their rhetoric, these fundamentalists justify their indiscriminate carnage by demonizing and dehumanizing nonbelievers. The differences shown in Table 2.2 result in the greater carnage per incident that characterizes recent years. As fundamentalists became the dominant terrorism influence, the number of transnational terrorist events fell, but their lethality rose (see charts in Chapter 3). Groups like al-Qaida and its associates are more interested in spectacular events with high casualty counts.

The fighting communist organizations ruled out suicide missions, while the fundamentalists have embraced them. Since 1968, a terrorist attack results in one fatality on average. A suicide attack, however, leads to thirteeen fatalities on average, because the suicide terrorists can choose to mount their attacks when casualties will be the greatest (Pape, 2003). In Figure 2.7, we display the number of suicide terrorist attacks – domestic and transnational – per quarter for the period 1981–2001. There were 32 suicide attacks in the 1980s, 109 in the 1990s, and 83 in 2000–2001. Attacks

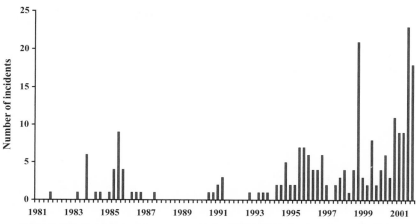

Figure 2.7. Suicide incidents: quarterly, 1981–2001. *Source:* Pape (2003).

in the 1980s were associated with Hezbollah's campaign to remove foreign troops from Lebanon. From the 1990s on, suicide attacks corresponded to campaigns by the Liberation Tigers of Tamil Eelam (LTTE) for a Tamil state in Sri Lanka, by the Kurdistan Workers' Party (PKK) for a Kurdish homeland, by al-Qaida for the United States to vacate the Saudi peninsula, by Kashimir rebels for India to leave Kashmir, and by Chechen rebels for Russia to grant Chechnya autonomy. The number of victims per quarter is displayed in Figure 2.8.

In a recent article, Pape (2003) argued that suicide attacks possess a strategic logic and are not the random acts of deranged individuals. Figure 2.7 shows the clustering of acts in apparent campaigns, which can be verified by looking at the raw data. According to Pape, terrorists resort to suicide missions because such attacks have induced moderate concessions from liberal democracies in the past (for example, the Israeli withdrawal from Lebanon in 1985 and the US troop withdrawal from Beirut in 1983, following the 23 October bombing of the US Marine barracks). *All suicide campaigns* have been *against liberal democracies*, where pressures are felt by elected officials to protect lives. Past concessions will encourage future campaigns as terrorists see that they pay.

The motivation of the terrorists who gave up their lives in suicide attacks is an important consideration. If terrorists are rational, as we believe, then there must be a rationality-based explanation for their willingness to make the ultimate sacrifice for the cause. To date, the best theoretical analysis is that of Azam (2005), who modeled suicide terrorists as altruists who highly value the well-being of the next generation. Their

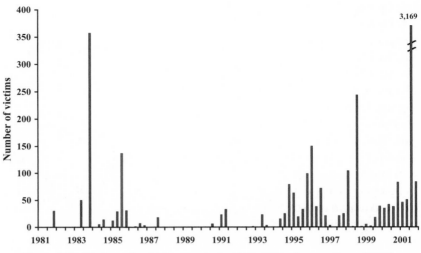

Figure 2.8. Victims of suicide: quarterly, 1981–2001. *Source*: Pape (2003).

act of sacrifice is an investment in a public good – the sought-after political change – that benefits the current and all future generations. Thus,
Azam characterized suicide bombings as an "intergenerational investment." Azam argued that, since education is usually positively correlated
with investment behavior, it is not surprising that a recent study (Krueger
and Maleckova, 2003) uncovered this correlation. From a policy viewpoint, the willingness of terrorists to make the ultimate trade-off means
that changes in policy that make some actions more difficult are unlikely
to influence suicide attacks.[11]

CONCLUDING REMARKS

Because of their openness and their duty to protect lives and property, liberal democracies are especially vulnerable to terrorist attacks. The recent
targeting of suicide terrorist attacks on liberal democracies underscores
this vulnerability. As liberal democracies are singled out for attack, they
must decide how much in civil liberties to trade away for increased security. Clearly, terrorism presents countries with a real dilemma; they are the

---

[11] That is, a policy-induced price rise need not alter a "corner" decision, because some
discrete changes in the constraint may have no effect. At a corner solution, the price
change would have to be of sufficient magnitude to change a choice variable. Corner
decisions or solutions involve nontangencies of the objective and the constraint at the
axis or a boundary point. See a fuller analysis in Chapter 5.

loser no matter how they respond. The final choice must try to minimize the losses, given society's preference for freedom versus security. In the new era of religious terrorism, when fundamentalist terrorists are bent on causing the greatest damage possible, the trade-offs are even grimmer. As attacks escalate, liberal democracies will sacrifice further freedoms as their constituencies become more willing to exchange liberties for a greater sense of security.

There are a number of unanswered questions that merit further analysis. For example, there is a need to quantify how much terrorism is exported from more autocratic regimes. Any export is motivated by the more conducive environment for terrorism in liberal democracies, including greater media coverage. Such exporting represents a negative externality. Another question concerns competition for political change among terrorist groups within the same country. Such groups may, nonetheless, have common (complementary) interests, because attacks by any group may weaken government resolve. Thus, competitive groups may form alliances so that an adversarial representation may not always capture the situation.

Terrorism represents an excellent area to which to apply economic tools – theoretical and empirical. Researchers need, however, to become familiar with stylized facts associated with modern-day campaigns if theoretical models are to inform policymakers. For example, the rise of fundamentalist terrorism alters the manner in which terrorists respond to counterterrorism measures. If, for example, terrorists are not interested in claiming responsibility, then some media bans may prove fruitless. Moreover, today's religious terrorists may view some logistical failures as successes if the body count is sufficiently high, which means that greater protective barriers may be required. Empirical models that include some countries with leftist terrorists and other countries with fundamentalist terrorists may give an average representation, not descriptive of either set of countries. This suggests that samples should be chosen carefully so that sample countries face *similar* terrorist threats.

THREE

Statistical Studies and Terrorist Behavior

Our eyes are wonderful at detecting associations in data because our brains are wired to simplify complicated patterns and relationships. Within a few seconds, you should be able to figure out that 25 is the next number in the sequence 1, 4, 9, 16. A computer program may need to make millions of calculations just to detect a pattern in the chess pieces that is readily visible to an accomplished player. The problem is that the patterns we perceive in the data may not meaningfully characterize its actual behavior. In the same way that our brains are able to "see" elaborate paintings in the clouds, we are sometimes able to "recognize" what are spurious relationships in economic data.

This chapter will present the time plots of various types of terrorist incidents, including bombings, assassinations, kidnappings, and skyjackings. Some features of the data will be clear even to the casual observer; for example, there is no decidedly upward trend in any of the incident series. However, many other features of the data may not be readily apparent, so that statistical analysis is required to draw inferences about the data. Toward this end, the chapter uses the basic tools of spectral analysis and intervention analysis to formally analyze data about terrorist incidents. Spectral analysis enables us to estimate the cyclical patterns in the various terrorist incident series, while intervention analysis allows us to measure the effects of important structural changes on the incident series. For example, using intervention analysis we can examine the effects on skyjackings of the introduction of metal detectors in airports, and the behavior of terrorists since the attacks of 9/11.

WHY USE STATISTICAL ANALYSIS?

Statistical analysis is a way of making precise mathematical statements about the interrelationships among variables and the behavior of variables over time. To illustrate some of the key points, consider the data in Figure 3.1 showing the annual number of sunspots from 1700 to 1995. The number of sunspots may, at first, seem to be quite erratic; however, closer examination reveals that there appears to be a cycle of approximately eleven years in *average* duration. A cycle can be as short as the eight years from 1761 to 1769 or as long as the cycle from 1787 to 1804. What you may not see is that the cycles are asymmetric. From the low part of the cycle (that is, from a trough), it takes about four years to reach a peak and then approximately seven years to fall back to a trough.

Scientists have long used the obvious patterns in the data to forecast sunspot activity. In fact, the regularities in this particular series are such that scientists have been able to predict future sunspot activity without fully understanding the type of nuclear reaction actually causing the sunspots to occur. This is easily done by noting that in 1995, the last observation in the data set, there were 17.5 sunspots (some began in 1994, and others were not completed by the end of 1995). The observed patterns in the data are sufficiently clear that you should be able to predict subsequent sunspot activity. Since 1995 seems to be at a trough, you might predict four successive increases in sunspot activity. Most people would predict about thirty-five sunspots for 1996, fifty-five for 1997, fifty-seven

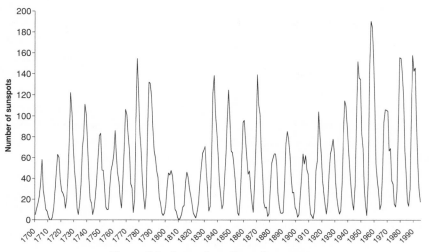

Figure 3.1. Annual number of sunspots.

for 1998, and fifty-nine for 1999. Thereafter, most people would predict seven subsequent declines.

Of course, the forecasts will not be exact, since the series is not perfectly predictable. Some of the peaks are clearly higher than others, and the number of years from one peak to the next changes over time. For example, the first peak (58 spots) occurred in 1705, the second (63 spots) occurred in 1717, and the third (122 spots) occurred in 1727. Even though such forecasts will contain errors, the forecasts made using the observed pattern in the data should be far better than those obtained using some other method. What if you wanted to make very long-term forecasts, such as predicting the number of sunspots that will occur in the year 2400? A reasonable guess is that the number will be just equal to the sample average of fifty sunspots per year. Since the pattern does not follow a precise eleven-year cycle, a long-term forecast will not benefit by using the patterns in the data or the current value of the number of sunspots.

The discussion points out the following:

1. *An observed pattern in the data can be used for forecasting.* If sunspots have a fairly regular cycle every eleven years, this eleven-year pattern can be projected into the future.
2. *Short-term forecasts are likely to be more accurate than long-term forecasts.* Since a series will not be perfectly regular, the cumulated errors will mean that long-term forecasts will be associated with rather large errors.
3. *Mathematical methods can aid simple observation.* Some people might not recognize the fact that there are typically four years of increasing sunspot activity followed by seven years of decreasing activity. Mathematical methods applied to data (that is, statistical methods) can often find patterns that are not readily apparent. Since the movements in the data are somewhat random, any description of the data and any predictions of the future are necessarily probabilistic. Statistics is the branch of mathematics dealing with the calculation of such probabilities.
4. *A series can be forecast without knowing why the variable changes.* As mentioned, you do not need to be an astronomer or a nuclear physicist to forecast sunspots. In the same way, we do not need to know all the details about the way terrorists operate to make predictions about their behavior.
5. *Our eyes can "see" patterns not actually present in the data.* Notice that the peaks in 1705 and 1717 are low relative to those during subsequent periods. Similarly, the peaks in 1804 and 1816 are low,

as are the peaks that occur in 1883, 1893, and 1909. Do you see the episodes of relatively low sunspot activity occurring every 100 years? In addition to the eleven-year cycles, there is a second type of cycle with a duration of 100 years or so. In actuality, there is no evidence to indicate that such cycles are real; instead, they are the result of flukes in the data that appear real. This points out the need to use statistical methods to verify (or refute) patterns suggested by casual inspection of the data.

These ideas are important for understanding the way in which social scientists apply statistical methods to the study of terrorism. In the next section, we will present some time-series data on the incidence of transnational terrorism. Just as in the sunspot data, the patterns in the time series, such as skyjackings, bombings, or assassinations, can be investigated. The time-series plot of any such series can be used to characterize the way it behaves over time for forecasting purposes. It is especially important to keep in mind that we do not need to know the actual causes of the terrorists' behavior in order to estimate their behavior. Remember that "eyeballing" the data may not reveal the actual patterns present in a series. Without a formal statistical model, such casual inspection may "reveal" nonexistent patterns.

THE DATA

The data that we use to analyze transnational terrorist incidents is drawn from *International Terrorism: Attributes of Terrorist Events* (ITERATE). ITERATE uses information from the print media to construct a chronology of transnational terrorist events. ITERATE relies on a host of sources for its information, including the Associated Press, United Press International, Reuters tickers, the Foreign Broadcast Information Service (FBIS) *Daily Reports*, and major US newspapers. Mickolus (1982) first developed ITERATE for the period running from 1968 through 1977. The year 1968 corresponds to the rise in transnational terrorism resulting from the 1967 Arab-Israeli war. This data set now covers 1968–2003 (Mickolus, Sandler, Murdock, and Flemming, 2004). Unless otherwise noted, the time series used in this book run through the end of 2003. The easiest way to explain the nature of the data is to consider the following excerpts drawn from the chronology by Mickolus, Sandler, and Murdock (1989, pp. 297, 300).

November 4–5, 1985 – **BELGIUM** – In early morning hours of November 4, a bomb exploded at the Brussels-Lambert Bank. Prior to the blast, a car with a loudspeaker warned occupants to leave. One night watchman was shot in the arm when he emerged from the building. Property damage was described as extensive. Around 11 A.M., a second bomb caused extensive damage to the Societe Generale in Charleroi. Leaflets of the Communist Combatant Cells (CCC) left at the bank gave the occupants 30 minutes to leave prior to the explosion. One person was slightly injured and damage was extensive.

On November 5, bombs exploded at the Manufacturers Hanover Bank in Charleroi and at the Kredietbank in Louvain. Damage was extensive, but no injuries were reported.

In a seven-page letter sent to the AGENCE FRANCE-PRESSE office in Brussels, the CCC claimed credit for the four bombs at banks, which they described as "major havens for the financial oligarchy in this country."

In December 1985 four alleged CCC members – Pierre Carette, Bertrand Sassoye, Didier Chevolet, and Pascale Vandegeerde – were arrested. The four were suspected of being the ringleaders of the CCC. On January 14, 1986, they were charged with the attempted murder of the night watchman at the Brussels-Lambert Bank.

November 5, 1985 – **GREECE** *–* Police discovered a bomb in a suspicious-looking cloth bag planted between the first and second floors of an Athens building at 8 Xenophon Street. The building housed the offices of Trans World Airlines. Bomb experts removed the bomb and detonated it without mishap.

November 5, 1985 – **USSR** *–* In Moscow, Mexican diplomat Manuel Portilla Quevedo and his domestic servant were found murdered in Quevedo's apartment. Quevedo had been shot in the neck, and the servant had been beaten to death. Quevedo had given frequent news interviews.

November 5, 1985 – **PERU** *–* A booby-trapped car exploded in front of the US Citibank in the San Isidro neighborhood of Lima. The 10:30 P.M. blast damaged the bank's doors and neighboring buildings but caused no injuries. Slogans painted on the bank's walls attributed the attack to the Tupac Amaru Revolutionary Movement (MRTA).

November 5, 1985 – **SOUTH KOREA** *–* In Seoul, 14 students armed with incendiary devices occupied the American chamber of commerce for two and a half hours before being overpowered and arrested by police. One of those arrested – Kim Yong-hui – told police that the students had originally planned to occupy the US embassy but changed plans owing to the tight security. The police were seeking three others connected to the incident.

November 6, 1985 – **PUERTO RICO** *–* US Army Maj. Michael S. Snyder, 37, was seriously injured by two .32 caliber pistol shots. The incident occurred in San Juan at 7:50 A.M. while Snyder was riding to work at Fort Buchanan. Two gunmen on a motorcycle pulled beside Snyder, who was on a motorscooter, and fired two shots hitting Snyder in the hip and side. He was listed in stable condition following surgery.

At 11 A.M. a self-proclaimed spokesman phoned the Spanish news agency EFE and took credit on behalf of Los Macheteros. A second anonymous caller claimed credit on behalf of the Volunteers for Revolution in Puerto Rico.

November 6, 1985 – **ARGENTINA** – At 1:30 A.M., a bomb damaged the Xerox Corporation branch office at the corner of Libertad Avenue and Jaramillo Street in Buenos Aires. Windows throughout the seven-story building were shattered. No injuries were reported.

November 6, 1985 – **EGYPT** – According to Interior Minister Ahmad Rushdi, security forces thwarted an attempt by four Libyan suicide commandos to assassinate former Libyan prime minister Abdul Hamid Bakoush and former Libyan cabinet official Muhammad al-Muqaryaf. The four would-be assassins drove across the western desert after entering the country from Libya on November 2. From the time that they entered, security forces put the men under surveillance. The assassination was planned for November 6 at the King Marriott Restaurant, 19 kilometers west of Alexandria. At the time of the planned assassination, Bakoush dined with a group of Libyan exiles; al-Muqaryaf was out of the country. Security forces moved in and arrested the four assailants – Yusuf al-Madani (a corporal in the Libyan Jamahariyah security organization), Muhriz Muhammad 'Umar (a corporal in the same organization), Muhammad Siddiq (a sergeant in the organization), and Saqr 'Abdallah Maydun (an official in the organization) – as they sped towards the restaurant in their Toyota. Some reports said that a short-lived gun battle erupted between the security forces and the assassins, but no casualties were reported. The security forces seized four machine guns, four pistols, four silencers, eight hand grenades, and a supply of ammunition. In November 1984, another Libyan-backed attempt on Bakoush was thwarted by Egyptian security. Minister Rushdi warned of six other commando squads trained in Libya that may be sent to Egypt. According to the assassins' confession, each was paid 1.5 million Libyan dinars to assassinate the two men. On November 11, the four were charged with attempted murder.

There are several noteworthy features of the descriptions of these incidents.

1. Despite the perception in the popular press that there is relatively little terrorism, many terrorist incidents occur in a single day. Although there were five separate incidents on November 5 and another five on November 6, there were thirty-two incidents on 24 June 1993. A skyjacking or an incident with substantial property damage and many victims will be reported on the nightly news. Other intense incidents will be reported in mainstream newspapers; however, "less newsworthy" incidents will escape the attention of the general public.

2. At times, it may not be clear if an incident is a simple crime or an act of terrorism. Despite the first incident in Belgium, terrorists do not typically leave any hard evidence proving their involvement. The bomb found outside the Trans World Airlines (TWA) office and the assassination of the Mexican diplomat and his servant may

have had nothing to do with political motives. Nevertheless, anyone constructing a complete set of terrorist incidents must make a judgment call regarding the second and third incidents.

3. The assignment of responsibility for a particular act to a specific terrorist group may be difficult. Sometimes, no one takes responsibility for having committed a terrorist act. In other cases, such as the shooting of Major Snyder in Puerto Rico, multiple groups claim credit for the same act.

4. In most instances, the date and location of a terrorist incident are recorded in ITERATE. When possible, the various attack modes (for example, bombings, assassinations, skyjackings, and shootings), the number of deaths and casualties, and other key incident characteristics are recorded.[1]

5. Some of the incidents are far more logistically complex than others. Most incidents require preparation, funds, some form of weaponry, and personnel willing to undertake a risky act. However, some incidents require far greater resources than others. Placing a bomb outside the TWA office in Athens took some careful planning: it was necessary to acquire and assemble the various parts of the bomb, gain access to the building, and plant the device without being detected. Nevertheless, it must have been far more difficult to plan the failed assassination attempt on Ahmad Rushdi and to obtain the necessary equipment, weapons, funding, and personnel.

Coders use the descriptions of the various events to construct time-series data for forty key variables common to all transnational terrorist incidents from the first quarter of 1968 (denoted by 1968:Q1) to the fourth quarter of 2003 (denoted by 2003:Q4). Coding consistency for ITERATE events data was achieved by applying identical criteria and maintaining continuity among coders through the use of overlapping coders and monitors. ITERATE excludes guerrilla attacks on military targets of an occupying force and all terrorist incidents associated with declared wars or major military interventions.

For our purposes, the key variables in ITERATE are given in Table 3.1. The time and place of each incident must be known, along with the type of incident. ITERATE classifies incidents into the twenty-five different categories shown in Table 3.2. For the period 1968–2003, there were 12,559 total transnational terrorist incidents recorded. You can clearly see that

---

[1] ITERATE includes additional files, called HOSTAGE and SKYJACKING, containing detailed information on these two important incident types. The file called FATE contains information concerning the outcome of the various incidents and the fate of the terrorists.

Table 3.1. *Key Variables in ITERATE*

Incident Characteristics
　　Date of start of incident: year, month, day
　　Location start: country
　　Location end: country
　　Type of incident
Victim Characteristics
　　Number of victims
　　Nationality of victims
Life and Property Losses
　　Total individuals wounded
　　Total individuals killed
　　Terrorists killed
　　Types of weapons used

Table 3.2. *Number of Incidents by Type (1968–2003): ITERATE Data*

Code	Incident Type	Number of Incidents
1	Kidnapping	1,186
2	Barricade and hostage seizure	178
3	Occupation of facilities without hostage seizure	76
4	Letter or parcel bombing	441
5	Incendiary bombing, arson, Molotov cocktail	1,017
6	Explosive bombing	4,003
7	Armed attack involving missiles	48
8	Armed attack – other, including mortars and bazookas	1,322
9	Aerial hijacking	362
10	Takeover of a nonaerial means of transportation	58
11	Assassination, murder	1,078
12	Sabotage, not involving explosives or arson	32
13	Pollution, including chemical and biological agents	25
14	Nuclear-related weapons attack	1
15	Threat with no subsequent terrorist action	1,120
16	Theft, break-in of facilities	111
17	Conspiracy to commit terrorist action	278
18	Hoax (for example, claiming a nonexistent bomb)	318
19	Other actions	402
20	Sniping at buildings, other facilities	130
21	Shoot-out with police	46
22	Arms smuggling	92
23	Car bombing	182
24	Suicide car bombing	27
25	Suicide bombing	26
	Cumulative Total:	12,559

7,066 bombings (that is, the sum of types 4, 5, 6, 7, 8, 23, 24, and 25) account for more than half of the incidents. Since logistically complex incidents utilize far greater resources, they tend to be fewer in number. ITERATE also reports information about the victims: for example, the number and nationalities of the victims are recorded, along with the number of people killed and wounded.

Before proceeding further, we need to point out that ITERATE has some shortcomings, since it relies on the world's print and electronic media for its information. As such, ITERATE is better at chronicling the actions of terrorists than at recording those of the authorities. ITER-ATE picks up *newsworthy* transnational terrorist incidents, so there is some bias, which must be recognized. Given the steady increase in the severity of terrorism, some incidents (for example, the unexploded bomb in Greece on 5 November 1985, and the bombing of the Xerox office in Argentina on 6 November 1985) might not be reported in today's newspapers. Thus, ITERATE might suggest that certain types of terrorist events have declined simply because they are no longer reported. Despite these difficulties, ITERATE is suited to a wide range of empirical tasks.

THE BEHAVIOR OF THE TERRORISM TIME SERIES

As we did with the sunspot data, it is instructive to plot the time path of the various terrorist incident types. Although ITERATE reports the specific date for each incident, the essential features of the data are easier to visualize by using quarterly totals. Figure 3.2 shows the time paths of the quarterly totals of all transnational incidents (ALL) and bombings (BOMBINGS) contained in ITERATE. The solid line represents the ALL series, and the dashed line represents the BOMBINGS series. An examination of Figure 3.2 suggests that there are periods during which the number of incidents is quite high and others during which it is low. For example, the number of incidents generally increased from 1968 to the early 1970s. There were forty incidents in the first quarter of 1968. By contrast, the average was ninety-three incidents per quarter from the first quarter of 1970 through the end of 1975. In the early 1980s, there was another upward surge lasting until 1987. Terrorism remained low until the early 1990s, when a three-year wave of terrorism began. The number of incidents then fell until the late 1990s. The shaded area contains incidents that have occurred since 9/11. The post-9/11 period seems to be characterized by an upward drift (possibly due to al-Qaida) that actually began in the first quarter of 2000.

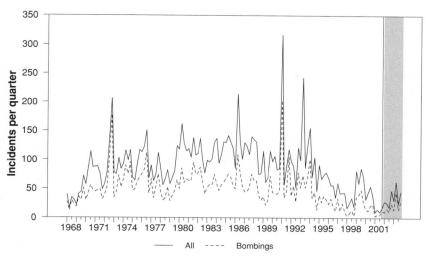

Figure 3.2. All incidents and bombings.

The seeming persistence of high-terrorism versus low-terrorism periods is helpful to social scientists trying to predict the behavior of terrorists. If any theory of terrorism is to be successful, it must capture the reasons why incidents tend to cluster. Moreover, the fact that terrorism seems to wax and wane is useful to forecasters. When the number of incidents is currently high, the number of incidents during the next period is also likely to be high. Similarly, when there is a current lull in terrorism, the number of incidents during the successive period will also tend to be low. Thus, the number of incidents during the current period can help forecast the number of incidents in the near future.

The BOMBINGS series shown in Figure 3.2 consists of various types of bombings and armed (explosive) attacks (incident types $4 + 5 + 6 + 7 + 8 + 23 + 24 + 25$ in Table 3.2). This series seems to track the total number of incidents reasonably well in that the two tend to rise and fall together. Over the years, BOMBINGS have been the most common incident type, accounting for 56.3% of all incidents. During many periods, BOMBINGS account for far more than half of the overall total. However, the large spikes in the ALL series are generally due to spikes in BOMBINGS, which account for a large share of all incidents. Terrorists can quickly increase the number of bombings, since a typical bombing incident is not logistically complex – a relatively small investment of terrorists' resources can set off a spate of bombings – so that sharp increases in bombings can occur at a relatively low cost. By contrast, it is far more costly for terrorists

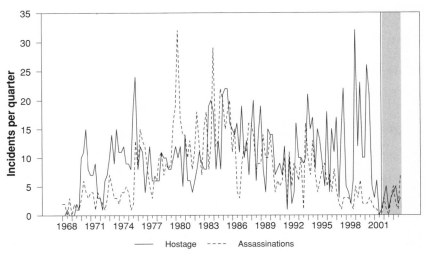

Figure 3.3. Hostage takings and assassinations.

to sharply increase incident types such as kidnappings, assassinations, and aerial hijackings (skyjackings). An interesting change in the proportion of bombings appears to begin at the end of 1999. A close examination of the figure reveals that the proportion of bombings relative to the total number of incidents has increased sharply since then.

Hostage Takings and Assassinations

Figure 3.3 shows the time series of assassinations (incident type 11) and various types of hostage takings (incident types $1 + 2 + 9 + 10$). Assassinations (ASSASSINATIONS) account for about 8% of all incidents, and the constructed hostage-taking series (HOSTAGE) accounts for just over 14% of all incidents. Over the very long run, the two series seem to move together. Both start from very low levels in the late 1960s and fluctuate in the neighborhood of eight incidents per quarter in the middle to late 1970s. Notice that the ASSASSINATIONS series begins to experience a long and gradual decline in the 1990s, but the drop in HOSTAGE incidents in 1999 is quite dramatic.

Assassinations and hostage incidents are quite resource-intensive. Nearly all assassinations and many hostage incidents require substantial amounts of planning. Victims and locations need to be chosen far in advance of the actual incident. In the case of the Mexican ambassador and his servant who were found murdered on 5 November 1985, someone had to acquire access to the apartment at a time when the ambassador was home. The timing had to be such that there was no one capable of thwarting the killing or preventing escape. Similarly, the shooting of Major Snyder might have been spontaneous, or the would-be assassins might have known that the major always rode to work on a scooter around 8 o'clock in the morning. The mechanics of staging an assassination or of obtaining and holding victims can also be quite complex. In comparison to most bombings, terrorists put themselves in great jeopardy during an assassination attempt, a kidnapping, or when holding hostages. These two incident types are logistically complex in that they require large amounts of the terrorists' time, personnel, and weaponry.

Since both kinds of incidents are similarly sophisticated, both understandably display the same long-run behavior. During short time spans, the two series can, however, move in very different ways. Notice the sharp jump in HOSTAGE incidents in 1970 and the sharp decline in 1999. During the 1990s, HOSTAGE incidents increased, while assassinations declined. A full theory of terrorism must be able both to explain the similarities in the long-run behavior of the series and to account for the discrepancies in the short-run patterns.

Threats and Hoaxes

On 26 September 2001, a caller, alleged to be Adam Ray Elliott, used his cell phone to threaten that the *jihad* would destroy the US Post Office in Suwannee County, Florida. The next day, the same caller indicated that a bomb and other explosives had been placed at the base of the Buckman Bridge in Duval County, Florida. Even though *jihad* is unlikely to ever be concerned about a post office or bridge in rural Florida, the authorities must respond to such threats and hoaxes. On 21 November 2003, Virgin Atlantic flight VS010 headed for London was rerouted back to New York when a passenger found a note indicating that there was a bomb aboard. There is no question that the hoax had to be taken seriously, despite the disruption in the passengers' travel schedules. On a larger scale, airport closings arising from terrorist threats are relatively costless for the terrorists, yet cause major disruptions to air passengers around the world. Government agencies charged with protecting the public must respond to all such incidents. After the fact, a threat or a hoax is nothing but a scare, but until the incident is resolved, the outcome is never clear.

Figure 3.4 shows how the quarterly totals of threats (incident type 15) plus hoaxes (incident type 18) have behaved over time. Notice the dramatic spikes of sixty-three and sixty-four incidents in 1986:Q1 and 1991:Q1, respectively. Since threats and hoaxes (denoted by the

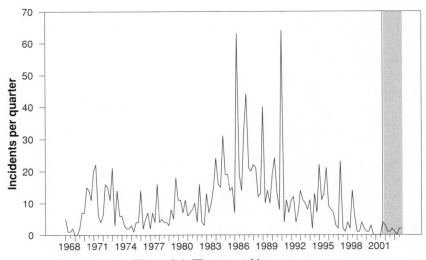

Figure 3.4. Threats and hoaxes.

THREATS series) entail few resources, such dramatic changes can occur
at the will of terrorists. However, for all practical purposes, threats and
hoaxes have virtually disappeared as a major weapon for transnational
terrorists. There are several causes for the decline. Remember that ITER-
ATE records specific events; the very general threats issued by groups
such as al-Qaida are often too vague to be recorded as an incident. Moreover, in mid-1996 the FBIS's *Daily Reports* became unavailable to ITER-
ATE coders, so that threats and hoaxes chronicled in the *Daily Reports*,
but not in other sources, are now missed. Another reason for the decline
is that the media are now less interested in reporting a threat or a hoax
unless it turns out to have serious economic consequences. Over time,
individuals have become less sensitive to reports of a small bomb or an
unspecified attack; thus, some transnational terrorist groups feel little
need to employ such tactics. Groups such as al-Qaida have been steadily
intensifying their activities by conducting attacks likely to result in large-
scale property damage and deaths. As a result, most threats and hoaxes
come from isolated individuals, such as the perpetrator of the Florida incidents, with no connection to a transnational terrorist group. Such domestic
incidents are not covered by ITERATE.

Deaths and Casualties

Obviously, some bombings are more lethal than others. Many skyjacking incidents end with no casualties; the hostages are released, and the

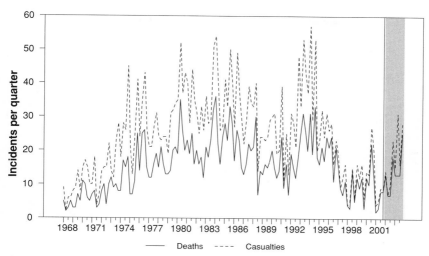

Figure 3.5. Incidents with deaths and casualties.

terrorists surrender. Others, including the skyjackings of 9/11, may involve great carnage. Hence, instead of looking at incidents by type, it is useful to look at the severity of the various incidents. The solid line in Figure 3.5 shows the time series of the number of incidents involving one or more deaths (the DEATH series). The dashed line shows the number of incidents with at least one casualty. An incident is classified as a casualty incident (CAS) if it involves at least one death or one wounded individual. Notice that both series rose fairly steadily from 1968 until early 1980. In the 1980s, the CAS series fluctuated around a mean of thirty incidents per quarter, and the DEATH series fluctuated around a mean of twenty incidents per quarter. For the 1980s, the exact proportion of CAS incidents involving deaths was 61.4%. The early 1990s saw a jump in both series. Since the jump in CAS was much larger than the jump in DEATH, the proportion of DEATH to CAS incidents actually fell. However, in the mid 1990s both incident types began a decline that lasted until the end of the decade. From this period on, there is little difference between CAS and DEATH because most incidents with a casualty involved a death, implying that the typical incident has been getting more lethal.

In the first quarter of 2000, both series turned upward. The heightened severity of the typical CAS incident is still clear. The increase in CAS is primarily due to an increase in the number of incidents with deaths. Another way to make the same point is to consider Figure 3.6, where the time-series plot shows the proportion of incidents with deaths as a proportion of all incidents. Until the early 1970s, only 9% of the terrorist

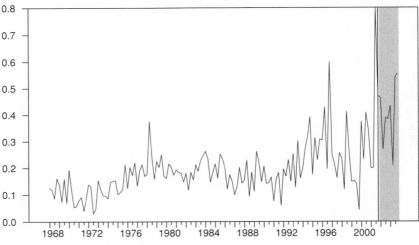

Figure 3.6. The proportion of lethal incidents.

incidents in ITERATE involved a death. From the late 1970s through the early 1990s, DEATH incidents were about 18% of all incidents. The proportion ratcheted up to 28% in the mid-1990s and ratcheted up again in the late 1990s. The evidence is consistent with the notion that terrorists are continuing to escalate the level of violence. As we become familiar with terrorism, terrorists need to become more daring and sensational in order to attract media attention. Moreover, the rise of religious fundamentalism, discussed in Chapter 2, is associated with an increase in the number of terrorist incidents with deaths and injuries.

Terrorist groups within Israel have also stepped up the number of deadly incidents. Figure 3.7 shows the number of suicide bombings in Israel for the period 2000–2003. Since these are domestic incidents, they are not reported in the ITERATE totals. After a lull in the late 1990s, the number of suicide bombings jumped sharply with the decline of the peace process.

SPECTRAL ANALYSIS: THE ANALYSIS OF CYCLES

Time-series analysis traditionally breaks down the movements in a variable into three separate parts:

Trend. The trend refers to long-run movements in the series, which is the portion of a time series that you would predict far into the future.

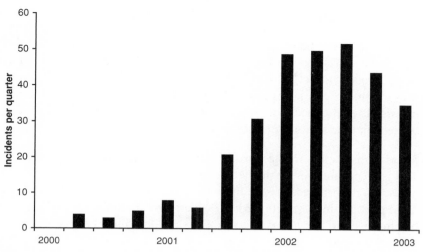

Figure 3.7. Suicide bombings in Israel. *Source:* Israeli Ministry of Foreign Affairs [http:// www.mfa.gov.il/mfa/home.asp].

Of course, what constitutes the long run for one data series may be very different from that for a second series. The long-run movements for the sunspot data might be a fifty- or hundred-year span. For terrorism, the long run is necessarily shorter. For example, beginning in 1993, it appears that the ALL series (see Figure 3.2) exhibited a decidedly downward trend that can be associated with the decline in state-sponsored terrorism discussed in Chapter 2.

Short-run dynamics. Any series will temporarily diverge from its long-run level or trend. Notice how the ALL series shows a positive jump at the end of 1998 and seems to remain away from the trend for several quarters. This type of movement is considered to be part of the short-run dynamics of the series. These short-run movements are often called irregular or cyclical.

One series might deviate from its long-run mean or trend for a substantial period of time, while another might revert back very quickly. We would hope that the lulls in terrorism are long-lasting and that high-terrorism periods are short-lived. If the nature of the short-run movements is known, the observed discrepancies from trend can be helpful in forecasting. A crucial issue for social scientists is to examine the persistence of the various terrorism series from their mean or trend. Knowledge of the persistence in a series can be helpful in predicting the number of future incidents.

For some series, the short-run movements can be quite regular. For the sunspot data, cycles are clearly present even though they are not perfectly regular. A plot of daily temperatures for Alabama would show that the highest temperatures always occur in August and the lowest in February, thus giving rise to a regular cycle. If there are cycles in the terrorism series, they are not as regular as those for sunspots or temperatures. Although not visible to the casual observer, as we will discuss, there are reasons to believe that the various terrorist series have regular cyclical components.

Noise. Noise refers to the portion of a series that cannot be predicted. This is the smallest error that a forecaster can make.

Do not be dismayed if you cannot see the separate trend, irregular, and noise portions in the terrorism series. Statistical methods usually have to be employed to decompose a variable's time path into these constituent parts. Also, many people are under the misconception that the trend portion of a series is a straight line; in fact, none of the terrorism series display a linear trend. For some series, the trend is nonlinear, and for others, there is no clear trend. Whenever the form of the nonlinearity is unknown, statistical methods can be applied to capture the long-run movements in the data. To be a bit more formal, let y_t denote the number of incidents occurring during some time period t. For example, there were six transnational skyjackings in 1981:Q1 and three in 1981:Q2. For the skyjacking series, we can thus write $y_{1981:Q1} = 6$ and $y_{1981:Q2} = 3$. If we use this notation, the three constituent parts can be written as:

$$y_t = \text{trend} + \text{cyclical} + \text{noise}. \tag{1}$$

Different time series display each of these components to different degrees. A series with a decided trend tends to evolve smoothly so that its long-run movements are predictable. The sunspot data is clearly cyclical in nature. The HOSTAGE and ASSASSINATIONS series are highly volatile in that they contain large noise components. Such series are especially difficult to forecast.

A standard procedure for estimating the trend in a series is to fit a polynomial time trend to the data. Everyone is familiar with a linear time trend, and most people are aware that a quadratic time trend looks like a parabola. None of the terrorist series displays the type of sustained upward trend often implied by the media. Based on the number of incidents, the claim that terrorism is steadily increasing is clearly false. Thus, a linear trend is inadequate to characterize the trend in terrorism. However, a high-order polynomial trend is capable of mimicking a wide variety of functional forms. The estimation methodology involves fitting a polynomial trend in time (t) and adding successive trend terms (for example, t, t^2, t^3) until the associated coefficient is no longer statistically significant.[2] In Sandler and Enders (2004), we formally investigated the nature of trends in the various incident series and found that they were either nonlinear or nonexistent.

Cycles in terrorism can be attributed to various factors that result in the bunching of incidents on a regular basis. To the extent that these factors affect various terrorist groups concurrently, there will be wavelike patterns in the overall time series. Copycat effects are one such reason for the clustering of events. A successful event can induce others to copy the attack until the authorities devise the means and acquire the resources necessary to develop effective countermeasures. As the new antiterrorism measures become increasingly successful, new terrorist attacks will be inhibited. Terrorists learn of the government's innovation and begin to develop other types of attack modes. Similarly, other governments will incorporate the successful antiterrorism measures into their own plans. Thus, there can be extended periods when there is relatively little terrorism. During such times terrorists can make new plans, recruit new members, and acquire weapons and funding. This rebuilding of the terrorists' resources can occur until an event occurs that precipitates another round of attacks.

Economies of scale can induce particular terrorist groups to bunch their attacks. When terrorists are able to spread the fixed costs of planning and executing a campaign over a large number of incidents, the resulting economies of scale reduce per-incident costs. The large number of suicide bomb-jackets captured from Saddam Hussein's cache is testimony to the ability to produce the weapons of terrorism in large quantities. On 29 March 2004, *USA Today* reported a story with the headline: *Second Uzbek explosion rips bomb-making factory*:

TASHKENT, Uzbekistan (AP) – A series of bombings and attacks linked to Islamic militants, including the first known suicide missions in Uzbekistan, killed 19 people and injured 26, officials said Monday in this nation closely allied with Washington in the war on terrorism.

---

[2] In much of the applied time-series literature, a variable is said to be "statistically significant" if the researcher can be 95% confident that the variable's estimated regression coefficient differs from zero.

Bomb-making factories can turn out a large number of explosive devices, all produced at the same time. The risks involved with obtaining the materials and plans for making a single bomb are similar to those for making many bombs at once. The unidentified terrorist group in the story was able to create, plant, and explode a number of bombs at various times and places around Uzbekistan.

Faria (2003) develops a theoretical cat-and-mouse model of the attack-counterattack process, where the government has many objectives, including the goal of maximizing national security by investing in enforcement. A key feature of the model is that terrorists have a budget constraint, so they cannot sustain a campaign indefinitely. Terrorists utilize weapons, financial resources, and personnel to plan and stage attacks. Thus, when enforcement is high, terrorists find it desirable to replenish material and financial resources, and to recruit personnel. Once there is a lull in terrorism, the public's attention begins to wane, and there is little pressure on politicians to undertake new antiterrorism initiatives. In response to the electorate's new concerns, politicians direct their efforts toward other social ills and away from antiterrorism policies. Terrorists view these lax times as ideal for launching a new round of attacks. The cycle is completed once the public demands a government crackdown on terrorists.

Enders and Sandler (1999) and Enders, Parise, and Sandler (1992) argue that each kind of attack mode has its own characteristic cycle. Since BOMBINGS and THREATS require relatively few resources and can be initiated quickly, they should have short cycles. On the other hand, logistically complex events (e.g., skyjackings, hostage takings, and assassinations) are expected to have long cycles. The countermeasures taken by the authorities against such events may take a long time to develop. Although the business community has seen relatively little cyber terrorism, we would expect such a process to result in rather long cycles. For example, the Technical Support Working Group (2003) is developing cyber security projects that[3]

focus on preventing or mitigating threats to computer networks vital to defense and transportation.... The complexity and sophistication of information technologies and widespread integration in other infrastructures increases the likelihood of unforeseen vulnerabilities. Unprecedented opportunities are created for criminals, terrorists, and hostile foreign nation-states to steal money or proprietary data, invade private records, conduct industrial espionage, or cause vital infrastructure elements to cease operations.

[3] This information was obtained from their web page: [http://www.tswg.gov/tswg/ip/ip_ma.htm].

Such technological improvements necessarily take a long time to develop and innovate. The appropriate hardware and software need to be developed, tested, and installed on the computer networks of businesses and government agencies. Of course, once cyber security is enhanced, we would expect terrorists to try to thwart its effects. Once terrorists develop the means to circumvent the new technology, the cycle would begin to repeat itself as the authorities begin a new round of enhanced cyber security. Therefore, a testable hypothesis concerns the length of the cycles in simple events relative to complex events.

A number of variants of this theme have appeared in the literature. For example, Feichtinger, Hartl, Kort, and Novak (2001) develop a model demonstrating the interrelationship between tourism and terrorism. The cycle begins when a tourist area develops its infrastructure to a level sufficient to accommodate large numbers of visitors. Hotels, restaurants, a major airport, and reasonable local transport all characterize most of the popular tourist destinations. As the area increases in popularity, it becomes more attractive to terrorists seeking media attention. Once terrorists target the area, tourists flock to alternative destinations. There are literally hundreds of beaches with white sand and warm water in areas with a great climate. When tourists turn to these alternative destinations, investment in tourism falls. No new hotels are built or remodeled in an area with already high vacancy rates. At this point, the area is no longer strategically important for terrorists, and the cycle repeats itself.

Spectral analysis is a statistical tool ideally suited to study cyclical phenomena. The method entails removing the trend (that is, the possible nonlinear trend) from an incident series. The resulting detrended series is then examined to uncover any underlying cycles. Specifically, the researcher estimates the cyclical behavior of a series by fitting sine and cosine terms to the detrended data. These trigonometric terms are able to capture the regular increases and decreases in a series. This procedure seems perfectly natural for the sunspot data, since the series looks like a sine (or cosine) wave. Given that terrorists randomize their behavior, the cycles in the terrorist series will not be as pronounced as those in the sunspot data. Hence, in comparison to the sunspot data, a large number of sine and cosine terms with various amplitudes and frequencies must be used to capture the cyclical nature of the terrorism series. The frequency of a cycle indicates how often the cycle repeats itself. Series with long durations will have most of their variance explained by low frequencies, and series with short cycles will have most of their variance explained by high frequencies. You might find it helpful to think of the pitch of a singer's voice. Very

Table 3.3. *Cyclical Properties of the Terrorist Time Series*

Series	Frequency	Period (in years)	Percent[a]
THREATS	36.70	0.98	21.3
BOMBINGS	5.60	6.43	29.1
HOSTAGE	4.76	7.56	35.2
ASSASSINATIONS	8.96	4.02	37.6
DEATH	3.64	9.88	43.6
CAS	4.20	8.56	43.8
SKYJACKING	5.04	7.13	46.4

[a] The proportion of a series' total variance accounted for by the lowest 15 percent of the frequencies.

high-frequency components will dominate a soprano's voice, and very low-frequency components will dominate the voice of a basso. The point is that very short cycles (high pitch) are high-frequency phenomena, and very long cycles (low pitch) are low-frequency phenomena.

The precise methodology used in spectral analysis is not reported here. Interested readers can consult Sandler and Enders (2004) for the details. Here, our goal is to update Sandler and Enders (2004) so as to use post-9/11 data. For each series, Table 3.3 reports the proportion of its total variance accounted for by the lowest 15% of the frequencies (in percent). Because a series with a long cycle should have most of its variation explained by the low frequencies, we expect the entries in Table 3.3 to be high for the logistically complex series. The table also reports the most significant frequency and the implied period (in years) of the cycle. The series are listed in descending order according to the entry in the percent column.

Notice that the lowest 15% of the frequencies explain only 21.3% of the THREATS series. This is consistent with the notion that threats and hoaxes are relatively simple to conduct and use small amounts of terrorists' resources. The most important frequency, 36.70, implies that the length of the cycle is about one year (about 36 cycles in 36 years). Just 29.1% of the variance of BOMBINGS is explained by the lowest frequencies, while almost 44% of the variance of the DEATH and CAS series is explained by the lowest frequencies. Moreover, the most important frequencies for each of these two series are much lower than those of BOMBINGS. Skyjackings display longer cycles than threats and hoaxes, bombings, and assassinations. The lowest 15% of the frequencies account for 46.4% of the variance of skyjackings, which is more than for the other series displayed. As expected, the low frequencies also explain a relatively large proportion of the HOSTAGE and ASSASSI-NATIONS series, which is consistent with the notion that these incident types are more complicated to stage and execute than THREATS and BOMBINGS.

INTERVENTION ANALYSIS

If you turn back to Figure 3.2, you can see that the ALL and BOMBINGS series seem to move in tandem, which should not be surprising, since bombings are the favorite attack mode of terrorists. Notice that there is nothing particularly telling around 9/11, in that both series seem to continue the upward movement that began around the first quarter of 2001. By contrast, Figure 3.3 indicates that the number of HOSTAGE incidents fluctuated around twelve incidents per quarter during the 1970s and 1980s and began to increase in the early 1990s. In 1999, the number of incidents suddenly dropped sharply. The behavior of the series in the two figures leaves the impression that ALL incidents and BOMBINGS did not change as a result of 9/11 but that the number of hostage takings fell (see Chapter 8 and Enders and Sandler, 2005a). Notice that Figure 3.6 suggests that there have been several instances in which the proportion of incidents with deaths ratcheted up. To the naked eye, the proportion appears to have permanently shifted upward in the late 1970s and again in 1992.

Intervention analysis is a statistical technique that allows us to ascertain whether these impressions are valid. The technique allows us to determine whether an abrupt change in the pattern of a series is due to a force, such as the rise of Islamic fundamentalism in the late 1970s, or to a particular event, such as 9/11. Moreover, the same statistical method permits a measurement of the long-run and short-run changes in the behavior of the various terrorist series. To briefly explain the technique, intervention analysis models the cyclical (or irregular) component of a time series using its previous values. Unlike spectral analysis, which models the short-run movements in a series using sine and cosine functions, intervention analysis uses the lagged values of the series itself. If y_t denotes the value of a series during the current time period t, then y_{t-1} represents its value during the previous period and y_{t-2} its value two periods ago. The short-run dynamics of the series can be captured by fitting the lagged values of $y_{t-1}, y_{t-2}, \ldots, y_{t-p}$ to the series and retaining those lagged values that are statistically significant. In this way, the relationship between the current and past values of the series can be determined.

A typical time-series model given by equation (1) might have the specific functional form:

$$y_t = a_0 + a_1 t + b_1 y_{t-1} + b_2 y_{t-2} + \varepsilon_t, \tag{2}$$

where the expression $a_0 + a_1 t$ denotes a linear trend; $b_1 y_{t-1} + b_2 y_{t-2}$ represents the expression for the short-run dynamics; and ε_t stands for the pure noise. Of course, some series might have more complicated trend and/or cyclical components than those specified in equation (2). Nevertheless, anyone familiar with a basic regression model should have little trouble understanding the essentials of the technique.[4]

Intervention analysis augments equations in the form of (2) in that it allows for permanent or temporary breaks in the series. Panel *a* of Figure 3.8 depicts a permanent intervention, called a *level shock* (or *level shift*), where the intervention is effective in all periods after its introduction. A temporary intervention, called a *pulse*, is depicted in Panel *b* of Figure 3.8., where for all periods, except intervention period three, the value of the pulse is zero. A temporary tightening of airport security would be represented by a pulse, while the permanent installation of an explosive-detection device would be represented by a level shift. In either case, the airport security enhancement would result in *fewer* incidents. Similarly, if 9/11 represented a temporary change in terrorist behavior, it would be represented as a pulse. If, however, 9/11 represented a permanent phenomenon, it would be shown as a level shift. Of course, more intricate intervention variables are possible. Although a level-shift intervention will have a permanent effect on the variable of interest, the intervention variable may not immediately jump to its long-run value. Since the installation of metal detectors in US airports occurred throughout the year 1973, this type of gradually increasing intervention could be represented by panel *c*. Even though the pulse is a one-time phenomenon, it can have prolonged effects on the variable of interest. Panel *d* illustrates a situation where the effect of a pulse on the variable of interest slowly fades away.

---

[4] A regression tries to capture the relationship between a variable of interest (that is, the dependent variable) and a set of explanatory variables called the "independent variables." In so doing, the regression uses observed values to estimate how the variation of a dependent variable is explained by a linear representation of independent variables. In the process, a dependent variable is expressed as a linear equation of a constant and independent variables, whose coefficients, if significant, indicate how a change in the independent variable impacts the dependent variable.

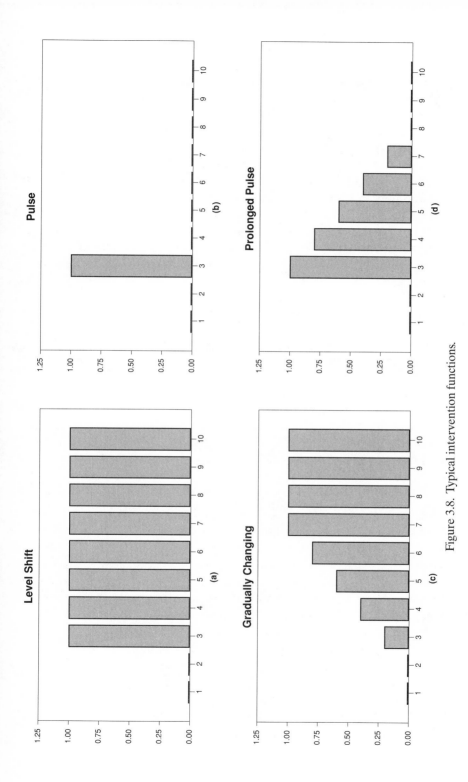

Figure 3.8. Typical intervention functions.

Intervention analysis actually allows for a rich variety of interventions with various response patterns. For those wishing to utilize the technique, the technical details are provided in Chapter 5 of Enders (2004). However, the introduction to intervention analysis provided here should be sufficient to explain its use in the study of transnational terrorism. The key point to note is that we modify equation (2) to allow for the various types of interventions. To take a numerical example, let y_t denote the values of the ALL series; let D_L represent a level shift variable for 9/11; and let D_P represent a pulse. Specifically, as suggested by panel b of Figure 3.8, we let the variable $D_P = 1$ for 2001:Q3 and $D_P = 0$ for all other periods. As indicated in panel a of Figure 3.8, we also let $D_L = 0$ for all values prior to 9/11 and $D_L = 1$ thereafter. We estimated the regression equation:

$$y_t = 34.07 + 0.222y_{t-1} + 0.190y_{t-2} + 0.217y_{t-3}$$
$$- 22.66D_P - 15.31D_L + \varepsilon_t. \tag{3}$$

We found no significant trend in the data, the short-run dynamics are given by the expression $0.222y_{t-1} + 0.190y_{t-2} + 0.217y_{t-3}$, and the noise term is represented by ε_t. Neither intervention variables were found to be statistically significant. As a result, we can conclude that 9/11 had no statistically significant effects on the ALL series (see Chapter 8). If, however, either intervention variable had happened to be significant, we would have analyzed the pattern it imparted on the data.

Estimating the Effect of Metal Detectors on Skyjackings

Aerial incidents such as the explosion of Pan Am flight 103 over Lockerbie, Scotland, on 21 December 1988 and the four skyjackings of 9/11 dominate newspaper headlines and the airwaves. Nevertheless, skyjacking incidents have actually been quite common. In an effort to offset a surge in skyjackings, US airports began to install metal detectors on 5 January 1973. Other international authorities soon followed suit. The quarterly totals of all transnational and US domestic skyjackings from 1968 through 1988 are shown in Figure 3.9. Although the number of skyjacking incidents appears to take a sizable and permanent decline in January 1973, we might be interested in actually measuring the effects of installing the metal detectors.

In Enders, Sandler, and Cauley (1990a), we were interested in the effects of metal detectors on US domestic skyjackings, transnational

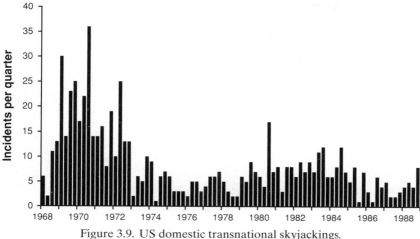

Figure 3.9. US domestic transnational skyjackings.

skyjackings (including those involving the United States), and all other skyjackings. We began by viewing the installation of metal detectors as an immediate and permanent intervention. Seeing it as such, we used a level-shift intervention to represent metal detectors. As suggested by panel *a* of Figure 3.8, we let the level-shift variable equal zero prior to 1973:Q1 and one in 1973:Q1 and thereafter.

The results of the estimations are reported in Table 3.4. Prior to 1973, the average quarter contained 3.03 transnational skyjackings. We estimated that metal detectors reduced the quarterly number of transnational skyjackings by 1.29 incidents on impact. We also estimated the long-run effect of metal detectors to be −1.78 incidents per quarter. Thus, the time path of the effects of metal detectors on transnational skyjackings looked something like panel *c* of Figure 3.8. The long-run effect of the permanent intervention exceeded the short-run effect. Overall, metal detectors prevented about seven transnational skyjackings per year. As you can see from Table 3.4, the installation of metal detectors reduced each type of skyjacking incident. The most pronounced effect was on US domestic skyjackings, which immediately fell by 5.62 incidents per quarter (see Table 3.4). The short-run and long-run effects were identical, as domestic skyjackings immediately fell from 6.70 to the long-run value of 1.08 incidents per quarter. On impact, other skyjackings (that is, domestic skyjackings in countries other than the United States) fell by 3.9 incidents per quarter. The long-run effect was estimated to be 5.11 fewer incidents per quarter.

Table 3.4. *Impact of Metal Detectors on Skyjackings:*
Intervention Analysis

Series	Pre-Intervention Mean[a]	Impact Effect[a]	Long-Run Effect[a]
Transnational	3.03	−1.29	−1.78
US Domestic	6.70	−5.62	−5.62
Other Skyjackings	6.80	−3.90	−5.11

[a] Incidents per quarter.

We also considered the possibility that metal detectors were gradually installed in non-US airports and, even when installed, that the enforcement was sporadic. As a check, we modeled the intervention as gradually increasing over the year 1973. Although the coefficients were nearly identical to those reported in Table 3.4, the fit of the overall regressions was superior when using a gradually increasing process to capture the effect of the interventions. Hence, we conclude that metal detector adoption was more gradual outside of the United States.[5]

United Nations' Conventions and Resolutions

A second aim of Enders, Sandler, and Cauley (1990a) was to examine how actions by the United Nations affected skyjackings and crimes against protected persons (for example, ambassadors, diplomats, and embassy personnel). The UN Convention on the Prevention and Punishment of Crimes against Internationally Protected Persons, Including Diplomatic Agents (CAPP), was adopted by the United Nations on 14 December 1973 and signed into law by the United States on 20 February 1977. We chose the first quarter of 1977 as the intervention date, since most of these crimes involved the United States. The UN also took measures to reduce hostage takings. On 18 December 1985, the UN Security Council Resolution against Taking Hostages was adopted by a 15 to 0 vote. During the period December 1969 through December 1970, there were several UN and international conventions against hijackings. These included UN General Assembly Resolution 2551 (XXIV): Forcible Diversion of Civil Aircraft in Flight, the Hague Convention on the Suppression of Unlawful

---

[5] In Chapter 5, we consider the effects of metal detectors in a multi-equation framework. A multivariable framework allows us to estimate the effects of metal detectors on several of the incident series simultaneously.

Seizure of Aircraft, and UN General Assembly Resolution 2645 (XXV): Aerial Hijacking. After some experimentation, we settled on 1971:Q1 as a single break date for these three resolutions and conventions.

UN conventions require that a nation use its own judicial system to implement and enforce the agreement. UN resolutions, on the other hand, are simply agreements on a particular set of principles or goals. Hence, conventions are more binding than resolutions, since resolutions do not imply a commitment to enforcement. Nevertheless, the United Nations has no direct power to force a nation to abide by any of its agreements.

The key finding is that none of these interventions had a significant effect in thwarting terrorism. Specifically, we obtained the number of crimes undertaken against protected persons from ITERATE. Neither the CAPP nor the UN Security Council Resolution against Taking Hostages had any significant effects on this series. Next, we constructed a time series of hostage events (that is, kidnappings, barricade and hostage taking, and skyjackings). Neither the CAPP nor the UN Security Council Resolution against Taking Hostages had any significant effect on this series. Even though the combined resolutions and conventions represented by 1971:Q1 specifically targeted aerial hijackings, we found that they had no significant effect on any of the skyjacking series.

More recently, the International Convention for the Suppression of Terrorist Bombings was signed on 15 December 1997 and entered into US law on 23 May 2001. We applied the methods used in Enders, Sandler, and Cauley (1990a) to determine whether this UN convention had any effect on bombings, deadly bombings, or the proportion of bombings relative to ALL incidents. Specifically, we used values of ITERATE running through 2003:Q4 to construct time series of these three types of bombings and used 2001:Q3 as a level-shift intervention. Not surprisingly, we found no significant effects of the convention on any of these series. As discussed in more detail in Chapter 6, without any enforcement mechanism, nations are unlikely to change their behavior as a result of a UN convention. Moreover, after a UN agreement, terrorists still have the same resolve and wherewithal to engage in violence. UN conventions and resolutions do little to reduce the terrorists' resource base or to deflect terrorists toward peaceful activities.

Estimating the Effect of the Libyan Bombing

The third aim of Enders, Sandler, and Cauley (1990a) was to consider the effects of the US bombing of Libya on the morning of 15 April 1986.

The stated reason for the attack was Libya's alleged involvement in the terrorist bombing of the La Belle discotheque in West Berlin. Since eighteen of the F-111 fighter-bombers used in the attack were deployed from British bases at Lakenheath and Upper Heyford, England, the United Kingdom implicitly assisted in the raid. The remaining US planes were deployed from aircraft carriers in the Mediterranean Sea. We considered the effects of the bombing on all transnational terrorist incidents directed against the United States and the United Kingdom. A plot of this incident series showed a large positive spike immediately after the bombing; the immediate effect seemed to be a wave of anti-US and anti-UK attacks to protest the retaliatory strike. This spike in each of the two series is apparent in Figure 3.2 (shown previously).

We considered two possible patterns for the intervention series. We initially allowed the intervention to have a permanent effect on attacks against the United States and the United Kingdom. Using this specification, we obtained an estimate of the level-shift variable that is not statistically significant. Alternatively, when we used a pulse intervention equal to one only in the second quarter of 1986, we found that the coefficient on the pulse term is highly significant. The fit of this second specification is far superior to that obtained when we viewed the attack as a permanent intervention. Our conclusion was that the Libyan bombing did not have the desired effect of reducing terrorist attacks against the United States and the United Kingdom. Instead, the bombing caused an immediate increase of over thirty-eight attacks per quarter. Subsequently, the number of attacks quickly declined; attacks were only 12.7 incidents per quarter above the pre-intervention mean in the third quarter of 1986.

Is Terrorism Becoming More Threatening?

In Enders and Sandler (2000), we tried to determine whether transnational terrorist incidents have become more threatening. Our aim was to determine whether several intervention variables account for the behavior of the DEATH and CAS series shown in Figure 3.5. Although we had access only to data running through 1996:Q2, the results are still relevant. To be a bit more specific, we examined the effects of metal detectors, two separate bouts of embassy fortifications, the Libyan raid, the rise of religious fundamentalism, and the break-up of the Soviet Union on the DEATH and CAS series. We set our multiple intervention variables as shown in Table 3.5.

Table 3.5. *Interventions*

Intervention	Description	Starting Date/ Intervention Type
METAL	Metal detectors installed in US airports in January 1973, followed shortly thereafter by their installation in airports worldwide.	1973:Q1 level shift
EMB 76	A doubling of the spending to fortify and secure US embassies beginning in October 1976.	1976:Q3 level shift
FUND	The rise of religious-based terrorism starting with the 4 November takeover of the US embassy in Tehran, Iran. The last quarter of 1979 coincides with the Soviet invasion of Afghanistan in December 1979.	1979:Q4 level shift
EMB 85	Further increases in spending to secure US embassies authorized by Public Law 98–533 in October 1985.	1985:Q4 level shift
LIBYA	US retaliatory raid against Libya on 15 April 1986 for its involvement in the terrorist bombing of La Belle discotheque in West Berlin.	1986:Q2 pulse
POST	The start of the post–Cold War era with the official demise of the Warsaw Pact on 1 July 1991 and the breakup of the Soviet Union on 20 December 1991. This date also corresponds to a decline in state sponsorship of terrorism by countries in Eastern Europe and elsewhere.	1991:Q4 level shift

Although our primary focus was on the effects of the rise of fundamentalism (FUND) and the demise of the Soviet Union (POST), we included the other interventions to control for other possible breaks. We used all of the interventions to estimate the short-run and long-run movements in the DEATH and CAS series. Remember that the CAS series includes incidents in which individuals were killed or wounded; hence, it is necessarily broader than the DEATH series. The results are summarized in Table 3.6.

Although Chapter 5 specifically addresses the substitution between attack modes, it is interesting to note here that the installation of metal

Table 3.6. *Effects of the Interventions (in incidents per quarter)*

Intervention	Casualties Series		Death Series	
	Short-Run	Long-Run	Short-Run	Long-Run
METAL	8.83	12.38	5.56	9.27
EMB 76	Not significant		Not significant	
FUND	7.75	10.86	4.17	6.95
EMB 85	−9.904	−13.90	−5.92	−9.87
LIBYA	Not significant		Not significant	
POST	9.90	13.89	6.77	11.12

detectors actually increased the number of incidents with casualties and the number of incidents with deaths. The short-run impacts on CAS and DEATH are 8.33 and 5.56 more incidents per quarter, respectively. The long-run effects are even more substantial: 12.38 and 9.27 more incidents per quarter. An unintended consequence of metal detectors was that terrorists substituted out of skyjackings and into more deadly events. Skyjackings are necessarily newsworthy and, until 9/11, were not usually associated with large numbers of deaths except when a rescue mission failed. After metal detectors made skyjackings more difficult to initiate, terrorists substituted into similarly newsworthy events. Unfortunately, events with casualties and deaths provided the media attention desired by terrorists.

We found very different results concerning the two different attempts at embassy fortifications. The security enhancements of 1976 may have protected US embassies, but they had no significant effect on the total number of CAS or DEATH incidents. The enhancements of 1985 were associated with a short-run reduction of about ten CAS incidents and six DEATH incidents. The long-run effects were even more substantial.

It is interesting that the Libyan retaliatory raid had no significant effect on either series. In light of our other estimates that the raid increased the total number of incidents directed against the United States and the United Kingdom, the overall effect of the raid was to increase noncasualty incidents, but not incidents with casualties or deaths.

The rise of fundamentalism and the demise of the Soviet Union were both associated with increases in CAS and DEATH incidents. The short-run impact of FUND was to increase CAS incidents by 7.75 per quarter and DEATH incidents by 4.17 per quarter. The long-run effects were 10.68 and 6.95 extra incidents in a typical quarter, respectively. The short-run impact of POST was to increase CAS incidents by 9.90 and DEATH incidents by 6.77. The long-run effects were 13.89 and 11.12 extra incidents in a typical quarter, respectively. Clearly, these two watershed incidents were associated with more threatening and more deadly forms of terrorism. In June 2000, a full fifteen months before 9/11, we stated that:

This shift toward greater religious-based terrorism is traced to a structural change ... at the time of the takeover of the US Embassy in Tehran. From this point, terrorism became more CAS prone and dangerous. ... The rise in religious terrorism in which massive civilian casualties are a goal poses a potential dilemma for government counterterrorism policy. If a government responds by tightening security at official sites (embassies and government buildings) as is currently being done in the United States, its civilian targets ... will become relatively less secure and attractive. (Enders and Sandler, 2000)

When the Enders and Sandler (2000) paper was being reviewed, one reviewer strongly objected to our analysis suggesting that terrorism was posing a greater threat to society!

CONCLUSION

Statistical analysis can either substantiate or refute "observed" patterns in a time-series plot or patterns suggested by a particular political or economic model. Unlike the perception given by the media, there is no decided upward trend in any of the terrorism series. Instead, the ALL series and its subcomponent series vary over time in predictable ways. Spectral analysis is a specialized branch of statistics that is particularly well suited to analyze cyclical phenomena. Spectral analysis indicates that logistically complex terrorist incidents (such as HOSTAGE and DEATH) have much longer cycles than simpler incidents (BOMBINGS and THREATS). Intervention analysis can be used to study how terrorists respond to particular events, such as the rise of religious fundamentalism, or to policy initiatives, such as the installation of metal detectors in airports. The statistical evidence suggests that terrorists responded to metal detectors and embassy fortifications, but not to UN conventions and resolutions. The demise of the Soviet Union and the increase in religious fundamentalism are both associated with increases in the severity of terrorism.

FOUR

Counterterrorism

Counterterrorism consists of government actions to inhibit terrorist attacks or curtail their consequences. Such policies can limit attacks by confronting terrorists directly. For example, intelligence and police investigations resulted in the capture of the entire leadership of Direct Action (DA) in France between 1982 and 1987 (Alexander and Pluchinsky, 1992, p. 135; Hoffman, 1998). Italian authorities captured most of the Red Brigades after responding to a tip-off in the kidnapping of Brigadier General James Lee Dozier, the senior US officer at NATO's southern European command who was abducted from his home on 17 December 1981. He was freed unharmed in a daring police rescue on 28 January 1982.[1] Based on state's evidence obtained from Antonio Savasta, captured during the raid, the police later apprehended 200 Red Brigade suspects, which resulted in further arrests and the eventual demise of the group. Other counterterrorism actions can safeguard potential terrorist targets by reducing an attack's likelihood of success or its expected payoff. The installation of metal detectors in US airports on 5 January 1973 decreased terrorists' probability of success, as did the fortification of US embassies in the mid-1970s and beyond. After 9/11, the deployment of federal screeners at US airports, the reinforcement of airplane cockpit doors, and the designation of no-fly zones in Washington, DC, and other American cities were intended to limit terrorists' success and, thereby, to prevent attacks.

---

[1] For a detailed account of the Dozier kidnapping and its aftermath, see Mickolus, Sandler, and Murdock (1989, vol. 1, pp. 234–9), which is compiled from newspaper accounts at the time of the kidnapping.

The purpose of this chapter is to investigate and evaluate the two primary categories of counterterrorism policies – proactive and defensive. Proactive or offensive measures attack the terrorists, their resource base, or those who support them. By contrast, defensive or passive policies erect a protective barrier around potential targets – physical or human. Such measures dissuade terrorists by decreasing their anticipated gains from attacks. This can occur if their costs are raised or their anticipated benefits are reduced. Defensive actions may also limit attacks if alternative nonterrorist actions are made more attractive.

This chapter casts light on two puzzles. First, we explain why there appears to be a proclivity for most countries to rely on defensive rather than proactive policies when addressing transnational terrorism, and why this tendency does not appear to characterize actions with respect to domestic terrorism. Nations are quite proactive in pursuing domestic groups when they harm interests at home – either directly or indirectly, through collateral damage. European action to dismantle many of the fighting communist organizations, such as the Combatant Communist Cells and the Red Brigades, in the 1980s is testimony to this proactive stance with respect to domestic terrorism. Israeli aggression against the Hezbollah and Hamas leadership in recent years also exemplifies this orientation. Second, for transnational terrorism, we explain the tendency for the world community to rely on one or two nations' proactive responses. To accomplish these goals, we employ some elementary game theory to identify strategic differences among participants. We are particularly interested in the strategic interaction among targeted governments, which may actually work at cross purposes as they independently make policy choices.[2]

Both this chapter and the next focus on counterterrorism. A conclusion common to both chapters is that an inappropriate level of antiterrorist actions often results especially when addressing *transnational* terrorism, because countries do not account for the costs and benefits that their independent choices imply for other countries. There is a marked tendency to engage in too much defensive action and not enough proactive

---

[2] The relevant literature on strategic interaction among targets includes Arce and Sandler (2005), Heal and Kunreuther (2003, 2005), Kunreuther and Heal (2003), Lee (1988), Lee and Sandler (1989), Sandler and Arce (2003), Sandler and Enders (2004), Sandler and Lapan (1988), and Sandler and Siqueira (2005). Interaction between target and terrorists, when policies are decided, is addressed by Enders and Sandler (1993, 1995), Jain and Mukand (2004), Lapan and Sandler (1993), Rosendorff and Sandler (2004), and Sandler, Tschirhart, and Cauley (1983).

measures. This follows because defensive measures often transfer the attack to softer targets abroad. Chapter 5 gives an in-depth treatment of this transference phenomenon. In the case of proactive policies, too little is done as countries wait for others to act. Given the suboptimality of counterterrorism responses to transnational terrorism, there is a need for international cooperation – the subject of Chapter 6.

PROACTIVE POLICIES

Proactive policies are offensive, since a government confronts the terrorists or their supporters directly. If action can curtail terrorists' resources, their finances, safe havens, infrastructure, or sponsors, then the ability of terrorists to engage in activities is curtailed. Terrorists' resources can be reduced by capturing or killing group members or by destroying their non-human resources – for example, weapons, ammunition, training camps, communication networks, or safe houses.

Consider the terrorist group's resource constraint,

$$P_T T + P_N N = I, \tag{1}$$

where P_T and P_N are the unit costs of generic terrorist (T) and nonterrorist (N) actions, respectively, and I is the group's income or resources for the current period. During each period, equation (1) indicates that the terrorist group allocates its resources between terrorist and nonterrorist activities, thereby exhausting its resources for the period. This constraint is displayed as AB in Figure 4.1, where terrorist attacks are measured along the y-axis (vertical axis) and nonterrorist attacks along the x-axis

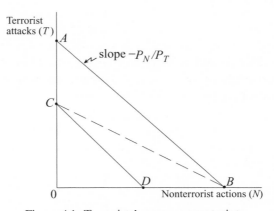

Figure 4.1. Terrorists' resource constraints.

(horizontal axis). If the terrorists devote all of their resources to terrorist attacks, then they can accomplish at most I/P_T attacks, which is found by setting $N = 0$ and solving for T in equation (1). As such, I/P_T represents the y-intercept of resource constraint AB. Similarly, the x-intercept, I/P_N, of constraint AB is found by setting $T = 0$ and solving for the maximal number of nonterrorist attacks in equation (1). To find the slope of the resource constraint, we rewrite it, by solving for T, as

$$T = \left(\frac{I}{P_T}\right) - \left(\frac{P_N}{P_T}\right) N. \tag{2}$$

The coefficient, $-P_N/P_T$, in front of N is the slope of the resource constraint, which indicates the change in T resulting from a unit change in N. Some proactive measures may reduce terrorists' resources, thereby shifting the resource constraint down in a *parallel* fashion to CD. The downward shift is parallel because a fall in I does not affect the ratio of unit costs in equation (2), thereby leaving the constraint's slope, $-P_N/P_T$, unchanged. Each intercept – I/P_T and I/P_N – falls by the same amount as I is reduced.

Proactive policies may, instead, raise the price of terrorist actions by making such activities more risky, thereby pivoting the resource constraint down in a nonparallel fashion to dashed line CB, if terrorists' resources are unaffected.[3] For example, the risk of being infiltrated by the government makes terrorist acts more costly without necessarily changing the terrorists' resource endowments. Group infiltration increases the relative attractiveness of nonterrorist acts. Finally, if the proactive measures raise the unit cost of terrorism and also reduce terrrorists' resources, then the resource constraint shifts downward in a nonparallel fashion (not shown) from AB, so that there is a greater fall in the y-intercept compared to the x-intercept of the new resource constraint. In any of these scenarios, proactive policies reduce the terrorists' choices and may result in reduced levels of both kinds of activities. When the governmental policy increases the relative costliness of terrorist actions, the tendency is for terrorists to switch to nonterrorist activities. If, however, a threatened government represses freedoms and raises the unit costs of nonterrorist acts, including legitimate protests, then the government may force the terrorists to rely on terrorism to a greater extent (Frey, 2004; Frey and Luechinger, 2003; Lichbach, 1987).

---

[3] As P_T rises alone from the proactive policy, the intercept along the y-axis falls from A to C in Figure 4.1.

Proactive policies can assume many forms, including a retaliatory raid against a state sponsor that provides resources, training, safe haven, logistical support, or intelligence to a terrorist group. An example of such a raid was the US bombing of targets in Libya on 15 April 1986 for its alleged involvement in the terrorist bombing of the La Belle discotheque in West Berlin on 4 April 1986, where 3 died and 231 were wounded, including 62 Americans.[4] Targets in the US raid included the Azizyah barracks in Tripoli, the Jamahiriyah barracks in Benghazi, the Sidi Bilal port west of Tripoli, the military side of the Tripoli airport, and the Benina military airfield.[5] The Azizyah barracks was the residence of Muammar Qaddafi. During the raid, two of his sons were seriously injured and his adopted one-year-old daughter was killed. Another example of a retaliatory raid was the Israeli attack against Palestine Liberation Organization (PLO) bases in Syria in response to the Black September attack on Israeli athletes at the 1972 Olympic Games.

Another type of proactive response is a preemptive attack against a terrorist group or a country harboring it, as in the case of 7 October 2001 US attack on the Taliban and al-Qaida in Afghanistan. A preemptive attack differs from a retaliatory raid because the former is more sustained and intended to severely compromise the capabilities of the terrorists. In June 2005, the US and Pakistani military were still attacking al-Qaida leaders and members in Afghanistan and Pakistan. Israeli assassinations of Hamas leaders and operatives in 2003 and 2004 also represent preemptive actions. Many past retaliatory raids merely lashed out at the terrorists or their sponsors without greatly limiting their ability to operate (see remarks in Chapter 3). As such, these raids served more as a vehicle for the government to send a signal to its citizens than as punishment for the culprits.

Less drastic but effective proactive measures include infiltrating the terrorist group and gathering intelligence. Infiltration can compromise the group's security and lead to arrests. To limit these consequences in light of the Red Brigades' experience, many terrorist organizations now rely on a cellular structure, where members know little about the identities of others outside of their small cell of four to six persons. The use of bloodlines and long-term friendships limits the possibility of infiltration. Effective intelligence can identify planned attacks and allow for countermeasures. Another proactive policy is to go after the financial resources

---

[4] Details of the La Belle discotheque bombing can be found in Mickolus, Sandler, and Murdock (1989, vol. 2, pp. 365–7).

[5] Details of the US raid are contained in ibid., pp. 373–4.

of the terrorists by freezing assets. Since 9/11, countries have frozen $200 million of terrorists' alleged assets (White House, 2003). At the international level, freezing assets raises problems of international cooperation addressed in Chapter 6 and in Sandler (2005).

George W. Bush's war on terror is a broad-based action that involves both proactive and defensive measures to protect the country and its citizens at home and abroad against terrorism. There is, however, a reliance on military power and proaction. The motivation for this extreme response is a realization that modern-day terrorism is a form of asymmetric warfare in which the terrorists rely on unconventional, irregular, and decentralized methods to confront a superior adversary – that is, the military and police of targeted industrial nations.[6] To counter the terrorist threat, the government deploys its military to destroy terrorists' bases of operation and assets. There are criticisms leveled against a military response (see, for example, Wilkinson, 2001). By characterizing the response as a war, the proactive government gives a false impression of a possible victory in which terrorism is eventually defeated. Some groups or sponsors may indeed be defeated or severely compromised, but terrorism, especially transnational terrorism, remains a tactic that will be embraced by new members and groups. Any "victory" will be temporary. A military response may also result in collateral damage to innocent individuals – for example, the victims of a smart bomb that misses its mark. In addition, a military response may turn world opinion against the offensive country if operations appear excessive or brutal. One of the greatest drawbacks is the possibility that a military response will attract new recruits to the cause, which, in turn, could result in a wider conflict.[7]

There is also the problem of measuring success associated with military operations. Following the October 2001 preemptive strikes by coalition forces in Afghanistan, there were al-Qaida-linked attacks in 2002 and thereafter – for example, the 12 May 2003 suicide truck bombings in Riyadh, Saudi Arabia, and the 16 May 2003 suicide car bombings in Casablanca, Morocco – that led critics to conclude that the Afghan war of

---

[6] This characterization comes from Schulze and Vogt (2003).

[7] To date, there are few theoretical analyses of the process of recruitment to terrorist organizations. Recruitment can be stimulated by past incident successes or by governments' draconian measures (see, for example, Rosendorff and Sandler, 2004). To properly address recruitment, a multiperiod dynamic model is required, whereby terrorist attacks and government countermeasures influence the stock of operatives in a terrorist campaign. This stock is also affected by retirements and casualties incurred in missions. The government must be sufficiently vigilant to limit successful incidents, but not so harsh as to encourage grievances and new recruits.

2001 did not achieve much. What we cannot know is how many additional attacks would have occurred had action not been taken in Afghanistan. This counterfactual problem is particularly acute with military operations because of the mistaken expectation that terrorism will cease. Measurement is also difficult owing to the cyclical nature of terrorist attacks; a lull may be due to a natural cycle rather than military actions taken. And fewer attacks may not even signal success, if attacks become bloodier or are transferred to other countries.

Proactive measures often represent pure public goods as defined in Chapter 1. A preemptive operation that reduces the capabilities of a common terrorist threat *confers nonexcludable and nonrival benefits on all potential targets.* If asked to contribute to the operation after the fact, most targets will understate their true derived benefits so as to free ride on the support of others. This tendency will lead to underprovision as targets wait for others to act. At the national level, the free-rider concern is addressed by assigning to the central government the authority to protect domestic targets with financing from tax revenues. When necessary, the central government coordinates the state and local jurisdictional responses. The free-rider problem is a major worry for combating transnational terrorism, because there is no supranational government that can provide a unified proactive policy *underwritten by taxes from target countries.* Since 9/11, the world community has relied on the United States to coordinate the proactive response, which other nations can voluntarily support. At the transnational level, some proactive policies may result in public bads as costs are imposed on other countries. If, for example, a proactive operation augments grievances and leads to recruitment of terrorists, then these public costs must be weighed against the public benefits in order to ascertain the net consequences (Rosendorff and Sandler, 2004). A particularly heavy-handed operation may conceivably do more to jeopardize other countries than to safeguard them. This is particularly true when the proactive country is also hardening its own targets at home so that grievance-inducing terrorist attacks occur abroad, where other interests are impacted. The result is a "forced ride," where a nation endures a consequence that it prefers to forgo (Tanzi, 1972).

DEFENSIVE POLICIES

Defensive measures protect potential targets either by making attacks more costly for terrorists or by reducing their likelihood of success. When an attack occurs, effective defensive action also limits the losses. Many defensive policies are reactive in the sense of being imposed after past incidents reveal vulnerabilities. The installation of metal detectors to screen passengers at airports is an instance. Prior to their installation on 5 January 1973 at US airports, there were on average approximately twenty-seven hijackings each year in the United States (Enders, Sandler, and Cauley, 1990a, p. 95). The installation of bomb-sniffing equipment to screen luggage on commercial flights came after bombs brought down planes – for example, Pan Am flight 103 over Scotland on 21 December 1988 and UTA flight 772 over Niger on 19 September 1989. Both metal detectors and bomb-sniffing devices are examples of technological barriers, which are especially effective when authorities continuously upgrade the technology to stymie attempts by terrorists to circumvent the barriers – for example, the development of plastic guns or non-nitrogen-based explosives.

Some defensive actions may involve hardening a target, such as efforts in 1976 and 1985 to fortify US embassies. Since the 19 April 1995 bombing of the Alfred P. Murrah Federal Building in Oklahoma City, barriers have been put around other federal buildings to create a safety perimeter to curtail the damage from a car or truck bomb. The decision to allow fighter jets to shoot down hijacked planes that could be used to destroy buildings as on 9/11 is another defensive policy. The deployment of sky marshals on airplanes is yet another defensive action, as are DHS terror alerts to warn the public of a heightened state of risk.

Some actions are intended to deter or hinder an attack by stiffening penalties for convicted terrorists. For example, the so-called Reagan get-tough policy on terrorism was expressed in two public laws (PL) passed by the US Congress and signed by President Reagan. These laws are PL 98–473 (signed on 12 October 1984) and PL 98–533 (signed on 19 October 1984). The first required up to life imprisonment for individuals taking US hostages, either within or outside the United States. Penalties for destroying aircraft or airport facilities within the United States were also raised, as were penalties for acts committed with a bomb or other weapon on a US aircraft. The second bill authorized the US attorney general to pay rewards for information leading to the apprehension or conviction, inside or outside the United States, of terrorists who targeted US interests (Pearl, 1987, p. 141; Mickolus, Sandler, and Murdock, 1989).

At the international level, the United Nations and other multilateral bodies (for example, the International Civil Aviation Organization, the International Maritime Organization, and the Council of Europe) have passed conventions and treaties outlawing certain acts of terrorism – for example, seizure of commercial aircraft, the taking of hostages, and the use of explosive bombs. Unlike domestic laws, these international conventions suffer from the absence of an enforcement mechanism. In Chapter 6, we present an evaluation of their effectiveness.

Effective defensive measures have a public good aspect that generally differs from proactive policies. A defensive action may deflect an attack from a hardened to a softer target and, in so doing, impose a public cost on other potential targets; thus, a negative externality is associated with this transference. Unlike proactive measures, which may be undersupplied, defensive measures may be oversupplied.

GAME THEORY PRIMER

We now apply simple game theory to compare and contrast how national governments strategically interact with one another in a noncooperative framework that involves acting independently to decide their counterterrorism policies. The need for cooperative behavior for some transnational interactions then becomes apparent. A noncooperative game is fully identified by four factors: the rules of the game, the set of players, their available strategies, and the payoffs for all possible strategy combinations. To simplify the analysis, we display games in their normal or matrix form as described below.

The Prisoners' Dilemma game is relevant for many antiterrorism decisions and is thus described in detail. A story line behind the Prisoners' Dilemma game is as follows. In the vicinity of an armed robbery, two individuals in a vehicle are stopped on suspicion of being involved. Not only do the suspects appear to match eyewitnesses' vague descriptions, but a search of their car turns up an unregistered handgun. The district attorney realizes that she has insufficient circumstantial evidence to convict them of the robbery unless she can get a confession from one of the suspects. Without a confession, she can only convict them of possessing an unregistered handgun, which carriers a one-year sentence. Her strategy is to separate the two suspects and offer each a deal. If just one of them confesses, then the confessor walks free, while the nonconfessor receives the maximum four-year sentence for the robbery. If both confess, then they each receive a reduced two-year sentence for cooperating with the district attorney.

In panel *a* of Figure 4.2, the relevant payoffs for the two suspects – prisoners *A* and *B* – are displayed in the four cells of the game box, where each prisoner has two strategies: confess or not confess. Given that each

	B	
	Confess	Does not confess
Confess	**2 years, 2 years**	0 years, 4 years
Does not confess	4 years, 0 years	1 year, 1 year

A (row label)

a. Prisoners' Dilemma in jail sentence terms

	B	
	Confess	Does not confess
Confess	**2, 2**	4, 1
Does not confess	1, 4	3, 3

A (row label)

b. Prisoners' Dilemma in ordinal form

Figure 4.2. Prisoners' Dilemma.

player has two choices, there are four possible strategy combinations for the two suspects: both confess, in the top left-hand cell; *A* confesses alone, in the top right-hand cell; *B* confesses alone, in the bottom left-hand cell; and neither confesses, in the bottom right-hand cell. In each of the four cells, the first payoff or prison sentence is that of prisoner *A* or the row player, whereas the second payoff is that of prisoner *B* or the column player. The payoffs in each cell correspond to those associated with the deal offered by the district attorney – for example, when both confess, they each receive a two-year term. To examine the strategic dilemma from *A*'s viewpoint, we must compare his payoffs from his two strategies. When prisoner *B* confesses, prisoner *A* gets a lighter sentence of two years by confessing, as compared to the maximum four-year sentence for not confessing. If, however, prisoner *B* does not confess, prisoner *A* is still better off by confessing, since he then is released rather than serving a one-year term for not confessing. Prisoner *A*'s payoffs in the confessing row are better than the corresponding payoffs in the not confessing row. A strategy such as confessing, which provides a greater payoff regardless of the other player's action, is a *dominant strategy* and should be played. By the same token, a strategy whose payoffs are less than some other strategy's corresponding payoffs is said to be a *dominated strategy* and should *not* be chosen. In panel *a* of Figure 4.2, suspect *B*'s dominant strategy is also to confess when the corresponding payoffs in the two columns are compared – that is, a two-year sentence is better than four years, and walking free is better than a one-year term. As both suspects apply their dominant strategies, the outcome is mutual confession with two years of jail time. The dilemma arises because keeping silent is better for both suspects.

The confession outcome represents a *Nash equilibrium* (with boldfaced payoffs), which is a collection of strategies – one for each player – such that no player would *unilaterally* alter his or her strategy if given the opportunity.[8] This can be seen by focusing on the confession cell in panel *a*, where both players confess. If suspect *A* (or *B*) alone changes to not confessing or withdrawing the confession, then this suspect's payoff is worsened by the addition of two years of jail time. As a consequence, the suspect will not change his or her strategy unilaterally. Of course, both suspects would have been better off if they had formed an agreement from the outset to stay silent and had stayed with the arrangement. Even if such an agreement had been made, problems arise when the district attorney tempts them separately with the deal. Given the dominant strategy that her deal places before each suspect, neither can be sure what the other will do – promise to keep silent or no promise. Even if suspect *A* is sure that *B* will not confess, *A* is better off confessing and playing his buddy for a sucker.

An alternative representation of the payoffs in panel *a* of Figure 4.2 distinguishes the so-called Prisoners' Dilemma from myriad other payoff configurations. This is done by rank ordering the payoffs from best to worst in panel *b* of Figure 4.2. The best payoff (the walk-free sentence) is assigned the highest ordinal rank of 4, the next-best payoff (the one-year sentence) is given an ordinal rank of 3, and so on. Any two-person game box that possesses precisely the same ordinal payoff array as in panel *b* is a Prisoners' Dilemma. There are seventy-eight distinct 2×2 arrays of ordinal payoffs, but only one of them corresponds to the Prisoners' Dilemma. The ordinal depiction captures the essential strategic features of the game, including the presence of dominant strategies and Nash equilibrium(s). In panel *b*, confessing remains the dominant strategy, since $2 > 1$ and $4 > 3$; and mutual confession is the Nash equilibrium, whose payoffs are boldfaced. If the columns and rows are interchanged so that confess is in the bottom row for *A* (left column for *B*), then a Prisoners' Dilemma still results, with the (3, 3) payoffs switching position with the (2, 2) payoffs along the diagonal, and the (1, 4) and (4, 1) payoffs switching positions along the off-diagonal.

---

[8] Another characterization of a Nash equilibrium is that each player chooses his or her best strategy as a counter to the other player's best response or strategy.

	B	
	Straight	Swerve
Straight (A)	1, 1	**4, 2**
Swerve (A)	**2, 4**	3, 3

a. Chicken game in ordinal form

	B	
	Does not retaliate	Retaliate
Does not retaliate (A)	**2, 2**	3, 1
Retaliate (A)	1, 3	**4, 4**

b. Assurance game in ordinal form

Figure 4.3. Chicken and assurance games.

Before we apply game theory to the analysis of antiterrorist policy choices, we examine two additional game forms. In panel *a* of Figure 4.3, we indicate the *chicken* game in ordinal form. The James Dean movie *Rebel without a Cause* popularized the game's story line of two hot rods speeding toward one another from opposite directions. Each driver – *A* and *B* – has two strategies – keep driving straight or swerve to avoid a collision. The payoffs reflect the following preferences. The greatest perceived payoff derives from driving straight when the other driver swerves, because the driver who holds the course appears strong to his peers. The next-best payoff occurs when both drivers swerve, which is better than swerving alone and being branded the "chicken." Of course, the worst outcome is for both drivers to hold their course and have a collision. This game has no dominant strategy: the payoffs associated with swerving are not both greater than the corresponding payoffs associated with driving straight, since $2 > 1$ but $3 \not> 4$. Similarly, the driving-straight strategy does not dominate swerving, insofar as $4 > 3$ but $1 \not> 2$. Nevertheless, there are two Nash equilibriums indicated in boldface, where a single driver swerves. At these equilibriums, neither player would unilaterally change his or her strategy. From an ordinal viewpoint, chicken and Prisoners' Dilemma differ by having the 1s and 2s switch positions. This small change has large strategic consequences – the failure to coordinate the proper response can be disastrous for chicken. A situation in which taking no action against a terrorist threat spells disaster may be characterized as a chicken game.

An *assurance* game is indicated in panel *b* of Figure 4.3, where two countries – *A* and *B* – must decide whether or not to retaliate against an alleged state sponsor of terrorism following some spectacular terrorist incident that creates grave losses for both countries. The ordinal payoffs in panel *b* of Figure 4.3 differ from those of the Prisoners' Dilemma in panel *b* of Figure 4.2 in one essential way: the 3s and 4s have switched positions, so that the greatest ordinal payoff comes from joint action, while the next-best payoff arises from free riding. To obtain this game, we assume that both countries *must join* forces to get the job done – a single retaliator cannot hurt the terrorists sufficiently to outweigh the associated costs. Free riding on the country's retaliation effort is the second-best outcome, because revenge, though inadequate, is better than no response by anyone. Retaliating alone is the worst outcome, because it is costly without accomplishing a net positive payoff, despite some political gain from taking action. The second-smallest payoff is mutual inaction.

The assurance game in panel *b* of Figure 4.3 has no dominant strategy, because the payoffs in either row (column) are not both greater than the corresponding payoffs in the other row (column). There are, however, two Nash equilibriums whose payoffs are boldfaced along the diagonal of the game box, where countries match one another's responses – either no one retaliates, or both retaliate. If one country takes the lead and retaliates, as the United States did following 9/11, then the other country is better off retaliating, since an ordinal payoff of 4 is more desirable than one of 3. The game is called the *assurance game*, since – unlike the Prisoners' Dilemma, where agreements are not honored – pledged (assured) action will elicit a like response by the other player.

The heinous nature of the 9/11 attacks and its human toll on American and British citizens at the World Trade Center altered the ordinal payoffs depicted in panel *b* of Figure 4.3. For the United States and the United Kingdom, the worst payoff was associated with no one retaliating, followed by retaliating alone. That is, the 1s and 2s switch positions in panel *b* of Figure 4.3, while the 3s and 4s remain as displayed. The resulting game matrix (not shown) has a dominant strategy for both countries to retaliate. The sole Nash equilibrium is for joint retaliatory action, which began on 7 October 2001; thus, the Prisoners' Dilemma is not always descriptive of the decision to retaliate. If a country is sufficiently hurt in a terrorist attack, retaliation may be a compelling response.

PROACTIVE VERSUS DEFENSIVE POLICIES

For a proactive policy, we consider preemption when two targeted countries must decide whether or not to launch a preemptive attack against a common terrorist threat. The preemptive strike is intended to weaken the terrorists so that they pose a less significant challenge. Suppose that each country taking the preemptive action confers a public benefit of 4 on itself and the other country at a cost of 6 to itself. The game payoffs are indicated in the matrix of Figure 4.4. When no one acts, so that the status quo is preserved, nothing is gained. If, say, the United States (US) preempts but the European Union (EU) does not, then the US nets $-2 (= 4 - 6)$ as costs of 6 are deducted from benefits of 4, while the EU receives free-rider benefits of 4. The payoffs in the top right-hand cell are reversed as these roles are interchanged. When both countries preempt, each gains 2 as its preemption costs of 6 are deducted from benefits of $8 (= 2 \times 4)$, derived from the preemptive efforts of both countries. If these payoffs are ordinally ranked, then the game is immediately identified as a Prisoners' Dilemma. The dominant strategy is to maintain the status quo (that is, $0 > -2$ and $4 > 2$), and the boldfaced Nash equilibrium is mutual inaction. Thus, a classic pure public good scenario emerges, with nothing happening as each country prefers to rely on the other.

In Figure 4.5, we extend this same scenario to six identical countries and examine the alternative outcomes from the viewpoint of nation i, whose payoffs are indicated. The columns denote the number of nations other than i that preempt. In the top row, nation i attempts to free ride.

	EU	
	Status quo	Preempt
US — Status quo	**0, 0**	4, −2
US — Preempt	−2, 4	2, 2

Figure 4.4. Two-target preemption game.

	Number of preempting nations other than nation i					
	0	1	2	3	4	5
Nation *i* does not preempt	**0**	4	8	12	16	20
Nation *i* preempts	−2	2	6	10	14	18

Figure 4.5. Six-nation preemption game.

If, say, two other nations preempt, then i receives $8 (= 2 \times 4)$. In general, nation i gains 4 times the number of preemptors as a free-rider payoff. The bottom row displays i's payoff when it preempts. Nation i nets -2 when no other nation joins its efforts, while i receives $2 (= 2 \times 4 - 6)$ when one other nation also preempts. In general, nation i gains $4n - 6$, where n is the number of preemptors including i.

The dominant strategy for this six-nation preemption game is not to preempt, because each payoff in the top row is higher than the corresponding payoff in the bottom row by 2, or the net loss from independent action. The boldfaced Nash equilibrium is where no nation preempts, as all nations exercise their dominant strategy of doing nothing. This outcome leads to a significant welfare loss to the six-nation collective. If all six nations engage in preemption, then each gains 18 for a cumulative total of 108. Thus, all-round free riding loses society 108 of potential benefits in this example.[9] As the number of nations in the scenario increases, this cumulative loss increases. For a worldwide network such as al-Qaida, these losses from inaction can be extremely large; thus, the need for international cooperation is highlighted. This example raises some interesting questions. Why is there more preemption for domestic terrorism? What explains situations in which there is preemption in light of a transnational terrorist threat?

For domestic terrorism, the target nation cannot rely on other countries, since it alone is the target of attacks. Quite simply, there are no free-riding opportunities, except among targets within the nations. A centralized response addresses any free-riding concerns within a nation. Moreover, the individual benefits from action often exceed the associated costs once the terrorist campaign surpasses some level of intensity. Thus, the net gain from acting alone is likely to be positive, not negative. As the terrorists turn up the heat – for example, the Tupamaros in Uruguay at the start of the 1970s – their enhanced brutality raises the government's perceived benefits from preemption and makes the net gain from action larger. Another factor may be the government's perceived payoff from inaction. Thus far, we have assumed it to be 0. If, instead, the government loses support by not responding, then the resulting negative payoff may transform the game into a chicken game where some action is taken.[10]

---

[9] The social optimum does *not* correspond to the payoff of 20 in Figure 4.5 associated with i free riding on the other five nations. In this scenario, i receives 20, but each of the preemptors gains just 14 from its efforts and those of the other four preemptors (see Figure 4.5). Society nets 90 $[= 20 + (5 \times 14)]$ instead of 108.

[10] This is the case when the losses from inaction exceed in absolute value the net loss from acting alone.

		EU	
		Status quo	Preempt
US	Status quo	0, 0	4, −2
	Preempt	**2, 4**	6, 2

Figure 4.6. Asymmetric preemption game.

For transnational terrorism, there are at least two strategic reasons for a nation to take preemptive measures. First, the underlying game form may be something other than the Prisoners' Dilemma – for example, chicken or assurance. If the terrorist campaign is sufficiently deadly, doing nothing may be politically unacceptable (for example, following 9/11 or the train bombings in Madrid on 11 March 2004), so that the maintenance of the status quo, where terrorists attack with impunity, may have high political costs. Second, the countries' payoffs may be asymmetric owing to the terrorists' targeting preferences. Consider the asymmetric preemption game in Figure 4.6 between the US and the EU. The payoffs for the EU are identical to those of Figure 4.4 – that is, it gains 4 from its own preemption or that of the US and must pay a cost of 6 when preempting. The US now gains more from its *own* preemption than it derives from EU preemption, because US action demonstrates to its citizens that it is striking back. US action still costs 6. Suppose that the US still derives just 4 in benefits from EU preemption but 8 from its own efforts. US payoffs in the bottom row are now 2 (= 8 − 6) and 6 (= 8 + 4 − 6) for acting alone and in unison, respectively. The dominant strategies in Figure 4.6 is for the US to preempt (2 > 0 and 6 > 4 for the row payoff comparison) and for the EU to do nothing (0 > −2 and 4 > 2 for the column payoff comparison).

The Nash equilibrium in Figure 4.6 involves the US preempting and the EU free riding. This example is not intended to point the finger at any country; rather, it indicates that a prime-target nation can be induced to preempt even if it has to do so alone. Only these prime targets may be sufficiently motivated to provide benefits to all potential targets by going after a common threat. This reaction is analogous to the situation where nations become more proactive for domestic terrorism once home attacks surpass a certain threshold. Despite US rhetoric prior to 9/11, it had seldom engaged in preemption, even through its interests sustained 40% of all transnational terrorist incidents. The 15 April 1986 Libyan retaliatory raid was a short-lived operation, as were the Clinton administration's

		EU	
		Deter	Status quo
US	Deter	**-2, -2**	2, -4
	Status quo	-4, 2	0, 0

Figure 4.7. Two-target deterrence game.

20 August 1998 strikes on Afghanistan and Sudan for their alleged involvement in the bombing of the US embassies in Tanzania and Kenya on 7 August 1998. There is a certain irony in this preemption asymmetry. Had the terrorists treated their targets more symmetrically and not concentrated attacks on a few countries' assets, no country would have resorted to preemption. Of course, the terrorists focus their attacks in order to win over a following by trading preemption risk off against the followers' support.

When two or more target countries engage in preempting the same terrorist threat, their level of action will be negatively related because preemption is a substitute – one country's action limits the need for the other to act (Sandler and Siqueira, 2005). Thus, prime targets easy ride on the preemption of others, which implies too little preemption unless decisions are made in a cooperative framework. If, for example, one country experiences more attacks, it will increase its preemption, which will decrease the other country's efforts. This is an instance where countries work at cross purposes when deciding upon antiterrorist activities.

Deterrence and Other Defensive Measures

For deterrence, a nation tries to limit terrorist attacks by making potential targets less vulnerable through protective measures.[11] A symmetric two-target – US and EU – deterrence game is displayed in Figure 4.7, in which each country can do nothing or deter an attack by hardening its

---

[11] We do not use deterrence in the Cold War sense of keeping an action from occurring through a threat of punishment that is also costly to the punisher. We instead use deterrence in its common definitional sense of dissuading an action. This is how it has been applied in the terrorism literature since Landes (1978), where deterrence affects the terrorists' constraint.

targets. Increased deterrence is assumed to give a private, country-specific gain of 6 to the deterring country at a cost of 4 *to both countries*. For the deterring country, costs arise from both the expense of deterrence and the increased likelihood of incurring damage to its assets abroad if the attack is deflected there. For the nondeterring country, the costs stem from the heightened risk that it assumes because it is now a relatively soft target that may draw the attack.

The payoffs in the matrix in Figure 4.7 are based on this scenario. If the US deters alone, it gains a net benefit of 2 ($= 6 - 4$) as its deterrence gains are reduced by the associated costs. The EU suffers external costs of 4 from attracting the attack. The payoffs are reversed when the roles are interchanged. If both countries deter, then each sustains a net loss of 2 $[= 6 - (2 \times 4)]$ as costs of 8 from both countries' deterrence are deducted from the deterrence benefits of 6. The status quo provides no gains or losses. The game is a Prisoners' Dilemma with a dominant strategy to deter and a Nash equilibrium of mutual deterrence. If this game were extended to n countries, then all countries would choose their dominant strategy to deter. Overdeterrence results as each country does not account for the external costs associated with its efforts to deflect the attack abroad. Globalization may reduce overdeterrence somewhat by tying countries' vulnerabilities together.

Countries' deterrence choices are usually complementary, since greater deterrence abroad encourages greater deterrence at home so as not to draw the attack. Defensive policies such as deterrence and proactive policies such as preemption may both result in a Prisoners' Dilemma when displayed as a simple game. Nevertheless, there are subtle, but crucial, differences. First, proactive decisions tend to be substitutes and under-supplied, while defensive decisions tend to be complements and over-supplied. Second, a greater variety of game forms is typically related to proactive policies (for example, Prisoners' Dilemma, chicken, assurance, and asymmetric dominance), while the Prisoners' Dilemma is typically tied to defensive policies (Arce and Sandler, 2005). Third, globalization may ameliorate the oversupply of defensive measures by making people equally vulnerable everywhere, whereas it may exacerbate the undersup-ply of proactive measures. Fourth, defensive measures may give rise to both negative and positive external effects. That is, deterring an attack by deflecting it abroad may result in external costs in the recipient country but external benefits to foreign residents in the deterring country. Proac-tive measures are typically associated with external benefits unless they create grievances and recruitment.

		EU		
		Deter	Status quo	Preempt
	Deter	**−2, −2**	2, −4	6, −6
US	Status quo	−4, 2	0, 0	4, −2
	Preempt	−6, 6	−2, 4	2, 2

Figure 4.8. Deterrence versus preemption − symmetric case.

The Choice between Deterrence and Preemption

We next examine the scenario where each of two targets – the US and the EU – must choose between deterrence and preemption.[12] Each target now has three strategies: deter, maintain the status quo, and preempt. The scenarios for deterrence and preemption are identical to the previously described 2 × 2 games in Figures 4.4 and 4.7, respectively. Thus, deterrence provides public costs of 4 to the two targets and a private benefit of 6 to the deterrer, while preemption provides public benefits of 4 to the two targets and a private cost of 6 to the preemptor. These payoffs are illustrative – any set of public and private benefits where the private benefit of deterrence exceeds the associated costs and the private cost of preemption exceeds the associated benefits will give the outcome presented. This pattern of payoffs ensures that each component 2 × 2 game is a Prisoners' Dilemma.

The 3 × 3 game matrix is displayed in Figure 4.8, where the embedded deterrence game is captured by the northwest bold-bordered 2 × 2 matrix, and the embedded preemption game is captured by the southeast bold-bordered 2 × 2 matrix. Only the payoffs in the two cells at the opposite ends of the off-diagonal need to be derived. If one target deters and the other preempts, then the deterrer gains 6 (= 6 + 4 − 4), while the preemptor nets −6 (= 4 − 6 − 4). The deterrer earns a private benefit of 6 from its deterrence and a public benefit of 4 from the other target's preemption, but must cover its deterrence cost of 4. The sole preemptor suffers a cost of 4 from the other player's deterrence and a cost of 6 from its preemption efforts, but achieves only a private preemption benefit of 4.

The Nash equilibrium for the embedded deterrence game is for both countries to deter, and that for the embedded preemption game is for both

---

[12] Material in this section draws from the analysis in Arce and Sandler (2005).

to take no action. Which of these two equilibriums, if any, now reigns in the 3 × 3 game scenario? For the US, the dominant strategy is to deter, since its payoffs in the top row are greater than the corresponding payoffs in the other two rows. Similarly, the EU's dominant strategy is also to deter when its column payoffs (the right-hand payoff in a cell) are compared to the corresponding payoffs in the other two columns. As both targets apply their dominant strategies, the Nash equilibrium of mutual deterrence results; thus, the deterrence equilibrium wins out. This outcome is unfortunate for two reasons. First, payoffs in the status quo outcome are higher for both targets than those in the mutual deterrence equilibrium. Second, the sum of payoffs from mutual deterrence is the *smallest* of the nine strategic combinations! Pursuit of one's self-interest by playing the dominant strategy leads to the worst social outcome in terms of total payoffs. If a nation has a choice between deterrence and preemption, deterrence often wins out – a situation reflective of nations' tendencies when confronting transnational terrorists to rely on defensive measures to deflect attacks rather than to go after the terrorists directly. This means that coordinating counterterrorism policies among countries can lead to significant gains. Elsewhere, Arce and Sandler (2005) examined alternative game forms – chicken, assurance, and others – when countries choose between defensive and proactive policies and demonstrated the general robustness of the tendency for targets to rely on defensive measures in symmetric scenarios. They also allowed governments a fourth option to use both deterrence and preemption to varying degrees. Once again, the sole reliance on deterrence wins out.

We next permit an asymmetric response for preemption identical to the earlier analysis, so that the southeast 2 × 2 matrix in Figure 4.9 is that of Figure 4.6. The northwest 2 × 2 deterrence matrix in Figure 4.9 is that of Figure 4.7. In terms of underlying payoffs, all that changes in Figure 4.9 compared to the symmetric scenario is that the US derives 8,

		EU		
		Deter	Status quo	Preempt
US	Deter	**−2, −2**	2, −4	6, −6
	Status quo	−4, 2	0, 0	4, −2
	Preempt	**−2, 6**	2, 4	6, 2

Figure 4.9. Deterrence versus preemption – asymmetric case.

rather than 4, in benefits from its own preemption owing to its prime-target status. Thus, only the US payoffs in the bottom row differ from those in Figure 4.8 by being 4 larger. The EU still has a dominant strategy to deter, so the only possible Nash equilibriums must be in the first column, where the EU deters. Given the payoffs of the specific example, there are now two boldfaced Nash equilibriums, where either both targets deter or the US preempts and the EU deters. If, however, the US receives even more benefits from its preemption, then the outcome will have the US preempting while the EU deters. After 9/11, US reliance on defensive measures would merely transfer the attack abroad, where its people and property are still targeted, thus limiting US gains from such reliance.

All of these simple games are conceptually enlightening in explaining why preferred-target countries resort to proactive *and* defensive measures against transnational terrorism, while less-targeted countries focus on defensive actions. In the latter case, the countries' assets may be hit abroad, but since their interests are not sought out per se by the terrorists, this likelihood remains small. Such countries are content to let some more at-risk country root out the terrorists and put its soldiers in harm's way to make the world safer. These strategic incentives bode ill for international cooperation and a united stance against transnational terrorism.

WEAKEST-LINK CONSIDERATIONS

In some cases, risks are interdependent so that securing one vulnerability without securing another does not achieve much (if any) safety.[13] Consider upgrades to airport screening to counter terrorists' ability to circumvent current measures. Suppose that the screening upgrade is introduced in just one of two vulnerable airports. The risk to the flying public may not be curtailed, because the terrorists can exploit the vulnerability at the other location where the device is not installed. The security upgrade is a *weakest-link public good*, whose effective supply is measured by the smallest provision level (Hirshleifer, 1983).

Consider the game depicted in Figure 4.10, where each target has two strategies: introduce a security upgrade to its airport screening or maintain current screening devices and procedures. Further suppose that the upgrade costs 6 but provides benefits of 8 to each country only when *both* targets adopt the upgrade. Unilateral adoption implies costs of 6 with no

---

[13] Interdependent risk is analyzed in Heal and Kunreuther (2003, 2005) and Kunreuther and Heal (2003).

		EU	
		Status quo	Security upgrade
US	Status quo	**0, 0**	0, −6
	Security upgrade	−6, 0	**2, 2**

Figure 4.10. Weakest-link security risk.

benefits. The resulting game is an assurance game. In Figure 4.10, there is no dominant strategy, because the payoffs in either row (column) are not both greater than those in the other row (column). There are, however, two Nash equilibriums along the diagonal where strategy choices are matched – either no upgrade is introduced, or both airports adopt the upgrade. Obviously, the mutual-upgrade equilibrium improves the well-being of both targets over the status quo. If the US leads and adopts the upgrade, then the EU is better off doing the same (a payoff of 2 exceeds that of 0). Matching behavior is the hallmark of weakest-link public goods, since it is senseless to exceed the smallest level of such goods: doing so incurs extra costs with no added benefits.

Next consider the case where each of two targets must choose among five levels of upgrade (including no upgrade), where each incremental upgrade gives 8 in additional benefits to both countries only when matched by the other player. Once again, suppose that every upgrade costs 6. The resulting game can be displayed in a 5 × 5 matrix (not shown) where all of the Nash equilibriums are along the diagonal where upgrade levels are matched. If, for example, each country adopts three upgrade levels, then each gains a net payoff of 6. Suppose that one target country has more-limited means than another. This country chooses the security level that it can afford, which may be a rather low standard of safety. The wealthier country can either match this level or subsidize the security upgrade of the other country.[14] If the level chosen by the poorer country is unacceptable to the richer country, then fostering the former's security is the logical choice. One of the four pillars of US counterterrorism policy is to "bolster the counterterrorist capabilities of those countries that work with the United States and require assistance" (US Department of State, 2003, p. xi). If, instead, two hundred countries must provide a weakest-link

[14] For an analysis of in-kind transfers of weakest-link public goods, see Vicary (1990) and Vicary and Sandler (2002).

security activity, then shoring up the many weakest links becomes an expensive proposition that we address in Chapter 6.

For domestic terrorism, the weakest-link issue is addressed by having the central government impose and coordinate acceptable standards countrywide. The training and deployment of professional federal screeners responded to the obvious vulnerabilities at Logan, Newark, and Dulles Airports demonstrated on 9/11. The creation of the Department of Homeland Security (DHS) was motivated, in part, by the goal of achieving acceptable levels of interdependent security risks countrywide.[15]

Interdependent risks abound in the study of counterterrorism. Many defensive actions involve such risks – for example, screening luggage transferred between airlines and airports, limiting the vulnerability of a network, and guarding ports of entry. Although weakest-link public goods tend to be tied to defensive measures, they may occasionally be associated with a proactive policy. For example, the least discreet intelligence-gathering operation may jeopardize everyone's efforts by putting the terrorists on notice. Moreover, efforts to freeze terrorists' assets can be severely compromised by inadequate action at some financial safe havens.

In some situations, the concept of a *weaker-link public good* may apply if efforts above the lowest level add some benefits to a counterterrorist action. If, on average, more luggage is transferred at airport A, then extra measures there may compensate somewhat for lower standards elsewhere. At a few airports, efforts to rescreen all transferred luggage limit interdependent risks and provide for greater payoffs from higher levels of vigilance. With weaker-link public goods, equilibriums may include some nonmatching policy combinations. The extent of nonmatching outcomes hinges on the degree to which extra efforts at one venue can compensate for inadequate actions elsewhere.

BEST-SHOT CONSIDERATIONS

Some counterterrorism policies are *best-shot public goods*, where the largest provision amount determines the benefits to all potential targets. Again, consider the case of transnational terrorism in which countries are confronted with a threat from the same terrorist network. The gathering of intelligence and the infiltration of the network – two proactive

[15] How well interdependent security risks are reduced in practice also depends on the screening technology given to the professional screeners. US government reports released in 2005 reveal that screening still has significant vulnerabilities as privacy is preserved.

		EU	
		Status quo	Innovate
US	Status quo	0, 0	**6, 2**
	Innovate	**2, 6**	2, 2

Figure 4.11. Best-shot security innovation.

measures – are often best-shot public goods whose benefits depend on the greatest effort. If, for example, the group is infiltrated, its security is compromised and the group presents a reduced threat for all targets. Often the greatest effort accomplishes this outcome; additional effort by others once the group is infiltrated adds no extra benefits. Another example is the development of a security innovation, such as stun grenades or a bomb-sniffing device. The best-performing innovation will be adopted by all at-risk nations; less adequate or identical innovations offer no additional benefits.

In Figure 4.11, we display a security-innovation game where each of two targets can maintain the status quo or discover a security breakthrough that can protect both targets. Suppose that the innovation costs the innovator 4 and provides benefits of 6 to each potential target. Further suppose that a second discovery of this innovation costs the discoverer 4, but yields no further benefits. In the game box, the sole innovator nets 2, while the other target gains a free-rider benefit of 6. If both innovate, then each receives just 2, as each must cover its innovation costs. The same kind of payoff scenario characterizes infiltrating a group, because a second infiltration is costly but does not necessarily weaken the terrorist group any more than the first. The same is true of redundant intelligence.

There is no dominant strategy in the two-target innovation game, but there are two Nash equilibriums in cases where there is a sole innovator. The boldfaced payoffs for these equilibriums lie along the off-diagonal. If the innovation scenario involves, say, twenty countries, then the equilibriums consist of just one country making the discovery and the others adopting it. The resulting game is a *coordination* game in which the countries must tacitly decide who is to expend the effort so that resources are not wasted in duplication. Often the innovation or group infiltration comes from the most threatened country. If the required effort is sufficiently large to surpass the capabilities of the prime-target country, then international cooperation and a pooling of effort may be necessary.

For domestic terrorism, the coordination is achieved by the central government orchestrating efforts to eliminate duplication. The rationale behind the creation of an intelligence czar and a single entity to coordinate the different intelligence-gathering agencies in the United States is to limit duplication and increase efficiency. Private firms play an essential role in developing technological innovations useful to counterterrorism. At times, their research and development are subsidized by the government in order to reduce investment risk to the firm. The best technology can then be sold by the firms to governments worldwide to increase safety. Currently, firms are developing biofeedback screening devices that can identify people based on their eyes or other unique features.

GETTING AT THE ROOTS OF TERRORISM

Another counterterrorism action is to address the grievances of the terrorists, thereby eliminating their rationale for violence. There are a number of difficulties with accommodating terrorists' demands. First, such accommodations may induce countergrievances and a new wave of terrorism from those who are harmed by the government's concessions. Second, granting concessions sends the message that violence pays and will encourage more terrorism. When deciding between legal and terrorist means, a terrorist group accounts for the likelihood of success of alternative techniques. By granting concessions, the government is raising the perceived likelihood of success of terrorist tactics (see Chapter 7). Third, terrorist grievances must be well articulated if they are to be satisfied; this is often not the case for modern-day transnational terrorism. For example, the grievances of al-Qaida are not clear and appear to evolve over time. Fourth, countries' responses to terrorists' demands are apt to work at cross purposes – for example, a country that removes its peacekeepers in response to a terrorist campaign makes it more difficult for other countries to continue their missions. After the 23 October 1983 bombing of the US Marine barracks in Beirut, Lebanon, President Reagan withdrew US forces from Lebanon and other countries followed suit. At the transnational level, one country's concessions create externalities for other countries as their policy options become more limited.

A more fruitful approach is to make nonterrorist activities less expensive and therefore more attractive, rather than to reward terrorist campaigns through concessions (Anderton and Carter, 2005; Frey, 2004). The latter policy goes against the principle of liberal democracies by allowing dissidents to circumvent the political process by extorting political change with the threat of violence. Such concessions reduce the payoffs to voting and utilizing legitimate institutions for change. By contrast, a government's encouragement of peaceful dissent raises the attractiveness of legal means. Ironically, when terrorism surfaces in a country, a common governmental reaction is to limit legitimate protest, thereby inducing more terrorism. Terrorist groups with political and military wings – for example, Hezbollah, Hamas, and the Irish Republican Army – pursue both legitimate and illegitimate means. Thus, actions to bolster the relative attractiveness of legitimate means can curb terrorism without compromising the ideals of a liberal democracy by rewarding terrorism.

CONCLUDING REMARKS

This chapter has applied simple game theory to analyze strategic differences between proactive and defensive policies. For transnational terrorism, the policy choices of a targeted government can have positive and/or negative consequences or externalities for other targeted countries. For instance, defensive measures taken by one country can deflect an attack to other, less protected countries. Following 9/11, industrial countries redoubled their efforts to harden targets; these efforts coincided with more attacks in other places – for example, Kenya, Morocco, Malaysia, Indonesia, and Turkey – where defensive measures were not increased. At the international level, there is a real need for cooperation or else countries will work at cross purposes with a tendency to undersupply proactive measures and oversupply defensive ones. Some defensive actions are weakest-link public goods, where the smallest precaution taken determines the level of safety for all. To shore up a weakest link, wealthy nations may have to bolster the defenses of other nations. In a globalized world, a country's interests can be attacked in places where defenses are inadequate, so weakest-link nations are everyone's concern. Many proactive policies are best-shot public goods, where the greatest action protects everyone. For such measures, coordination is important so that actions are not duplicated in a wasteful manner.

In the case of domestic terrorism, the central government can account for the strategic consequences arising from proactive and defensive policies. A central viewpoint allows the government to raise security to acceptable standards countrywide. The central government is motivated to pursue terrorists that target any of the countries' diverse interests. One essential question that calls for further research is the proper allocation of resources between proactive and defensive measures. This is an interesting issue, because the two sets of policies are interdependent. If, for example, proactive measures weaken the terrorist threat, then there is less need for defensive policy. As all targets are secured through defensive measures, there may be less need to go after the terrorists. In analyzing this allocation, the strategic interaction can be extended to include the terrorists along with the targeted countries.

FIVE

Transference

Contraband such as automatic and semiautomatic machine guns, bazookas, hand grenades, suicide vests, and hand-held rocket launchers can easily fit into a ship's cargo container. The Department of Homeland Security (DHS) is understandably worried about these potential terrorist weapons reaching US shores. The Container Security Initiative (CSI) is designed to secure US ports against the importation of these and other dangerous materials (see Chapter 10 on homeland security). With the cooperation of its trading partners, US inspectors in port cities such as Rotterdam, Singapore, and Hong Kong inspect and label cargo before it reaches US shores. The CSI is predicated, in part, on the notion that terrorists make choices by taking costs and benefits into account. If it is more difficult to smuggle weapons aboard a commercial plane or by airfreight, terrorists will seek out a "weaker link" or softer target. Thus, unless US ports of entry are made more secure, DHS predicts that enhanced airport security will make US ports a weaker link.

The bombing of the three train stations in Madrid on 11 March 2004 is another instance of terrorists finding a weaker link. The bombs, designed to explode during rush hour, left 191 dead and injured more than 1,200 others. The coverage in the Spanish press and the effects on the Spanish psyche rivaled the influence of 9/11 in the United States. One indirect consequence of the attack was the unanticipated victory of the Socialists over the ruling Partido Popular party. Why did al-Qaida decide to attack train passengers? One rationale given for the train station bombings was that terrorists found that skyjacking was too difficult and too risky to be successful. The main Atocha train station and the two smaller stations were a softer target.

As analyzed in this chapter, the search for weak links is an important type of policy-induced substitution. Social scientists refer to this behavior as "transference." In the two examples just mentioned, enhanced airport security resulted in a transference from airline-related crimes to those involving other forms of transportation. In a sense, the unintended consequence of many government policies designed to thwart one type of terrorist behavior is to cause an increase in another type of terrorism. As one type of attack declines, policymakers need to anticipate transference effects in order to protect the public against new attack modes.

MODELS OF RATIONAL TERRORISM

In order to forecast new types of terrorist attack modes, the number and severity of future incidents, or the likely behavior of terrorists in response to a shift in government policy, we must posit a rational-choice theory of terrorist behavior. If terrorists are completely irrational, there is no way of knowing how they will respond to future events. By contrast, the rational-agent model gives us a number of straightforward predictions that have proven to be correct. In Chapter 3, we saw that the installation of metal detectors in airports was associated with a reduction in the number of skyjackings. However, as we will consider in more detail, once skyjackings became more difficult, terrorists substituted into other, logistically similar attack modes. This transference follows directly from the assumption that terrorists are rational.

There are only two essential ingredients of rational behavior. The first is that the agent has a well-defined set of preferences, which requires that the individual is able to rank, or order, the alternative feasible choices. Consider an individual, say Justin, who has preferences over three baskets of goods, A, B, and C. For these rankings to be sensible, they must be internally consistent. If Justin prefers basket A to basket B and basket B to basket C, Justin must then prefer A to C in order for his preferences to be consistent – a condition of rationality. Unless this so-called "transitivity" condition is satisfied, the ordering is meaningless. The second essential ingredient of rationality is that the individual select the most preferred of the available choices. If, therefore, Justin is presented with the equally affordable choice of A or C, then rationality requires that he select A if he prefers A to C. Rationality does not require that we answer the question "Why does he prefer A?" or "Should he prefer A?" Moreover, a rational individual may have preferences that change over time.

The rational-choice model posits that terrorists will allocate their scarce resources so as to maximize the expected value of their utility. Landes (1978) was the first to explicitly model the behavior of a potential sky-jacker contemplating the forceful diversion of a commercial aircraft. To take a simplified version of his model, suppose there are three possible states of the world: the skyjacking is not undertaken, the skyjacking is successful, and the skyjacking fails. Landes is not especially concerned about the ultimate goals or motives of the terrorist. Simply, suppose that U^S is the terrorist's utility if the skyjacking is successful and that U^F is the terrorist's utility if the skyjacking fails. The utility of a success obviously exceeds that of a failure, so that $U^S > U^F$. A key aspect of the choice is that skyjackings have an uncertain outcome. The potential skyjacker believes that the probability of a successful skyjacking is π and that the probability of an unsuccessful skyjacking is $(1 - \pi)$.

The rational terrorist will compare the expected utility of the skyjacking to the next-best alternative. To highlight the risky nature of a skyjacking, we assume that utility in the no-skyjacking state is the certain value U^N. The decision tree for the terrorist's actions is displayed in Figure 5.1. If the terrorist chooses not to undertake the skyjacking, the payoff is U^N. If the skyjacking is undertaken, the terrorist receives U^S with probability π and U^F with probability $(1 - \pi)$. Hence, the expected utility from undertaking the skyjacking is

$$EU^{SKY} = \pi U^S + (1 - \pi)U^F, \tag{1}$$

where EU^{SKY} is the expected utility if the skyjacking occurs.

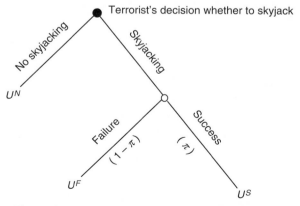

Figure 5.1. Expected utility of a potential skyjacker.

The skyjacking will be undertaken if the expected utility from skyjacking exceeds U^N.[1] Hence, the skyjacking will occur if

$$U^N < EU^{SKY} = \pi U^S + (1 - \pi)U^F. \tag{2}$$

An increase in U^N or a decrease in EU^{SKY} reduces the likelihood that the terrorist will attempt a skyjacking. A policy that reduces the utility of a skyjacking success, such as a guaranteed refusal never to concede to terrorists, reduces EU^{SKY}. If a terrorist group seeks media coverage for its cause, then government actions to limit such coverage also reduce U^S and, thus, skyjackings. A policy that reduces the utility of a failure, such as longer jail sentences, reduces EU^{SKY} and skyjackings. Given that $U^S > U^F$, a policy that reduces the probability of a success, such as enhanced airport security, reduces EU^{SKY}.[2] In addition, concessions granted to a terrorist can encourage future terrorist acts by raising terrorists' perceptions about the utility associated with a skyjacking success. Such concessions might also induce subsequent skyjackers to perceive that the probability of success is higher. A policy that increases utility in the no-skyjacking state, such as alleviating some portion of the terrorist's grievances, reduces the incentive for terrorism.

Landes (1978) obtained US Federal Aviation Administrative (FAA) data and estimated two regression equations for US skyjackings for the 1961–1976 period. The first empirically related (regressed) the quarterly total of skyjackings on policy variables such as the probability of apprehension, the probability of conviction, and a measure of the severity of sentencing. Recall from Chapter 3 that a regression uses data to explain the variation in a dependent or response variable (for example, the quarterly number of skyjackings) based on the values of a number of independent or control variables. Landes's second equation regressed the time interval between skyjackings on the same set of variables. Both regressions found the length of sentence and the probability of apprehension to be significant deterrents to skyjackings. The probability of conviction was only marginally significant. One of his key findings was that between forty-one and fifty fewer skyjackings occurred in the United States following the installation of metal detectors in US airports in 1973.

---

[1] Throughout, we assume that terrorists are risk-neutral in the sense that they are indifferent to taking a fair bet. Of course, if terrorists are sufficiently risk-averse (so that they would not undertake a fair bet), they might not undertake a skyjacking even if the expected utility from skyjacking exceeds U^N.

[2] Given that $EU^{SKY} = \pi U^S + (1 - \pi)U^F$, it follows that $dEU^{SKY}/d\pi = U^S - U^F > 0$. Hence, increasing (decreasing) π increases (decreases) EU^{SKY}.

Enders and Sandler (1993) generalize Landes's framework to allow for substitutions between terrorist and nonterrorist activities *and* for substitutions within the set of terrorist activities. Specifically, they use the household production function (HPF) model to analyze the behavior of a terrorist group whose utility is derived from a shared political goal. This shared goal is obtained from the consumption of a number of *basic commodities* such as media attention, political instability, popular support for their cause, and the creation of an atmosphere of fear and intimidation.

Each basic commodity can be produced using a number of political strategies that include various types of terrorist and nonterrorist activities. At one extreme, the group might simply choose to turn out voters for local elections or run their own candidates for office. Alternatively, nonterrorist acts of civil disobedience might be undertaken – protestors might block the entrance to a government building, or refuse to ride in the back of a bus in Selma, Alabama. At the other extreme, the group might resort to bombings, hostage takings, or assassinations. Some groups, such as the Irish Republican Army (IRA), simultaneously produce basic commodities using terrorist *and* nonterrorist means. The provisional wing of the IRA has engaged in numerous acts of domestic and transnational terrorism. Sinn Féin ("Ourselves Alone" in Gaelic) is generally considered to be the political wing of the IRA. Under Gerry Adams's leadership, Sinn Féin has moved away from serving as a support base for the Provisional IRA to become a professionally organized political party in both Northern Ireland and the Republic of Ireland.

The point is that the group can be modeled as having a well-defined set of preferences over terrorist activities (T) and nonterrorist activities (N). Increases in terrorist activities and nonterrorist activities both augment the production of basic commodities and, hence, the utility of terrorists. We can write these preferences in the form of the utility function U:[3]

$$U = U(T, N). \tag{3}$$

Terrorist activities are actually a composite good consisting of a number of different attack modes that can be substitutable if they are capable of producing the same basic commodities. Substitution is most likely between modes that are logistically similar and yield similar basic commodities. Kidnappings and skyjackings tend to be good substitutes, since both are

---

[3] An alternative way to present the model is to let the group receive utility from two basic commodities, B_1 and B_2. If the basic commodities are produced by T and N, the group's utility is an implicit function of T and N.

logistically complex incident types that can result in similar amounts of media attention (see Chapter 7). Attack modes will be complements if they are essential ingredients for the production of a single basic commodity or if they reinforce each other's effectiveness. Bombings and threats tend to be complementary. In response to a bombing campaign, terrorists often make threatening calls to the media and to the authorities, since these low-cost threats heighten the tension associated with the actual detonation of the bombs.

The Resource Constraint

A terrorist group has access to resources that may include direct financial wealth, capital equipment including weapons and buildings, personnel, and entrepreneurial skills. During any period, a group's total outlays cannot exceed the total of these monetary and nonmonetary resources. The terrorist group, thus, faces the same resource allocation problems as any household, because the selection of one set of activities precludes the group from selecting some other activities. The group must decide whether to produce basic commodities by terrorist or nonterrorist means, or by some combination of the two. The group must also choose among the various types of terrorist activities. For example, a group bent on attracting media attention can select a skyjacking, a kidnapping, or a suicide bombing. Since terrorists can expend or augment their resources in the current period or "save" their resources for future attacks, rational terrorists time their attacks in order to enhance their overall effectiveness. Moreover, terrorists are able to attack domestically or abroad. From the set of activities consistent with its total resource holdings, a rational terrorist group selects the one that maximizes its expected utility.

The choices made by the group will be influenced by the prices of the various terrorist and nonterrorist activities. The full price of any particular attack mode includes the value of the resources used to plan and execute the attack and the cost of casualties to group members. The simultaneous attack on the three Madrid train stations was a high-priced incident because it required a substantial amount of planning and coordination. Certain attack modes are more likely to expose the group's membership to capture than others. The price of a suicide bombing includes the direct cost of the bomb, the cost of grooming the perpetrator to ensure that the attack takes place, and the cost of protecting the group's security in case of a failed attack. At the other end of the spectrum, threats and hoaxes typically require few inputs. The effectiveness of an attack mode is not necessarily commensurate with its price. In the months following 9/11, a number of people opened packages containing various powders disguised as anthrax. The cost of some baby powder, an envelope, and a stamp caused recipients to feel the same fear, and caused the authorities to undertake the same precautions, as if the powder had been real.

Transference occurs because the prices and payoffs faced by terrorists can be influenced by a government's antiterrorism policies. Enhanced airport security increases the logistical complexity of a skyjacking and raises its price. If, at the same time, governments do not increase security at ports of entry, attacks relying on contraband become relatively cheaper. If, similarly, immigration officials make it more difficult for terrorists to enter the United States, a terrorist group might attack US interests located abroad (for example, tourists and firms). Hence, a government policy that increases the price of one type of attack mode will induce a substitution away from that mode into other logistically similar incident types. In order to induce the group to substitute from terrorist to nonterrorist activities, policymakers must raise the price of all types of attack modes or lower the price of nonterrorist activities (for example, by providing easier access to elections).

We conclude this section with the example of the 9 September 2004 car bombing outside the Australian embassy in Jakarta, Indonesia. At least 9 people were killed and more than 150 were wounded by an explosion that left a crater nine feet deep. Australia has been a strong US ally and has sent troops to support the war in Iraq. According to the *New York Times* (10 September 2004, p. A10), an Australian official stated that the al-Qaida-linked group Jemaah Islamiyah selected the Australian embassy as a target because "it was easier to hit than the US embassy."

A FORMALIZATION OF THE MODEL

We can formalize the HPF model by combining the group's indifference curves with its budget constraint. The indifference curve labeled 1 in Figure 5.2 shows the number of terrorist attacks (T) and nonterrorist actions (N) necessary to produce a given level of the group's shared political goal or utility. Each indifference curve has a negative slope, since T and N both aid in the production of the basic commodity. If, therefore, T increases, then N must decrease or else the terrorist group would produce more of the basic commodity and end up on a higher indifference curve. An increased use of one type of input allows the group to reduce its use of the other input and still maintain the same utility level. If a terrorist group

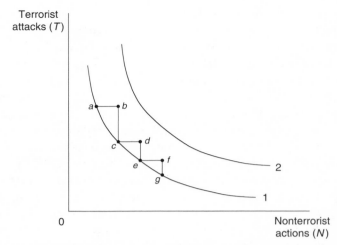

Figure 5.2. Indifference curves for terrorist and nonterrorist actions.

were contemplating increasing N by the amount ab, it could maintain the same level of utility by reducing T by bc units.

If the inputs were perfect substitutes, the indifference curves would be linear, since one unit of T could always be traded off for a fixed amount of N. All of the indifference curves in Figure 5.2 are, however, convex to the origin, because each extra unit of N has to replace ever smaller amounts of T if the terrorists are to maintain a given level of the basic commodity or utility. That is, the ability of one input to substitute for the other input diminishes as more of the former input is utilized. Notice that in moving from a to c and then from c to e, each equal increment in nonterrorist activities ($ab = cd$) releases successively smaller amounts of inputs from terrorist attacks, as $bc > de$. Similarly, a movement from e to g would require ef units of N but would free up only fg additional units of T. Since $ef = cd$ but $de > fg$, indifference curve 1 is intended to be convex to the origin throughout its entire range.[4]

The group's utility will increase if it can move from indifference curve 1 to indifference curve 2. If you compare the two curves, you will see that indifference curve 2 entails a greater utilization of inputs than does 1. For

---

[4] The convexity may be consistent with the law of diminishing marginal productivity. The marginal productivity of an input diminishes if its successive application results in smaller and smaller increments of the basic commodity. Beginning on indifference curve 1, the successive application of ab, cd, and ef units of N results in smaller and smaller additional units of the basic commodity. Thus, smaller and smaller amounts of T can be withdrawn from the production process if output of the basic commodity is to remain constant.

any point you select on indifference curve 1, there is a point on curve 2 with more *T* and *N*. Since both inputs contribute to the production of the basic commodity, the level of utility associated with indifference curve 2 is higher than the level associated with 1.

The issue for the terrorists is to choose the combination of *T* and *N* that maximizes their expected utility. Rational terrorists will combine the information contained in the indifference map with their budget constraint. As in Chapter 4, we can let the budget constraint of the terrorist group be

$$P_T T + P_N N = I, \qquad (4)$$

where P_T and P_N are the unit costs of a generic terrorist incident (*T*) or nonterrorist action (*N*), respectively, and *I* is the group's income or resources for the current period.

In Figure 5.3, we superimpose the budget constraint from Figure 4.1 on the indifference map of Figure 5.2. The budget constraint, *AB*, is like a menu in that it indicates the feasible combinations available to the terrorists. The terrorists can allocate all of their income to terrorist attacks (producing 0*A* attacks), all of their income to nonterrorist actions (producing 0*B* units of *N*), or some of their income to both activities (corresponding to some point on the line *AB*). As shown, the optimal or best choice for the terrorist group is point *R*, where the group engages in $0T_0$ units of terrorist attacks and $0N_0$ units of nonterrorist activities. A few moments reflection will show why *R* is the optimal choice. Any movement away from *R* along *AB* (so that total expenditures are maintained) results in a lower utility level than that enjoyed on indifference curve 2, as lower

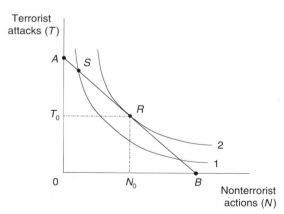

Figure 5.3. The optimal allocation.

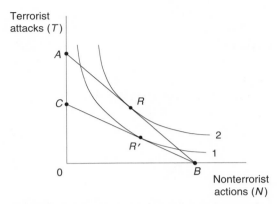

Figure 5.4. Increasing the cost of terrorist attacks.

indifference curves are reached. Given its budget constraint, the group would never select a suboptimal point such as S on indifference curve 1. Moreover, since the indifference curves further from the origin than curve 2 are unattainable with expenditure level I, the group can do no better than to select point R.

Now we are in a position to revisit the concept of proactive and defensive policies. Remember that defensive policies, such as the installation of metal detectors and bomb-sniffing devices in airports, protect potential targets either by making attacks more costly for terrorists or by reducing their likelihood of success. Figure 5.4 illustrates the situation in which a bomb-sniffing device raises the price of a terrorist act without reducing the level of the group's resources. Consequently, the budget constraint rotates from AB to BC. Notice that the original choice (R) is no longer attainable. Instead, the new rational choice for the terrorist group occurs at point R'. As drawn, the policy induces terrorists to reduce the level of terrorist attacks *and* to increase nonterrorist activities.[5]

---

[5] Notice that there is an ambiguity about the change in the level of N. In Figure 5.4, we could have drawn the indifference curves so that N falls. Because the relative price of nonterrorist activities decreases, there is a substitution into N and away from T. However, the group's opportunity set shifts inward from AB to BC. If we assume that T and N are normal goods, then the resulting negative "income effect" reduces the amounts of T and N produced. The amount of T unambiguously falls, since the relative price of T increases and the group's real income has fallen. The effect of the decrease in the relative price of N and the decrease in the group's real income have, however, opposing effects on the amount of N ultimately produced. The importance of this income effect increases as the group becomes increasingly specialized in terrorism.

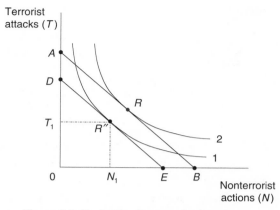

Figure 5.5. Reduction in terrorists' resources.

Some proactive policies also raise the price of terrorist actions. As mentioned in Chapter 4, an increased risk of being infiltrated by the government makes terrorist acts more costly without necessarily changing the terrorists' resource endowments. Rotating the budget constraint in Figure 5.4 from AB to BC represents such a circumstance. In that case, both a defensive and a proactive policy could induce a terrorist group to select R' instead of R. Unlike defensive measures, proactive policies can reduce the total income of the terrorist group. Certainly, the terrorists' resource holdings decline when the government captures or kills group members, cuts off the group's funding, or destroys weapons, safe havens, and infrastructure. In Figure 5.5, the reduction in the group's income is represented by the parallel shift of the budget constraint from AB to DE. The decline in total resources means that the opportunities to engage in both terrorist *and* nonterrorist acts have decreased. The terrorist group now chooses point R'', engaging in T_1 units of terrorism and N_1 nonterrorist activities.

Without a careful empirical investigation, there is no simple way to determine which type of policy (proactive or defensive) is the most appropriate. The success of any antiterrorism policy depends on how successful it is in restricting the terrorists' choice set. The HPF approach makes it clear that policies having no effect on the group's resource constraint or preferences will be completely ineffective. Consider the United Nations' International Convention against the Taking of Hostages that was open for signatures in 1973 (approved on 17 December 1979). The key provision of the convention is that:

Each State Party is required to make this offence [hostage taking] punishable by appropriate penalties. Where hostages are held in the territory of a State Party, the State Party is obligated to take all measures it considers appropriate to ease the situation of the hostages and secure their release. After the release of the hostages, States Parties are obligated to facilitate the departure of the hostages. Each State Party is obligated to take such actions as may be necessary to establish jurisdiction over the offence of taking of hostages. (United Nations, 2003)[6]

Although the goals of the convention are laudable, the United Nations itself has no direct enforcement mechanism; rather, it is left to each member to take "appropriate" actions to secure the release of hostages. As such, there may be different levels of enforcement depending on the signatories' attitudes toward terrorism. This results in an important loophole, since many nations have registered objections to one or more portions of the convention. For example, Lebanon worried that the convention's provision might compromise the means that a state can bring to bear on foreign occupiers. Given these circumstances, we might expect that the overall effect of the convention was nil, since it had no effect on terrorists' budget constraints. As mentioned in Chapter 6, past empirical tests have found no overall effect of this and similar conventions.

The model also allows for the possibility that the group fully specializes in one of the activities. If the group's preferences are such that the indifference curves are vertical (horizontal), it will devote all of its resources to N (T). The group's indifference curves would be perfectly vertical if it received no benefit from T, and they would be perfectly horizontal if it received no benefit from N.

So far, we have considered only substitutions between terrorist and nonterrorist activities. The household production function approach also allows for substitutions between the various attack modes. Notice that little would be changed if we redrew Figures 5.4 and 5.5 using two different attack modes as the decision variables. Instead of T and N, skyjackings (Sky) might be on the vertical axis and other terrorist actions (O) on the horizontal axis. Figure 5.4 would then show that an increase in the price of skyjackings would cause a substitution away from that attack mode and into other terrorist acts. The redrawn Figure 5.5 would show that a reduction in the group's expenditures on terrorist activities would be represented by a parallel shift of the expenditure line toward the origin.

---

[6] This representation of the treaty's key provisions splices together statements from the convention. The treaty's text can be found in United Nations (2003).

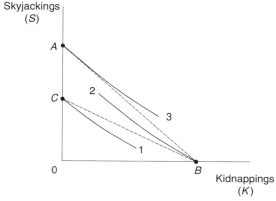

Figure 5.6. Substitutability between attack modes.

If both attack modes were normal, then the amount of *Sky* and *O* would decline.

A critical prediction of the HFP model is that a high degree of substitutability between attack modes reduces the effectiveness of antiterrorism policies directed to only one of the modes. Figure 5.6 depicts the trade-off between kidnappings (K) and skyjackings (S) for a hypothetical terrorist group seeking media coverage. The indifference curves are downward-sloping, since a reduction in S will necessitate an increase in K if the group is to maintain a particular level of utility from media attention. As drawn, indifference curves 1, 2, and 3 cut the horizontal and vertical axes, since neither attack mode is essential. If the group wants to spend an amount such that the budget constraint is the dashed line AB, then there will be a corner solution; the group selects point A on indifference curve 3, where it fully specializes in skyjackings. Now consider the effects of a defensive policy, such as the installation of enhanced screening devices, that makes it more costly to conduct a skyjacking. In particular, suppose that the increased cost of a skyjacking is such that the budget constraint becomes the dashed line BC. Given its total resource endowment, the terrorist group now fully specializes in kidnappings by producing on indifference curve 2 at point B. Total media attention falls (indifference curve 2 entails less media attention than 3), but not as much as in the case where substitutability is low. If the group could not substitute any kidnappings for skyjackings, it would necessarily produce at point C on indifference curve 1. Hence, when substitution possibilities are high, terrorists can readily circumvent a policy that raises the price of only one attack mode. An effective antiterrorism policy is one that raises the costs of *all* attack modes or reduces the overall resource level of the terrorists.

Enders and Sandler (1993) summarize the four main propositions of the model as follows:

Proposition 1: Relative Price Effects. An increase in the relative price of one type of terrorist activity will cause the terrorist group to substitute out of the relatively expensive activity and into terrorist and nonterrorist activities that are now relatively less expensive.

Proposition 2: Substitutes and Complements. Terrorist attack modes that are logistically similar and yield similar basic commodities will display the greatest substitution possibilities. Since the effects of complementary events are mutually reinforcing, an increase (decrease) in the price of one activity will cause that activity and all complements to fall (rise) in number.

Proposition 3: Terrorist-Nonterrorist Substitutions. An increase in the price of all terrorist activities or a decrease in the price of nonterrorist activities will decrease the overall level of terrorism.[7]

Proposition 4: Income Effects. For normal goods, an increase (decrease) in the resource base will cause a terrorist group to increase (decrease) the level of terrorist and nonterrorist activities.

SUICIDE BOMBERS AND RATIONAL BEHAVIOR

Some scholars argue that it is not possible to apply the notion of rationality to suicidal terrorist actions. Such acts are not rash or spontaneous outbursts of emotion; instead, they are carefully orchestrated incidents that are prepared far in advance of the actual attack. While in flight training school, for example, the pilots of the 9/11 planes knew that they were preparing for a single mission. The issue is whether rational agents can carefully prepare and execute a plan of action that calls for their own demise. If such behavior is irrational, the presence of suicide missions casts doubt on the entire rational-actor framework. As illustrated by Figure 3.7 (see Chapter 3), suicide bombings are not isolated incidents.

Suicide can be rational if the utility obtained from living with the current state of affairs is less than that obtained by a life-ending action. Few would question the rationality of a person living in substantial pain asking

---

[7] As discussed in note 5, we are assuming that income effects associated with relative price changes do not offset the direct substitution effects.

to have a life-giving medication withheld. In the same way, a suicidal terrorist mission can be rational if the utility associated with planning and contemplating the consequences of the suicide mission is at least as great as that of living with the status quo. The issue is why certain individuals gain utility from a suicide act. Wintrobe (2002) argues that suicidal terrorists are rational in that they engage in such acts in order to obtain a group "solidarity" or cohesiveness. He argues that individuals strive to belong to a group and that such solidarity is typically acquired through group-directed activity. Well-defined groups, such as gangs, cults, labor unions, political parties or movements, and religious sects, can provide this essential feeling of belonging. As terrorist group members, individuals are viewed by Wintrobe as gaining benefits from social cohesion as they adopt group-sanctioned beliefs. In a sense, there is a trade-off between being integrated into a group and a sense of self. All of us make certain sacrifices of our individual autonomy in order to be members of a well-functioning society. In some extremist groups, the belief system entails the willingness to sacrifice a few of the individual members. Wintrobe (2002) argues that for suicide attacks, there is a "corner solution" such that the individual sacrifices everything for the sake of the group.

The theory has a number of implications that seem to be borne out by terrorist groups. First, newcomers to the group are unlikely to be selected for a suicide mission – such individuals will have had scant time to bask in the camaraderie provided by group membership. Instead, the group's leadership will nurture young members, allowing them to consume the benefits of group membership. Such benefits would include the "feeling of belonging," the esteem accorded to a future martyr, and thoughts of the heavenly rewards of dying for the *jihad*. Second, a member selected for a suicide mission must be made aware that he will receive a strong group sanction if the attack is not carried out. Some groups will blackball, and others will harm, a member who "chickens out."

Azam (2005) argues that another motivation for suicide missions is purely altruistic. Many parents have placed themselves in harm's way in order to save their children from danger. More typically, individuals commonly sacrifice current consumption for the benefit of future family members. Actions such as the purchase of a life insurance policy, or the creation of a will or trust, indicate that members of the current generation are willing to sacrifice for future generations. Azam (2005) views suicide bombings as a form of intergenerational investment. Reducing current consumption to zero by conducting a suicide bombing is viewed as an extreme form of saving. Even in the circumstance where the bomber has no estate to pass on to descendents, the bombing can increase the probability that beneficial public goods will accrue to the next generation. In the case of Palestine, the public good might be an increased probability of an independent political state. Evidence of compensation paid to the families of suicide bombers by the government of Iraq and by members of the Saudi royal family provides some support for Azam's model. According to the BBC, during the Saddam Hussein regime a suicide bomber's family got $25,000, while relatives of militants killed in fighting received $10,000. Azam also notes that Israel punishes the suicide bombers' families by systematically destroying their houses.

Berman and Laitin (2005) provide a similar explanation. They allow a religious organization to supply social welfare benefits to members. Members of the group must adhere to group demands in order to attain the welfare benefits. They define a hard target as one that cannot be attacked without a high probability of apprehension. Suicide attacks are a favored tactic as they have the great advantage of not allowing the attacker to be apprehended, potentially exposing the other operatives.

We believe that revenge can motivate suicide attacks. On 25 August 2004, two flights left Domodedovo Airport near Moscow and exploded in midair. Two Chechen women, thought to be Amanat Nagayeva and Satsita Dzhbirkhanova, detonated the explosives that blew up the aircraft. A week later, Ms. Nagayeva's younger sister set off a bomb that killed eleven people, including herself, outside a Moscow subway. On 8 September 2004, at least two (and possibly four) women were among the terrorist group that killed at least 335 children, parents, and teachers at Middle School No. 1 in the city of Beslan. According to the *New York Times* (10 September 2004, p. A1), female Chechen suicide bombers have taken part in at least fifteen suicide attacks since 1999. In the Russian media, such women are referred to as "black widows" to denote their willingness to undertake a suicide mission avenging the death of a father, husband, brother, or son.

Thwarting suicide acts is especially difficult. In terms of Landes's (1978) model of a potential skyjacker, a person concerned about living and the quality of life in prison will have a relatively low value of U^F. However, a fanatical terrorist, who does not fear death (and might even welcome it), has a higher U^F. The point is that fanatical terrorism brings U^F closer to U^S. In the extreme, $U^S = U^F$, so that a change in the probability of success (π) has no effect on the terrorist's behavior. In the HPF model, such individuals opt for a corner solution so that they are fully specialized in terror. Such fanatical terrorists must be apprehended or killed in order to prevent the attack.

ESTIMATES OF THE SUBSTITUTION EFFECT

Vector autoregressions (VARs) have proven to be an important way to empirically measure the extent of substitution effects in transnational terrorism. You can think of a vector autoregression as a many-variable generalization of the intervention model discussed in Chapter 3. To explain VAR analysis, consider the following simplified system allowing for only two incident types:

$$Sky_t = a_{10} + a_{11}Sky_{t-1} + a_{12}Kidnap_{t-1} + \varepsilon_{1t}, \tag{5}$$

$$Kidnap_t = a_{20} + a_{21}Sky_{t-1} + a_{22}Kidnap_{t-1} + \varepsilon_{2t}, \tag{6}$$

where Sky_t (Sky_{t-1}) is the number of skyjacking incidents during time period t (period $t-1$), $Kidnap_t$ ($Kidnap_{t-1}$) is the number of transnational kidnapping incidents during time period t (period $t-1$), and ε_{1t} and ε_{2t} are shocks to each incident type that may be correlated. Since skyjackings tend to cluster, we would expect a_{11} to be strongly positive; that is, when the value of Sky_{t-1} is large, the value of Sky_t will tend to be large. Similarly, a positive value of a_{22} can capture the tendency of kidnappings to cluster. The interrelationships between the series are captured by the values of a_{12} and a_{21}. For example, if the incident types were complements, so that an increase in skyjackings were associated with a subsequent increase in kidnappings, the value of a_{21} would be positive. Alternatively, if increases in skyjackings come at the expense of future kidnappings, the value of a_{21} would be negative. The relationship between the contemporaneous movements in the two series is captured by the correlation coefficient between ε_{1t} and ε_{2t}. If this correlation coefficient is positive (negative), the co-movements between Sky_t and $Kidnap_t$ tend to be positive (negative).

The VAR represented by equations (5) and (6) can be extended in a number of different ways. Additional lags of the variables can capture the possibility of more sophisticated dynamic linkages among the variables, insofar as more than one period may be required for a change in the number of skyjackings (kidnappings) to affect the number of kidnappings (skyjackings). Similarly, there may be interactions among a much larger number of incident types. Increasing the number of variables used in the VAR could allow for the possibility that skyjackings, kidnappings, assassinations, and threats are all interrelated. For our purposes, a critical extension is to incorporate the effects of various intervention variables into the basic VAR. For example, the installation of metal detectors in US airports during the first quarter of 1973 (1973:Q1) can be treated as a permanent level-shift dummy variable. Suppose that the dummy variable $METAL_t$ is equal to zero for all time periods before 1973:Q1 and is equal to one beginning in 1973:Q1. After constructing such a variable, it is possible to write a VAR augmented with dummy variables as

$$Sky_t = a_{10} + b_{10}METAL_t + a_{11}Sky_{t-1} + a_{12}Kidnap_{t-1} + \varepsilon_{1t}, \qquad (7)$$

$$Kidnap_t = a_{20} + b_{20}METAL_t + a_{21}Sky_{t-1} + a_{22}Kidnap_{t-1} + \varepsilon_{2t}. \qquad (8)$$

The new VAR is similar to the original VAR except for the presence of the metal detector dummy variable. Since $METAL_t = 0$ for all periods prior to 1973:Q1, the two VARs should be identical for the pre–metal detector period. However, beginning with 1973:Q1, the value of $METAL_t$ jumps to one. Hence, for the post–metal detector period, the VAR becomes

$$Sky_t = a_{10} + b_{10} + a_{11}Sky_{t-1} + a_{12}Kidnap_{t-1} + \varepsilon_{1t}, \qquad (9)$$

$$Kidnap_t = a_{20} + b_{20} + a_{21}Sky_{t-1} + a_{22}Kidnap_{t-1} + \varepsilon_{2t}. \qquad (10)$$

Now, the difference between the VAR of equations (5) and (6) and the VAR of equations (9) and (10) is the intercept terms, so that the intervention variable acts as a change in the intercepts of the two regression equations. Prior to 1973:Q1, the intercepts are a_{10} and a_{20}; post-1973:Q1, the intercepts are $(a_{10} + b_{10})$ and $(a_{20} + b_{20})$. If b_{10} is negative (so that the new intercept for SKY_t is below a_{10}), the installation of metal detectors will have reduced skyjackings. The short-run substitution effect is captured by the magnitude of b_{20}. If b_{20} is positive (so that the new intercept for $Kidnap_t$ is above a_{20}), the installation of metal detectors is associated with an increase in the number of kidnappings. In this way, b_{10} represents the direct effect of the installation of metal detectors on skyjackings, and b_{20} represents the substitution between skyjackings and kidnappings.[8]

The long-run effects of the interventions account for the fact that lagged values of kidnappings affect Sky_t, and lagged values of skyjackings affect $Kidnap_t$. Due to the dynamic interactions between the series, the long- and short-run effects of the interventions can be quite different. Nevertheless, once the VAR equations have been estimated by a regression analysis, it is possible to shock $METAL_t$ by one unit and trace out the entire time path of the estimated effects of the installation of metal detectors on the

---

[8] The statistical significance of the coefficients b_{10} and b_{20} can be tested using a standard t-test.

two series. The difference between the initial mean values and the final mean values are the long-run effects of the intervention.

VAR Results

Enders and Sandler (1993) use the VAR methodology to estimate the impact of important policy interventions on the attack modes used by terrorists.[9] A number of different combinations of attack modes are examined in their VAR analysis. Enders and Sandler's findings using skyjackings, *other kinds* of hostage takings (including kidnappings) (*Hostage*), attacks against protected persons, and all other attacks are especially interesting. Attacks against protected persons (*APP*) is the time series of nonhostage crimes against diplomats and other protected persons. The United Nations' definition of an "internationally protected person" includes official representatives of a head of state, diplomats, ambassadors, and all accompanying family members. Attacks are counted if they occurred in a country that was a signatory to the UN convention on protected persons and involved a victim from a signatory country.[10] The time series of all other attacks (*OT*) consists primarily of bombings, threats, and hoaxes. The policy interventions include the installation of metal detectors in airports, two embassy fortifications, and the retaliatory raid on Libya. More-detailed descriptions of the interventions are provided in Table 5.1.

The actual quarterly incident totals of *Sky, Hostage, APP*, and *OT* are shown as the dashed lines in Figure 5.7. The solid lines are the estimated time paths of the effects of the various interventions. To construct these estimated paths, we took the predicted values of *Sky, Hostage, APP*, and *OT* from the estimated VAR, conditioned on the interventions alone.[11] As such, the shifts in these lines represent the effects of the interventions alone. As a visual aid, the vertical lines represent the starting dates of each of the four interventions.

---

[9] Each regression equation of a VAR can be estimated using ordinary least squares. The details of the estimation methodology are not especially important for our purposes here. Interested readers can find a detailed discussion of VAR estimation, testing, and analysis in Chapter 5 of Enders (2004).

[10] A complete description can be found in the United Nations (2003), Convention on the Prevention and Punishment of Crimes against Internationally Protected Persons, available at [http://untreaty.un.org/English/Terrorism.asp].

[11] As such, the predicted values are not one-step-ahead forecasts. Each series was initially set at its pre-1973:$Q1$ mean, and we traced out the time path of each using only the altered values of the intervention variables.

Table 5.1. *Description of the Intervention Variables*

Intervention	Description
METAL	The United States began to install metal detectors in airports on 5 January 1973. During the installation process, various screening techniques, including hand searches of carry-on luggage, were conducted. Other international airports worldwide followed suit shortly thereafter.
EMB76	A doubling of spending to fortify and secure US embassies beginning in October 1976. Security measures included the screening of visitors to US embassies.
EMB85	Additional resources were allocated to security in the 1980s as a result of the takeover of the US embassy in Tehran on 4 November 1979. A significant increase in spending to secure US embassies was authorized by Public Law 98–533 in October 1985.
LIBYA	On 5 April 1986, a bomb went off in the La Belle discotheque in West Berlin. It killed a Turkish woman and two US servicemen, and injured 230 people. Many of the injured were US servicemen. On the morning of 15 April 1986, the US undertook a retaliatory raid against Libya for its involvement in the terrorist bombing. At least fifteen people were killed, including the fifteen-month-old adopted daughter of leader Muammar Qaddafi. More than 100 people were injured in the raid.

From the figure with incidents per quarter on the vertical axis, one can see the abrupt changes in *Sky, Hostage,* and *APP* beginning in 1973:Q1. On impact, metal detectors decreased skyjackings by 12.2 incidents per quarter. This is an important effect and is consistent with Landes's (1978) results. However, as predicted by the HPF approach, an increase in the price of a skyjacking results in substitutions into similar incident types. We found that the impact effect of $METAL_t$ was to increase hostage incidents by 3.68 incidents per quarter. Notice that *Hostage* continued to increase for several quarters following 1973:Q1. The cumulated total effect (i.e., the long-run effect) of the intervention was to increase *Hostage* by 5.21 incidents per quarter.

An important aspect of the VAR study is that the installation of metal detectors is found to decrease *APP* even though the immediate impact is almost zero (the short-run coefficient is 0.032). We found that the long-run effect of $METAL_t$ on *APP* is −4.53 incidents per quarter. The rationale is that the installation of metal detectors reduced skyjackings and that the eventual extension of the metal detector technology helped to shield

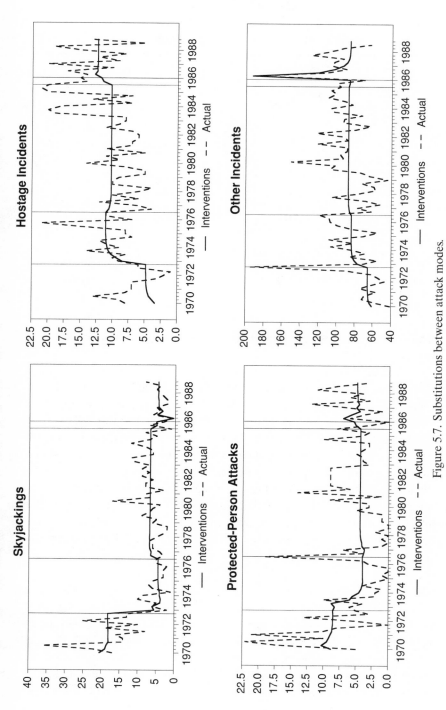

Figure 5.7. Substitutions between attack modes.

131

Table 5.2. *Results of the VAR*

Intervention	Skyjackings	Hostage Takings	APP	OT
Short-run Effect				
METAL	−12.20**	3.68*	0.03	12.20
EMB76	2.05	−0.44	−1.53	1.73
EMB85	−1.72	1.39	0.94	−1.48
LIBYA	−3.81	1.28	1.60	107.40**
Long-run Effect				
METAL	−13.70$^{\#}$	5.21$^{\#}$	−4.53$^{\#}$	18.20
EMB76	2.32	−0.80	0.40	4.10
EMB85	−2.19	2.10	0.54	−1.30
LIBYA	NA	NA	NA	NA

** denotes statistical significance at the 5% level.
* denotes statistical significance at the 10% level.
# denotes a significant intervention or that the effect is significant through its effects on an important explanatory variable in the VAR.
All effects for Libya are temporary.
NA denotes not applicable.

protected persons at various government buildings, embassies, and military bases.

There seems to be a slight increase in *OT* following the installation of metal detectors, but this increase is not statistically significant. The embassy fortifications seemed to have no significant effect on any of the series. Other than the installation of metal detectors, the only significant intervention was the Libyan bombing, which caused the number of other incidents (*OT*) to jump sharply before falling back to the series' pre-intervention mean. Since bombings, threats, and hoaxes are usually logistically simple and utilize few resources relative to the other types of incidents, it is fairly easy to ratchet up the number of such incidents. The calculated short-run effects and the long-run effects of the four intervention variables are summarized in Table 5.2. The entries are in terms of incidents per quarter.

CONCLUSION

Many social scientists view terrorists as rational actors who use their scarce resources to maximize their expected utility. Rational behavior is predictable and allows social scientists to formulate the terrorists' best response to any antiterrorism policy. The household production approach to terrorism indicates that an increase in the relative price of one type of terrorist activity will cause the terrorist group to substitute out of the relatively expensive activity and into terrorist and nonterrorist activities that are now relatively less expensive. Similarly, attack modes that are logistically similar and yield similar basic commodities will display the greatest substitution possibilities. Transference occurs because governments can alter the prices faced by terrorists. Even suicidal terrorists can be viewed as being rational. Unfortunately, suicidal attacks are unlikely to be deterred by a relative price change; the opportunity set of such terrorists must be reduced if suicidal attacks are to be prevented.

Transference means that the unintended consequence of government policies designed to thwart one type of terrorist behavior can induce increases in other types of terrorism. The empirical literature supports the importance of the substitution effect in transnational terrorism. Antiterrorism policies that do not constrain terrorists' behavior, such as UN conventions and resolutions, have no effect on the level of terrorism. Piecemeal policies, designed to thwart only one attack mode, are shown to induce a substitution into other, similar modes, whose unintended consequences may be quite harmful.

SIX

International Cooperation

Dilemma and Inhibitors

In a globalized world with a high volume of cross-border flows, transnational terrorism is a global public bad, while action to control or eliminate it is the quintessential global public good. As such, antiterrorism efforts yield nonrival benefits – enhanced security – received by all at-risk countries. The formation of far-flung terrorist networks has greatly increased the spatial dispersion of benefits derived from measures against these networks. The theory of public good supply teaches that as the dispersion of these measures' benefits increases, their underprovision worsens as providers fail to include the benefits that their efforts confer on others when deciding upon antiterrorism actions (see Chapter 4; Sandler, 1997, 2004).

The sheer volume of cross-border exchanges of all types makes it possible to monitor but a small fraction, thereby affording opportunities for terrorists to move personnel and equipment internationally. For example, over a half-billion people cross US borders each year. Also, 130 million motor vehicles, 2.5 million railcars, and 5.7 million cargo containers transit US borders annually (White House, 2004, p. 165). The combination of globalization and technological advances means that even the most secure borders may be penetrated by determined terrorists who utilize technologies (for example, communication advances) and apply innovative methods to circumvent security upgrades. Terrorists weigh relative risks to identify the least secure venue or weakest link at which to stage their attack against a targeted nation's assets. Thus, as we have seen in Chapter 2, most attacks against US interests occur outside of the United States, where defenses are weaker. The networking of terrorists facilitates their ability to identify vulnerable targets and to exploit governments' failure to act, except episodically, in unison.

134

The reach of 9/11 in terms of its financial consequences,[1] induced anxiety, and human toll indicates that global counterterrorism efforts are needed to fight today's terrorism. Although some coordinated actions occurred after 9/11, including the 7 October 2001 invasion of Afghanistan and some joint police operations in Europe, this coordination has waned over time. Basile (2004, p. 177) indicated that a much smaller amount of al-Qaida's funds has been blocked in recent years after a great deal of success during the year immediately following 9/11. This is due in part to al-Qaida finding nations that are not abiding by cooperative efforts. Nations rely on unilateral counterterrorism responses to maintain their autonomy over security and to limit their transaction costs, which can be high for transnational cooperation. US actions in Iraq in the name of counterterrorism have turned some nations away from US-led measures, which may have involved US-specific objectives – for example, the removal of Saddam Hussein. An indisputable link between al-Qaida and the Iraqi regime was never established before *or* after the US invasion. Terrorist groups, including al-Qaida, are now operating in Iraq. The 11 March 2004 attack against Spain was intended to send a warning to other nations that cooperation with the United States in its war on terror may carry additional costs. Such intimidation attacks may further hamper a united front against terrorism.

Transnational interdependencies with respect to counterterrorism policies often result in too much of some unilateral actions and too little of others. Unfortunately, terrorists are often motivated to address their collective action problems, while governments are not properly motivated to respond to their common concerns. As shown in Chapter 4, countries have a proclivity to rely on prime-target nations to take action against a collective terrorist threat. The associated collective action problems tend to fall into two game categories: Prisoners' Dilemma and coordination games. For the latter, the difficulty is particularly acute if a noncooperator can undo the joint efforts of the cooperators – for example, a nation that provides a secure haven for terrorists' financial assets cancels out the collective efforts of other nations to deny such a haven.

This chapter has a number of purposes. First, we explore why policy interdependencies among countries result in inefficient provision of counterterrorist action. This analysis goes beyond the presentation in Chapter 4. Second, we highlight the asymmetries between terrorists and

---

[1] On these financial implications, see Chen and Siems (2004), Eldor and Melnick (2004), Drakos (2004), Kunreuther and Michel-Kerjan (2004a, 2004b), and Chapter 9.

governments in order to explain why the two adversaries achieve such different results when addressing their respective collective security concerns. Third, we conceptualize some of the cooperators' dilemmas using elementary game theory – for example, the problems associated with shoring up the weakest link. Fourth, we evaluate past efforts at international cooperation. In particular, we explain why international conventions and resolutions – favored by President Reagan, Senator John Kerry, and others – have not accomplished as much as one would hope. Fifth, we review post-9/11 efforts to freeze terrorists' assets. Finally, we offer some policy recommendations regarding international cooperation.

TRANSNATIONAL EXTERNALITIES

In the fewest words possible, an *externality* is an uncompensated interdependency between two or more agents. If one nation's action or choice imposes a cost or benefit on one or more other nation(s) and no compensation is received or paid, then a *transnational externality* exists. A nation that imposes costs on another nation will not alter its behavior if doing so is costly and there is no mechanism to compel change. Thus, a nation whose electricity-generating plants create acid rain for downwind nations has no incentive to account for the external costs that it imposes on others. In fact, countries build high smokestacks for the purpose of transferring such pollutants abroad. By the same token, a country whose actions have favorable consequences beyond its borders may undersupply such actions because the associated external benefits are not supported or subsidized by recipient countries.

Proactive counterterrorism measures that reduce threats to other countries give rise to external benefits. By contrast, defensive counterterrorism actions can deflect terrorist attacks to less fortified countries, thereby generating external costs. After 9/11, the United States and many industrialized European countries instituted greater defensive actions; thereafter, there were numerous attacks on rich countries' interests in developing countries – for example, the Philippines, Indonesia, Malaysia, Kenya, Morocco, Pakistan, and Saudi Arabia. Because defensive measures may also confer external benefits on other countries by protecting foreign residents, both external benefits and external costs may derive from such policies (Sandler, 2005; Sandler and Siqueira, 2005).

In Figure 6.1, we depict the case where *only* external costs arise from defensive actions that deflect an attack onto softer targets abroad.[2] The

---

[2] The graph adapts the standard treatment of a negative externality – see Bruce (2001, Chapter 4) – to the case of defensive counterterrorism measures.

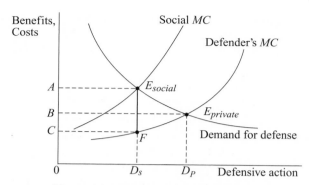

Figure 6.1. Transnational external costs.

demand for these actions is downward-sloping, indicating that a country's marginal (additional) willingness to pay declines as greater defensive measures are taken. This curve's shape reflects a diminished marginal gain as security is tightened around potential targets. To provide each level of defensive measures, the country incurs costs for guards, fortifications, and intelligence. The defending country's private additional or *marginal cost* (*MC*) rises as more actions are taken. Thus, the defender's *MC* curve is depicted to rise with increased measures. In essence, this curve represents the private supply curve. When a country determines its best level of defense, it equates its demand and supply curves. In Figure 6.1, this equality occurs at $E_{private}$, where D_P defensive measures are undertaken at a marginal benefit and marginal cost of $0B$.

Social inefficiency arises at $E_{private}$ because the country's independent action does not account for the marginal costs that its defense creates for other nations through transference (see Chapters 4 and 5). These third-party costs also increase with the level of these defensive efforts – that is, greater protection of home targets make foreign targets look softer so that they attract more attacks. If these third-party costs are added to the defender's *MC* curve, then the social *MC* results. This latter curve is above the defender's *MC*, because it is the vertical sum of private *and* third-party (external) *MC*. The social optimum occurs at the intersection of the defender's demand and the social *MC* curve – that is, at point E_{social}, where D_S is the efficient level of defensive effort that accounts for costs imposed on others. As seen in Figure 6.1, independent action results in too much defensive effort, where $D_P > D_S$, as claimed at the outset of this chapter.

There are a number of ways to "internalize" or adjust for these external costs. First, the countries can bargain to level D_S – where, say, the externality recipient compensates the providing country for lowering its defense from level D_P. The recipient is willing to pay the defender AC per unit for reducing defensive actions from D_P to D_S as the recipient's marginal damage falls from higher levels (that is, the difference between social MC and defender's MC) to AC. Moreover, the defender is willing to accept AC, since it equals the defender's unexploited marginal net gain (that is, the difference between its demand per unit and its MC) at D_S. A bilateral agreement, such as the US-Cuba Hijacking Pact of February 1973 in which the parties agreed to return the hijacked plane, passengers, crew members, and hijackers, attempts to internalize the associated external costs through bargaining. The bargaining solution may, however, fail when there are more than two countries involved, because the transaction costs of reaching a mutually acceptable agreement may be prohibitive.[3] Not surprisingly, nations have an easier time framing bilateral counterterrorism agreements as compared to multilateral accords. Second, a tax of AC per unit can be imposed on the defender country, where this tax equals the marginal external cost at a defensive level of D_S. This "fix" is fraught with difficulties, since the international community lacks a recognized institution with the authority to tax sovereign nations for their externally imposed costs. To preserve sovereignty, nations will likely oppose setting up such an authority unless the terrorism threat becomes more severe. Moreover, there is an information problem in ascertaining a recipient's marginal damage. The recipient country has perverse incentives to exaggerate its damages if compensation is to follow. Third, some supranational authority can set a quota on the defender's actions at level D_S. This solution also suffers from the absence of such an authority. Fourth, nations facing a common terrorist threat will account for the external costs if they take unified actions. Except in dire times, nations have insisted on maintaining independence over counterterrorism policies. Simply put, externalities are easier to conceptualize than to correct.

Transnational External Benefits

Some counterterrorism policies may give rise to transnational external benefits. For example, proactive measures that succeed in crippling or reducing the effectiveness of a terrorist group that poses a common threat to multiple countries yield external benefits to all at-risk countries. Thus, US efforts to capture or kill al-Qaida's leadership after 9/11 provided such benefits to other targeted countries. For external benefits, it is the demand

---

[3] On bargaining and externalities, see Cornes and Sandler (1996, pp. 86–91).

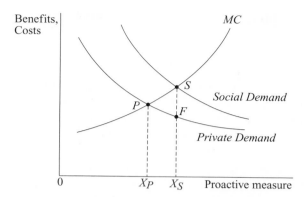

Figure 6.2. Transnational external benefits.

curve that must be adjusted to include the marginal external gains that a nation's counterterrorism confers on others. Thus, the social marginal-willingness-to-pay curve or social demand curve in Figure 6.2 lies above the providing nation's demand curve by the amount of marginal external benefits. As the level of the proactive response increases, marginal external benefits decrease owing to diminishing returns; that is, the marginal gains from proactive measures are greatest when there are few such actions, and decrease as more efforts are expended.

The nation's independent solution is at P, where the nation equates its private demand and MC and provides X_P. If, however, the social optimum is found, then the social demand must be equated to MC, and the optimum level is X_S, which exceeds X_P. With external benefits, independent action leads to too little of the action. Now, in order to internalize the externality, a nation must be made to include these marginal external benefits in its decision calculus. For example, a subsidy of SF per unit of proactive response to the providing nation would result in the social optimum, but this requires a supranational authority that currently does not exist.

In both cases of externalities, the difference between private and social solutions increases as the number of nations receiving the externality from counterterrorism increases. This follows because the relevant private and social curves are farther apart, thereby making the inefficiency of independent behavior greater. That is, X_P and X_S would lie farther apart in Figure 6.2 as the number of external benefit recipients increases. As a terrorism network expands its geographical reach, the number of targeted countries grows, and so the extent of external benefits (or costs) also increases. The al-Qaida network is more widely dispersed than earlier terrorist threats – for exampie, the Abu Nidal Organization (ANO) of the

1980s – so that proactive or defensive measures against al-Qaida result in more external benefits or costs than similar actions against the ANO. As a consequence, the extent of suboptimality from the failure of nations to cooperate today is greater than in past decades. The globalization of terrorism means that the externality problem has worsened. The internet, for example, permits the terrorists to widen their network and, in so doing, increases the inefficiencies resulting from lack of government cooperation with respect to counterterrorism against a global threat. Communication and transportation innovations will serve to worsen this concern.

In some cases, there may be both positive and negative externalities associated with counterterrorism. For example, a proactive response protects other countries' interests, but may also incite anger among terrorists and their supporters, thereby motivating harsh future attacks (Rosendorff and Sandler, 2004). If these attacks are visited on soft targets outside the nation taking the proactive measures, then an external cost arises. When there are both external benefits and costs, the relative position of independent provision vis-à-vis the social optimum depends on the relative strength of the associated external benefits on social demand and the relative strength of the associated external costs on social MC. If, for example, the external benefits dominate, then the providing country's action will be too small compared to the social optimal level.

Intertemporal Externalities

Externalities may also take on an intertemporal character, where action by an agent *today* may create uncompensated costs or benefits for agents *tomorrow*. A country that grants concessions to hostage takers – as France did during the 22 July 1968 El Al hijacking, or as the United States and Israel did during the 14 June 1985 hijacking of TWA flight 847[4] – creates an intertemporal externality by making terrorists believe that future hostage taking will be profitable, thus leading to more incidents (see Chapter 7). The terrorist escalation of carnage to attract media attention also creates intertemporal external costs by inducing terrorists to outdo past outrages. Thus, 9/11 means that terrorists may resort to even larger-scale events;

---

[4] A detailed description of this watershed hijacking can be found in Mickolus, Sandler, and Murdock (1989, vol. 2, pp. 219–25). On 30 June 1985, the Amal leader, Nabih Berri, in Lebanon released the remaining thirty-nine hostages in return for a US pledge not to launch any retaliatory strikes. Moreover, Israel agreed to release 735 prisoners from its Atlit prison. The hijackers were allowed to escape.

eventually, this escalation may lead terrorists to seek weapons of mass destruction (WMD).

On the more positive side, innovations in counterterrorism can yield intertemporal external benefits to nations that can capitalize on these innovations in future operations. An excellent example occurred during the rescue mission of Lufthansa flight 181, a Boeing 737 hijacked en route from Mallorca to Frankfurt on 13 October 1977.[5] Once it was hijacked, the plane refueled in Rome and then flew on to Dubai. After a stopover in Aden, Yemen, the plane landed in Mogadishu, Somalia, on 17 October. At 2 A.M. on 18 October, West German Grenzschutzgruppe Neun (GSG-9) commandos entered the rear of the plane after creating a diversion with an ignited oil canister at the front of the cockpit. Once in the plane, the commandos exploded British stun grenades that temporarily incapacitated the hijackers. Only four of the eighty-six hostages were slightly injured in the successful rescue. Both the stun grenades and commandos' operating procedures were copied in later rescue missions.

Intertemporal externalities are even more difficult to address than standard externalities, because tomorrow's agents who benefit or are harmed by an action may not be present to bargain with the externality generator. For example, a government that applies a new procedure for freeing hostages may not have been in office when the procedure was developed years before. Moreover, the developer of the procedure may no longer be in office. Thus, intertemporal beneficial externalities will be undersupplied, while intertemporal detrimental externalities will be oversupplied not only at some point in time, but over time.

ASYMMETRIES BETWEEN TERRORISTS AND GOVERNMENTS

Terrorist groups have displayed a tendency to cooperate in loose networks since the onset of modern-day terrorism (Chapter 2; Hoffman, 1998). Early terrorist networks cooperated on many levels, including training, intelligence, safe haven, financial support, logistical help, weapon acquisition, and the exchange of personnel (Alexander and Pluchinsky, 1992). For example, operatives were exchanged in the 21 December 1975 attack on the Organization of Petroleum Exporting (OPEC) countries ministerial meeting in Vienna and in the 27 June 1976 hijacking of Air France flight 139 (Mickolus, 1980). Loose ties existed among the European

---

[5] Based on newspaper accounts, this incident is described in detail in Mickolus (1980, pp. 734–40). The facts in this paragraph come from Mickolus' account.

fighting communist organizations (FCOs), which shared a common ideology. The FCOs also had ties to the Palestinian groups, which were connected as well. In addition, Euzkadi ta Askatasuna (ETA) and the Provisional Irish Republican Army (PIRA) had links. In more recent years, the al-Qaida network operates in upwards of sixty countries and stages its attacks worldwide. This network includes such groups as Abu Sayyaf (the Philippines), Al-Jihad (Egypt), Harakat ul-Mujahidin (Pakistan), Islamic Movement (Uzbekistan), Jemaah Islamiyah (Southeast Asia), and bin Laden's al-Qaida (Afghanistan).

By contrast, governments detest sacrificing their autonomy over security matters and so severely limit their cooperation. An exigency such as 9/11 fosters cooperation – for example, nations participated in various capacities in the US-led retaliation against the Taliban beginning on 7 October 2001 for harboring al-Qaida and Osama bin Laden – but this cooperation fades with time unless reignited by some new heinous terrorist attack. Why do governments have greater difficulty addressing their collective action concerns than their terrorist adversaries? There are at least three main factors at work. First, governments' strength provides a false sense of security, thereby inhibiting them from appreciating the need for coordinated action. By contrast, terrorists' relative weakness, compared to the well-armed governments that they challenge, means that terrorists have little choice but to pool resources to stretch limited means. Second, governments do not agree on which groups are terrorists – for example, until recently the European Union (EU) did not view Hamas, despite its suicide bombing campaign, as a terrorist organization. Although terrorist groups have different agendas and goals, these groups share similar opponents – for example, the United States and Israel – which provides a unity of purpose. Third, governments and terrorists have different time horizons. In liberal democracies, government officials' interest in the future is circumscribed by the length of the election period and their likelihood of reelection. Officials with one remaining term – for example, an American president in his second term – are likely to be unconcerned about the consequences of decisions beyond that term. Because governments change, agreements made with leaders of other countries to combat terrorism may be rather short-lived, and this detracts from the gains that might be attained from fostering such arrangements. For example, Spanish Prime Minister Zapatero pulled the country's troops out of Iraq following his victory in the 2004 national elections. Spanish support of the US-led war on terror, which had been very strong, weakened under Zapatero. By contrast, terrorist leaders tend to be tenured for life, so they view intergroup cooperative arrangements as continual. They consequently take a long-term viewpoint and place higher value than do governments on future benefits. Failure of one group to honor its commitments can lead to long-run retribution by other groups in terms of withholding cooperative action. This loss of future cooperative gains may outweigh any short-run payoff from reneging on a pact, thereby bolstering cooperation.

These three factors imply that terrorists are better able than governments to address collective concerns; in so doing, terrorists create synergistic gains. Through global networks, terrorists are able to identify and exploit a weakest link (softer target) whenever it appears. Moreover, terrorists can dispatch their best-equipped cell to this target of opportunity. The absence of sufficient intergovernmental cooperation means that these weakest links are always present (Sandler, 2003).

Other essential asymmetries distinguish governments from terrorists. Unfortunately, these asymmetries provide a clear tactical advantage to the terrorists. Governments and the nations that they protect are target-rich; terrorists and their safe havens are target-poor. Terrorists often hide among the general population in urban centers, thereby maximizing collateral damage during government raids. In other cases, terrorists reside in inaccessible places, such as the caves of Afghanistan or jungle tracts. Governments must guard everywhere, while terrorists can identify and attack the softest targets. This means that defensive measures by governments may be relatively expensive. Governments have to be fortunate on a daily basis, while terrorists only have to be lucky occasionally.[6] Hence, terrorists can wait and choose the most opportune time to act, as they did on 9/11. Democratic governments are restrained in their responses to terrorists (see Chapter 2), while fundamentalist terrorists are unrestrained in their brutality. Governments are organized hierarchically, whereas today's terrorist groups are organized nonhierarchically (Arquilla and Ronfeldt, 2001). Given their loose networks, terrorist cells and groups can operate independently. Infiltrators and spies can do great damage owing to the hierarchical structure of governments; by contrast, captured terrorists can provide only limited intelligence owing to the virtual autonomy of many of the network's components. Size can be a disadvantage to governments, as more targets require protection and more coordination is required. The looseness of terrorist networks can make greater size an advantage,

---

[6] This asymmetry paraphrases what IRA terrorists said in a letter after they learned that their 12 October 1984 bombing of the Grand Hotel in Brighton had narrowly missed killing Prime Minister Margaret Thatcher. Their letter said, "Today, we were unlucky. But remember we have only to be lucky once. You will have to be lucky always." See Mickolus, Sandler, and Murdock (1989, vol. 2, p. 115).

as there are more resources to draw on. Also, a farther-flung network means that the terrorists can better capitalize on soft targets.

Another asymmetry involves information. Governments are not well informed about terrorists' strength, whereas terrorists can easily discover the nature and extent of the government's antiterrorist activities. In many liberal democracies, such information is a matter of public record. This asymmetry is poignantly illustrated by US estimates of al-Qaida's size as "several hundred to several thousand members" just five months prior to 9/11 (US Department of State, 2001, p. 68). Experience during the US-led invasion of Afghanistan and intelligence gathered thereafter indicated that al-Qaida had far more members than the upper bound of the US estimate. Misleading intelligence can greatly compromise the planning and success of such an invasion. In June 2005, the US military is still trying to rid Afghanistan of al-Qaida and its supporters. Such misestimates inhibit the ability of a leader nation to encourage other countries to contribute to a preemptive strike. In the case of Aum Shinrikyo, Japanese authorities had no idea until after their raids in 1995 what a formidable threat this group posed.

In Table 6.1, we have gathered together the asymmetries for ready reference. The irony of these asymmetries is that they reverse somewhat the advantage from the strong (the governments) to the weak (the terrorists). The only way to minimize the disadvantage that some of these

Table 6.1. *Essential Asymmetries between Terrorists and Targeted Governments*

Terrorists	Targeted Governments
• Target poor	• Target rich
• Weak relative to adversary	• Strong relative to adversary
• Take a long-term viewpoint when interacting with other terrorist groups	• Take a short-term viewpoint when interacting with other governments
• Agree on common enemies	• Do not agree on common enemies
• Address their collective action concerns	• Do not address their collective action problems
• Can be restrained or unrestrained in their response	• Restrained in their response
• Nonhierarchical organization	• Hierarchical organization
• Size furthers interests	• Size may hamper interests
• Luck needed on occasion	• Luck needed always
• Reasonably well informed about government's strength	• Not well informed about terrorists' strength

asymmetries create for the governments is for them to rely less on security autonomy and to start cooperating more fully with their counterparts. Other asymmetries – for example, response restraint, the need for luck, and size considerations – derive from the adversarial roles associated with terrorism. Because such factors favor the weak, they resort to terrorism, which levels the playing field.

GAME-THEORETICAL ISSUES

We begin with an explanation, using some elementary game theory, of why the short and *fixed* time horizon of government officials hampers international cooperation among governments. We purposely construct the example to minimize computational complications. Suppose that two governments confronting the same terrorist threat must decide whether to preempt the terrorists through an attack on their base or sponsors. Unlike the analysis in Chapter 4, we further suppose that the two governments in our example can interact for only *two* periods owing to election-term considerations.

The procedure for solving such a game is to examine the Nash equilibrium for the second period and then to *condition* the Nash equilibrium solution for the first period on the solution value found for the second period. In technical parlance, this gives a *subgame perfect equilibrium* in which the players would not unilaterally change their strategies in the current *or* future period. This solution strategy is found by solving the game backward, starting at the last period. As we did in Chapter 4, we assume that the preemption game is a Prisoners' Dilemma. In Figure 6.3, we display the 2×2 game matrix for the two players – nation 1 (the row player) and nation 2 (the column player) – viewed from the standpoint of the second and last period of the two-period game. Recall that the left-hand payoff in each cell is that of nation 1, and the right-hand payoff is that of nation 2. The payoffs are based on the following assumptions. During each period, a preemptor confers a benefit of 8 on each of the two players at a cost of 10 to itself. If, therefore, only one country preempts, then the preemptor nets -2, while the free rider gains 8. If, however, both countries take action, then each receives 6 ($= 2 \times 8 - 10$) as cumulative benefits of 16 from two preemption actions are reduced by the country-specific provision costs of 10. When no one acts, there are no benefits. This is a classic Prisoners' Dilemma (see Chapter 4) with a dominant strategy of status quo, where the payoffs are greater than the corresponding payoffs of preempting (that is, $8 > 6$ and $0 > -2$). As each nation exercises

| | | Nation 2 | |
		Preempt	Status quo
	Preempt	6, 6	−2, 8
Nation 1			
	Status quo	8, −2	**0, 0**

Figure 6.3. Prisoners' Dilemma viewed from period 2 of a two-period game.

its dominant strategy, the second-period Nash equilibrium, whose pay-offs are boldfaced in Figure 6.3, is achieved, with neither nation taking measures against the terrorists.

We now use the second-period solution's payoffs to view the first-period game. This is done by adding the Nash equilibrium payoffs of 0 to each player's first-period matrix, whose payoff array is identical to that in Figure 6.3 prior to this addition. Since we are adding 0 to each payoff, the first-period matrix augmented by the second-period Nash payoffs remains identical to that in Figure 6.3 and so is not displayed. If, say, the Nash payoffs in the second period had been 2 for each player, then *every* payoff in the first-period matrix would be greater by two than those in the second-period matrix. Whether 0 or some other constant is added to every payoff of the first-period matrix, *the dominant strategy will not change and remains for each nation to maintain the status quo*. Thus, the subgame perfect equilibrium for the two-period repeated interaction is for each government to maintain the status quo in each period – hence, the absence of action or cooperation against a common terrorist threat.[7]

Suppose that the government officials in the two countries have any number of *known* periods to interact. The game is solved the same way, starting at the last period as in Figure 6.3 and finding the Nash equilibrium at mutual inactivity with payoffs of 0. These zero payoffs are then added to every payoff in the 2 × 2 matrix for the next-to-last period. The Nash equilibrium of the augmented next-to-last-period matrix is again mutual inactivity, as it was for the next earlier period, and so on. In short, the

---

[7] If preemption during the first period degrades the terrorists and, thus, reduces the ben-efits from action during the second period, then one would have to allow for different contingent matrices during period 2 depending on first-period actions. This complication need not change our conclusion, because the net benefits to a preemptor during the sec-ond period, *will remain negative* if preemption benefits have declined due to first-period actions. The transformed game remains a Prisoners' Dilemma during the second period, with a Nash equilibrium of no action. In fact, no action is also anticipated during the first period owing to the Prisoners' Dilemma.

game is "folded back" period by period to show that the subgame perfect strategy is to maintain the status quo in each and every period. The same result follows if there are more than two interacting governments (Sandler, 1992). Limited terms of office inhibit cooperative arrangements among governments when addressing a threat of transnational terrorism.

There are only two instances where cooperation develops: if the officials' number of terms in office is *unknown* (that is, if the officials can be elected for an indefinite number of terms) or if the officials are tenured for life. In either instance, the officials know that reneging on a cooperative arrangement may have repercussions as their counterpart punishes their misbehavior.[8] Because the last period in office is not known with certainty, there is no point at which cheating will necessarily go unpunished during the ensuing period. The presence of future periods is precisely what motivates a terrorist group with tenured leaders to honor its commitments to other groups. Quite simply, terrorists are interested in the future because failure to abide by understandings has consequences for future interactions.

Coordination Games

Many alternative game forms can reflect countermeasures against transnational terrorism (see Chapter 4; Arce and Sandler, 2005; Sandler and Arce, 2003). An important game form for select counterterrorist policy choices is a "Stag Hunt" coordination game, where both nations are better off taking identical measures. When one nation takes the measure alone, this nation receives the smallest payoff, and the nation that fails to act earns the second-greatest payoff. This kind of scenario is descriptive of a host of counterterrorism policies where two or more nations must act in unison for the best payoffs to be achieved. Instances include freezing terrorist assets, denying safe haven to terrorists, or staying with a no-negotiation policy. Even a sole defector can spoil the policy's effectiveness for all nations abiding by the policy. We use agreements to freeze terrorists' assets to illustrate such games.

For illustration, we assume just two nations – 1 and 2 – and a situation in which each can either freeze the assets of the terrorists or take no action (status quo). In Figure 6.4, the highest payoff, *F*, results from mutual

---

[8] This assumes a tit-for-tat strategy, where a nation cooperates in the first period and then matches its counterpart's strategy in the preceding period. If, therefore, nation 1 does not preempt in some period, then nation 2 will withhold preempting until nation 1 preempts. For more on repeated games, see Sandler (1992) or any game theory text.

| | Nation 2 | |
	Freeze	Status quo
Freeze	*F, F*	*B, E*
Status quo	*E, B*	*A, A*

Nation 1

$$F > E > A > B$$

Figure 6.4. Freezing assets: coordination game.

action, followed by a payoff of E from doing nothing when the other nation freezes assets. This scenario implies that the nation that does not join the freeze can profit by providing a safe haven for terrorists' funds. The nation may be so inclined if it does not view its own people and property as likely targets. Nevertheless, F exceeds E because this nation may risk negative ramifications if discovered. Moreover, the noncooperator cannot be positive that its people and property will never be attacked, which limits the size of E. The third-lowest payoff, A, is from mutual inaction, while the worst payoff, B, is the "sucker" payoff of acting alone. This follows because the sucker bears the costs and gains no added safety, because the terrorists can still safeguard their assets through the other nation's duplicity.

The game in Figure 6.4 has three Nash equilibriums. If both nations freeze terrorists' assets, this is a Nash equilibrium because neither nation would switch strategies on its own, insofar as $F > E$. Another Nash equilibrium is for both nations to do nothing. Once again, neither nation will unilaterally change its strategy, because $A > B$. Obviously, there is no dominant strategy. These first two equilibriums are known as pure-strategy Nash equilibriums, because a nation exercises the same strategy all of the time. A third Nash equilibrium involves mixed strategies in which each pure strategy is played in a probabilistic fashion. For example, nation 1 may freeze assets p percent of the time and do nothing $(1 - p)$ percent of the time, while nation 2 may freeze assets q percent of the time and do nothing $(1 - q)$ percent of the time. To identify this mixed-strategy equilibrium, we determine nation 2's q probability for freezing assets that makes nation 1 indifferent between freezing terrorist assets and doing nothing.[9] Similarly, we can determine nation 1's p probability for freezing assets. These probabilities identify the mixed-strategy equilibrium. For

---

[9] The calculation for q (or p, not shown) goes as follows: $qF + (1 - q)B = qE + (1 - q)A$, so that nation 1's expected gain from freezing assets, based on nation 2's uncertain action, equals nation 1's expected gain from not freezing assets, again based on nation 2's uncertain action. This equality indicates nation 2's indifference. This equation yields: $q = (A - B)/(F - B)$. This expression and an analogous one for p give the influences described in the text. See Sandler (2005) for details of further calculations.

example, p represents the uncertain belief that nation 2 has of the likelihood that nation 1 will freeze assets; similarly, q denotes the uncertain belief that nation 1 has of the likelihood that nation 2 will freeze assets. If nation 2 (nation 1) believes that there is a greater than p (q) chance that its counterpart will freeze terrorists' assets, then nation 2 (nation 1) will follow suit. Anything that reduces these "adherence probabilities" serves to make cooperation more likely. For example, an increase in the gain from mutual action, F, or a smaller mutual status quo payoff promotes coordination by reducing the required adherence probabilities. An increase in the payoff, B, associated with unilaterally freezing terrorists' assets promotes cooperation, while an increase in profitable opportunities, E, from hiding terrorists' assets serves to inhibit cooperation. Although the mathematics appear complicated, these outcomes are quite intuitive.

A fascinating extension, which we will not show analytically, is to allow for more nations. Suppose that all n nations are required to freeze assets so that the terrorists cannot circumvent the restriction through some safe haven. The greater the number of required adherents for effectiveness, the larger the adherence probabilities required by each nation to participate. Even for a relatively small number of nations, near-certain adherence is required (Sandler and Sargent, 1995), which is not an encouraging result. Hence, nations will not join freezes unless the actions of others can be guaranteed. This is of particular concern in the case of freezing assets, because even one nonadherent nation can be the spoiler when one realizes that the 1993 World Trade Center bomb cost only $400 but caused over $500 million in damages (Hoffman, 1998).

Weakest-link Problems

In Chapter 4, we introduced weakest-link security considerations, where the overall level of the associated public good hinges on the smallest provision effort. Consider the case of portable anti-aircraft missiles (MANPADs) that can shoot down commercial aircraft. Planes are especially vulnerable to MANPADs on takeoff and landing, when a terrorist on the ground near an airport can fire a heat-seeking missile at a plane. Currently, the US Department of Homeland Security is considering having MANPAD defenses, which fire flare decoys, installed on US planes at the cost of billions of dollars for the entire US fleet. If US planes are protected and other countries do not follow suit, then terrorists bent on using MANPADs will merely travel to a country where planes are not so equipped and try to shoot down a foreign plane full of Americans. The additional safety derived from MANPADs depends on the least effort taken. The need for international cooperation, so that all air carriers equip their planes with similar security methods, is evident.

Because countries have different capacities to respond owing to income considerations, there is a need in the case of MANPADs and other security upgrades to consider "*shoring up*" the defenses of some countries. A prime-target nation, such as the United States, may be expected to help bolster the defenses of some of these weakest links (Sandler, 2004, 2005). There are, however, a number of problems with this fix. First, the United States does not have sufficient resources to shore up all of the weakest-link situations, particularly since its own antiterrorism budget has grown so fast since 9/11 (see Chapter 10). Second, there is a proclivity for other countries to free ride on any nation that is inclined to shore up weakest links, because this action provides purely public benefits for all countries. Third, nations that take on the lion's share of this effort can be expected to have an agenda – that is, the assistance may involve conditions, such as a demand for military bases or political concessions. Fourth, there is a moral hazard problem because the recipient country may not use the money as intended unless the providing country supplies the assistance in-kind.

To shore up weakest links requires coordinated international action directed by some multilateral institution such as the United Nations. This institution would need to pass an assessment resolution, requiring member nations to share in the funding needed to shore up the the weakest links in a system similar to UN assessment accounts for underwriting peacekeeping expenditures.[10] Assessment would be based on member nations' ability to pay based on gross domestic product and benefits derived. Those developed countries attracting the most terrorist incidents – say, over the last ten-year period – would have the greatest assessment shares of expenditures to cover. To avoid the moral hazard problem, this institution would need to provide the actual security upgrades and train the country's personnel. Of course, nations would have to agree to such an assessment arrangement, and the recipient country would have to consent to the assistance.

INTERNATIONAL ACTIONS TO ADDRESS
TRANSNATIONAL TERRORISM

In Table 6.2, global and regional conventions and treaties related to controlling international terrorism are displayed. The table is set up as

---

[10] On UN assessment accounts, see Durch (1993) and Mills (1990).

follows: the convention/treaty is named in the first column; the supporting institution is given in the second column; the date and place of framing are listed in the third column; and its entered-in-force date is indicated in the fourth column. Only conventions are given in Table 6.2; there are myriad international resolutions – for example, UN General Assembly Resolution 2551 on the Forcible Diversion of Civil Aircraft in Flight (12 December 1969) and UN General Assembly Resolution 2645 on Aerial Hijacking (25 November 1970). A resolution typically expresses a declared position or intended action, while a convention indicates a mandated, but usually unenforced, response. We focus on the latter because resolutions are weaker and are often enacted as a convention later if deemed sufficiently important.

To date, there are twelve international conventions and seven regional ones that forbid a wide range of terrorist activities from bombing to hostage taking. International conventions prohibit actions against diplomatic missions, aircraft, ocean platforms, nuclear power plants, and ships. A 1998 convention makes terrorism more difficult by tagging plastic explosives in order to identify perpetrators, and another convention seeks to suppress terrorist financing. In contrast to their international counterparts, regional conventions outlaw all forms of terrorism that meet the convention-approved definition.

These conventions have been reactive, responding only after a spate of attacks. For example, the International Civil Aviation Organization (ICAO) conventions followed numerous hijackings and bombings of commercial airlines in the 1960s. The UN convention outlawing crimes against diplomats and other protected persons came only after many such attacks in the late 1960s and the beginning of the 1970s. All conventions rely on the ratifying countries to implement the stipulated prohibition or institute the required action using its own laws and resources. Essentially, conventions are a means of bolstering antiterrorist policy by coordinating national action through set guidelines. Varying levels of adherence are consequently anticipated, especially since none of these conventions possesses an enforcement mechanism and nations have differing counterterrorism capacities and resources. Conventions involving a weakest-link public good are particularly problematic, because success may be compromised by inadequate responses by nonratifiers or by ratifiers with limited capacity. Terrorists will take advantage of such vulnerabilities. For example, plastic explosives may not be traced following a bombing if terrorists acquire them in a country where the convention is not effectively implemented. For many international conventions, a single compliance failure

Table 6.2. *Global and Regional Conventions and Treaties Relating to Controlling International Terrorism*

Convention/Treaty	Supporting Institution	Date/Place Signed	Entered into Force
• Convention on Offences and Certain Other Acts Committed on Board Aircraft	International Civil Aviation Organization (ICAO)	14 September 1963 Tokyo	4 December 1969
• Convention for the Suppression of Unlawful Seizure of Aircraft	ICAO	16 December 1970 The Hague	14 October 1971
• Convention for the Suppression of Unlawful Acts against the Safety of Civil Aviation	ICAO	23 September 1971 Montreal	26 January 1973
• Convention on the Prevention and Punishment of Crimes against International Protected Persons, including Diplomatic Agents	UN General Assembly	14 December 1973 New York	20 February 1977
• International Convention against Taking of Hostages	UN General Assembly	17 December 1979 New York	3 June 1983
• Convention on the Physical Protection of Nuclear Material	International Atomic Energy Agency	3 March 1980 Vienna and New York	8 February 1977
• Protocol for the Suppression of Unlawful Acts of Violence at Airports Serving International Civil Aviation	ICAO	24 February 1988 Montreal	6 August 1989
• Convention for the Suppression of Unlawful Acts against the Safety of Maritime Navigation	International Maritime Organization (IMO)	10 March 1988 Rome	1 March 1992
• Protocol for the Suppression of Unlawful Acts against the Safety of Fixed Platforms Located on the Continental Shelf	IMO	10 March 1988 Rome	1 March 1992

Convention	Organization	Date and place of adoption	Entry into force
• Convention on the Marking of Plastic Explosives for the Purpose of Detection	ICAO	1 March 1991 Montreal	21 June 1998
• International Convention for the Suppression of Terrorist Bombings	UN General Assembly	15 December 1997 New York	23 May 2001
• International Convention on the Suppression of Financing of Terrorism	UN General Assembly	9 December 1999 New York	10 April 2002
• Arab Convention on the Suppression of Terrorism	League of Arab States	22 April 1998 Cairo	7 May 1999
• Convention on Combating International Terrorism	Organization of the Islamic Conference	1 July 1999 Ouagadougo, Burkina Faso	Not yet in force
• European Convention on the Suppression of Terrorism	Council of Europe	27 January 1977 Strasbourg, France	4 August 1978
• Convention to Prevent and Punish the Acts of Terrorism Taking the Form of Crimes against Persons and Related Extortion That Are of International Significance	Organization of American States	2 February 1971 Washington, DC	16 October 1973
• Convention on the Prevention and Combating of Terrorism	African Union	14 July 1999 Algiers	Not yet in force
• Regional Convention on Suppression of Terrorism	South Asian Association for Regional Cooperation	4 November 1987 Kathmandu, Nepal	22 August 1988
• Treaty on Cooperation among the States Members of the Commonwealth of Independent States in Combating Terrorism	Commonwealth of Independent States	4 June 1999 Minsk	Not yet in force

Source: United Nations (2002a, pp. 17–18; 2003).

153

can severely jeopardize the safety of all potential targets in a globalized world. Such noncompliance greatly limits the usefulness of the convention. For some conventions, universal ratification and implementation are necessary, but are never attained.

To investigate the effectiveness of some of these international conventions, Enders, Sandler, and Cauley (1990a) applied time-series analysis to various terrorist events. In the case of crimes against diplomats and other protected persons, they compared the pre-convention mean of the series for such attacks with its post-convention mean and *uncovered no significant differences*, suggesting that this convention was ineffective. For skyjackings, these authors performed the same test for the UN Security Council resolution of 1985 and earlier anti-hijacking resolutions and conventions (for example, the Hague Convention on seizure of aircraft), and again found no significant impact on the mean number of hijackings. In Chapter 3, we performed a test on the effectiveness of the 23 May 2001 International Convention for the Suppression of Terrorist Bombings and found no impact. Ironically, bombings as a proportion of terrorist incidents have been rising since about the time that the convention entered into force. Simply condemning a type of terrorist event is not going to hold any sway over individuals consumed by a purpose and willing to sacrifice themselves for a cause.

Regional conventions typically prohibit all forms of terrorism. These all-purpose condemnations are unlikely to lead to anything concrete, especially when the underlying definition of terrorism permits exceptions for campaigns of national liberation or other motives. Many regional conventions provide for cooperation among states confronting a common terrorist threat, usually in terms of sharing intelligence and other information about the terrorists (for example, preferred targets). On the surface, this cooperation should improve the situation, but this may not be the case if other policy decisions are not shared as well. Nations independently decide which targets to harden and determine their own budgets for deterring attacks. Shared intelligence may exacerbate nations' working at cross purposes as they spend even more money on deterrence after they learn of terrorists' strength and targeting predisposition from shared intelligence (Chapters 4–5; Enders and Sandler, 1995). This is a classic "second-best" problem, where cooperating on only one of two choice variables may reduce the well-being of everyone, as noncooperation on the second policy option more than offsets any gain achieved from the partial cooperation. Nations' insistence on making most security decisions on their own is highlighted by the wasted resources spent on maintaining commando squads for individual nations rather than developing a single network that can respond quickly to a terrorist crisis anywhere.

COLLECTIVE ACTION AGAINST TERRORIST FINANCING

Successful efforts that limit terrorists' resources curb their ability to engage in all forms of terrorism. Unlike antiterrorism policies that harden targets, actions that reduce terrorist resources do not merely change the terrorist attack mode from, say, hijacking to kidnapping. Since 9/11, select nations have tried to be more attentive to tracking the money trail as a way of inhibiting terrorist operations. In September 2003, the US Treasury reported that $135 million of alleged terrorists' assets had been frozen worldwide after 9/11 (*The Economist*, 2003). In February 2004, the White House (2003) increased this figure to $200 million.

In Table 6.3, some of these international initiatives are highlighted, starting with the creation of the Financial Action Task Force on Money Laundering (FATF), established in 1989 by the G-7 countries. FATF issues recommendations aimed at limiting terrorists' and drug cartels' abilities to move funds internationally. Key recommendations include freezing assets, adopting international conventions, generating accurate originator data on wire transfers, reporting suspicious transactions, fostering greater international cooperation, reviewing laws regulating nonprofits (including charities), registering businesses active in international remittances, and criminalizing the funding of terrorism (Levitt, 2003, p. 62).

Another development in stemming the funding of terrorism came with the creation of Financial Intelligence Units (FIUs) in November 1996. At the national level, FIUs monitor money transactions to spot and eliminate those supporting crimes, including terrorism. International cooperation and information exchange among the FIUs are bolstered by the Egmont Group, which began its efforts to link FIUs in April 2001. Because it is not a worldwide network, the Egmont Group provides terrorists with plenty of avenues (that is, weak links) to escape FIU surveillance. Moreover, the Egmont Group has no means to compel cooperation or universal participation.

Even before 9/11, the International Monetary Fund (IMF) and the World Bank pledged in April 2001 to increase anti–money laundering activities. IMF complements FATF's activities by providing technical assistance to countries needing enhanced capacity to cope with terrorist financial flows (IMF, 2001a). Primarily, IMF fosters the exchange of information among countries whose institutions are working to reduce

Table 6.3. *International Efforts against the Funding of Terrorism*

Action	Description
Financial Action Task Force on Money Laundering (FATF), 1989	This intergovernmental body, created by the G-7 countries in 1989, issues recommendations for reducing terrorist funding. It can merely make suggestions. Currently, the FATF is chaired by the United States and Spain and consists of twenty-nine countries.
Financial Intelligence Units (FIUs), November 1996	FIUs are national bodies established to limit money flows for illicit purposes, including terrorism.
Egmont Group and FIUs, June 2001 (Egmont Group established in 1995)	Through the exchange of intelligence, the Egmont Group promotes cooperation among FIUs to reduce money laundering and the financial resources of terrorists.
International Monetary Fund (IMF) Actions, April 2001	Bolster efforts at curbing money laundering by working with the major international anti–money laundering (AML) groups. Provide technical assistance to countries whose AML capacity is limited. Promote international cooperation and information exchange to reduce terrorist funding.
World Bank Executive Board, April 2001	In partnership with IMF, the Bank agreed to limit money laundering and funding for terrorism. The Bank also promised to implement the recommendations of the FATF.
UN Security Council Resolution 1373 and UN Counterterrorism Committee (CTC), November 2001	The resolution calls for global efforts to combat terrorism. It mandates three primary actions: to curb terrorist finances, to stop state sponsorship of terrorism, and to cooperate with other states' antiterrorist actions. The resolution instructs all nations to sign and implement the twelve international antiterrorist conventions. The CTC serves an advisory role for those countries actively seeking to curb terrorist funding.
International Convention on the Suppression of Financing of Terrorism, April 2002	Requires states to take appropriate actions to detect and freeze terrorist finances. The convention provides for no enforcement mechanism.

Sources: IMF (2001a), Levitt (2003), Organization of Economic Cooperation and Development (2003), United Nations (2002a, 2003), United Nations Security Council (2001).

terrorist and criminal money transfers. At the same time, the World Bank has indicated that it will work with the IMF to reduce money laundering while bolstering countries' ability to address the problem. Following 9/11, UN Security Council Resolution 1373 called for global cooperation to combat terrorism and formed the UN Counterterrorism Committee to serve in an advisory role to member states that sought its advice. Resolution 1373 also implored UN members to ratify and implement twelve international conventions, including the International Convention on the Suppression of Financing of Terrorism that eventually came into force in April 2002.

A Leaky Bucket

At first, efforts by the world community to go after terrorists' finances as reported in this chapter appeared impressive, but actions have waned compared to those in the year immediately following 9/11 (Basile, 2004, p. 177). All such efforts rely on nations to rigorously enforce standards of vigilance and best practice endorsed by FATF. As long as some countries lack the capacity or will to institute FATF's recommendations, terrorists will find ways to finance their heinous acts.

There are numerous means available to al-Qaida and other terrorist networks to circumvent international efforts to freeze their assets.[11] First, terrorists can hide their financial assets in nations that are noncompliant to agreements. Second, they can transfer their money in small transactions – under $5,000 – because only suspicious transfers above this ceiling must be reported under current guidelines. Multiple small transfers can fund most terrorist operations, including spectaculars – the 1993 World Trade Center bomb cost just $400, and the 9/11 attacks cost less than a half-million dollars (*The Economist*, 2003, p. 45). Third, terrorists use the *hawala* system of informal cash transfers, where bookkeeping balances are held and settled among a network of balance holders at a later time through a wire transfer or an exchange of commodities. This serves to disguise who is making the transfer to whom and the exact amount of the transfer (Basile, 2004, p. 176). Fourth, terrorists can convert their financial assets to precious commodities, such as diamonds, in order to underwrite operations. Fifth, terrorists can disguise their financial dealings through legitimate and illegitimate business transactions. Sixth, terrorists can rely on contributions to charitable organizations for some of their finances.

---

[11] This paragraph derives, in part, from the research of Basile (2004) and Levitt (2003).

The initial success in freezing terrorist assets came as the terrorist networks were caught unprepared. Since then, terrorists have found new means and venues to bypass restrictions.

An Assessment

Recent articles by Basile (2004) and Levitt (2003) suggest ways to address the problems with freezing terrorists' assets – for example, applying pressure on Saudi Arabia to control its charities, bringing more nations under FATF guidelines, lowering the limits on reporting money transfers, and monitoring the *hawala* system. Although these policy recommendations will temporarily improve efforts to freeze terrorists' assets, their long-run effectiveness is very limited. As loopholes are closed, the terrorists will innovate and find new ways to transfer the funds used to finance their relatively inexpensive operations. Freezing terrorists' assets is a moving target, and so the authorities must anticipate the next loophole. Additionally, international efforts will never involve a universal compliance to freezes; terrorist networks will always be able to counter some (much) of the collective efforts of others owing to the strategic (Stag Hunt) nature of the underlying interaction. Some nations will not go along with a freeze simply because they know its effectiveness is limited by nonuniversal subscription. Such freezes may prove an annoyance to terrorists, but freezes by themselves will not greatly curb terrorism, no matter what loopholes are closed. Freezes are not a panacea for terrorism, since the bucket will always leak by the very nature of the problem.

CONCLUDING REMARKS

Networked terrorists present a formidable threat to a globalized and technologically sophisticated world where target nations act largely independently to curb transnational terrorism. Our analysis of transnational externalities associated with counterterrorism demonstrated that there will be too little of some actions and too much of others so long as nations continue to preserve their autonomy over security. The cooperation asymmetry between terrorists and target governments, whereby terrorist groups cooperate while governments do not, permit terrorists to exploit government vulnerabilities. Watershed events – 9/11 and the 3/11 Madrid train bombings – foster cooperation temporarily until countries become complacent about the terrorist threat or else encounter a political disagreement (for example, over the US invasion of Iraq).

Although difficult to achieve, international cooperation will not only conserve resources but also make for more effective resource allocation. If international cooperation is to work, then an enforcement mechanism is needed, and that is unlikely at this time. Past resolutions and conventions have been shown to have little real impact in outlawing specific terrorist modes of attack. Recent efforts to freeze terrorists' assets have waned over time as terrorists find and exploit loopholes. More thought is required to engineer international cooperative arrangements on a par with those that have characterized terrorist networks since the late 1960s. Unless nations universally view the benefits from such arrangements as sufficient to support their efforts, noncompliant nations can be the spoilers by offsetting cooperative gains. As long as the terrorists do not pose a threat to all countries, international cooperation will remain partial and of limited effectiveness.

SEVEN

Hostage Taking

"He has pulled a hand-grenade pin and is ready to blow up the aircraft if he has to. We must land at Beirut. No alternative." These are the frantic words of pilot John L. Testrake to the control tower at the Beirut International Airport on 14 June 1985 during the hijacking of TWA flight 847 (Mickolus, Sandler, and Murdock, 1989, vol. 2, p. 219). Testrake's plea came after Lebanese officials had blocked the runway with fire trucks to keep the Boeing 727-200, with less than fifteen minutes of fuel remaining, from landing.[1] Flight 847 was hijacked en route from Athens to Rome with 145 passengers (including the two Lebanese hijackers) and 8 crew members. The hijackers, armed with a chrome-plated pistol and two hand grenades, stormed the cockpit and took over the plane ten minutes after takeoff; thus began a hijacking that would last until 30 June as the plane flew back and forth between Algiers and Beirut. In total, the plane made three landings in Beirut and two in Algiers. During the first three days of the incident, hostages were released sequentially in exchange for fuel and other demands. From 16 June until the end of the incident, the plane remained on the ground at Beirut, where most of the remaining hostages, but not the three-member crew, were hidden throughout the city to inhibit a rescue attempt. As the incident dragged on, the number of terrorists increased, thereby indicating state assistance. The world's media provided nonstop coverage of the seventeen-day ordeal, which captured the world's attention. In the end, the hijackers succeeded in pressuring Israel

---

[1] The information in this paragraph is derived from Mickolus, Sandler, and Murdock (1989, vol. 2, pp. 219–25), where the incident is described in detail using facts taken from a variety of news sources.

to release 735 prisoners from the Atlit prison. Moreover, the United States had to reaffirm its support for the sovereignty of Lebanon and to agree not to retaliate against the Amal militia that had aided the hijackers in Beirut. The hijackers were allowed to read a statement and then escaped. Flight 847 reflects the type of media coverage that only a few hostage-taking missions have achieved.

On 1 September 2004, roughly 25 Chechen and other terrorists held over 1,000 people hostage in a school in Beslan, Russia, for 52 hours.[2] Once again, the world's attention turned to Beslan, given the large number of children being held as hostages and the apparent ruthlessness of the terrorists. The outcome of past incidents involving Chechen rebels – for example, the October 2002 seizure of a Moscow theater – gave the world ample reason to be apprehensive. At 1 P.M. on 3 September, the incident ended horribly as emergency personnel were being allowed by the terrorists to retrieve the bodies of dead hostages. Apparently, the hostage takers mistakenly thought that a rescue mission was under way and began firing. Fire was returned by security forces and the townspeople as bedlam broke loose. Terrorist-planted bombs in the school also began going off. By the time the shootings and explosions had stopped, 340 people had perished and hundreds were injured.

Hostage-taking incidents come in four varieties: kidnappings, skyjackings, the takeover of nonaerial means of transportation (for example, a bus or a ship), and barricade and hostage-taking missions (henceforth, referred to as *barricade missions*). This last type involves the takeover of a building or venue and the seizure of hostages, as in the Beslan incidents. The riskiness of hostage-taking incidents differs by type: typically, kidnappings are the least risky, because the authorities often do not know the kidnappers' location or that of their hostages. As a kidnapping drags on, the authority's ability to learn the kidnappers' location increases. The other three types of hostage-taking events pose much greater risks to the terrorists, insofar as their location and that of their hostages are known from the outset. Skyjackings have become especially dangerous since the installation of metal detectors in January 1973, because would-be hijackers must now get their weapons past security barriers. The same is true of an embassy takeover, but may not be true of takeovers of other buildings.

This chapter has four purposes. First, the strengths and weaknesses of past theoretical approaches to the study of hostage taking are reviewed. Second, we evaluate the feasibility of a no-negotiation policy to limit

---

[2] The facts in this paragraph are drawn from *The Economist* (2004, pp. 23–5).

hostage taking, which is one of the four pillars of US counterterrorism action (US Department of State, 2003).[3] Third, we investigate past empirical tests of bargaining theory based on terrorist hostage-taking events. Data on hostage-taking incidents afford researchers an opportunity to test propositions regarding bargaining in intense situations. For example, does an increase in the number of dimensions over which the negotiations are conducted augment the likelihood of a negotiated success, as bargaining theory suggests? Fourth, we suggest some directions for future research. In the course of the chapter, we conclude that a game-theoretic analysis of hostage taking is particularly appropriate, given the intense interaction between the terrorists and the targeted government. The effectiveness of a no-negotiation policy depends on many unstated assumptions that may not hold in practice, thus leading governments to renege on their pledge in practice. The outcome of the hijacking of TWA flight 847 indicates that the Reagan administration, along with the Israeli government, made some concessions to the hostage takers – a situation that often encourages more hostage taking

WHY HOSTAGE TAKING?

Terrorists can resort to many alternative attack modes – ITERATE, for example, identifies twenty-five types of attacks – and new types may arise in the future. Hence, one must wonder why terrorists use hostage-taking missions that are not only logistically very complex, but also costly in terms of resource expenditure and associated risks. Terrorists will be drawn to such events provided that the expected payoffs – taking into account the probability of success – equal or exceed the expected costs. Thus, the terrorists must perceive there to be a reasonable chance of high gains in terms of media exposure and potential concessions if they are going to engage in such costly attacks. Since the rise of modern terrorism in the late 1960s (see Chapter 2), terrorists have viewed hijackings and other hostage-taking events as having the potential for huge gains. Based on ITERATE data for 1968–2003, just 14.2% of all terrorist attacks were hostage-taking missions. The individual percentages corresponding to each type of hostage-taking event are: 9.44%, kidnappings; 2.88%, skyjackings; 1.42%, barricade missions; and 0.46%, takeovers of nonaerial

---

[3] The four pillars are as follows: (i) make no concessions to terrorists; (ii) bring terrorists to justice; (iii) make states end their sponsorship of terrorism; and (iv) bolster the counterterrorist capabilities of target countries that require assistance.

means of transportation. These percentages indicate that terrorists choose the type of hostage-taking event by responding to risks, because the least risky kind of hostage operation represents two-thirds of all such operations. The higher percentage of skyjackings compared to barricade missions can be explained by the greater difficulty of ending a skyjacking compared to the takeover of a building. In a skyjacking, it is often difficult for the rescuers to approach the plane unseen. Moreover, in the confined space of an airplane, hostages are in great peril during rescue missions. The capability of the terrorists is aptly illustrated by their relatively high logistical success rate – 75.7% (1,350 of 1,784) of all hostage missions ended in the terrorists securing one or more hostages.

A much smaller percentage of hostage-taking missions ends in a successful negotiation where one or more demands are met. In a study using US government data on 549 transnational hostage events from July 1968 to July 1984, Sandler and Scott (1987) found that 87% of such attacks resulted in logistical success, while only 27% ended in successful negotiation. The lower percentage of successful negotiations is understandable for two reasons: an event must first be logistically successful in order to move into the negotiation phase; and governments realize that giving in to terrorists' demands encourages more hostage taking.

Despite the difficulties and risks posed by hostage operations, terrorists have good reason to turn to them some of the time. Hostage-taking missions can stay in the news longer than other types of events, with the sole exception of "spectacular" attacks such as those of 9/11 and 3/11 where there were massive casualties and widespread fallout. Hostage attacks not only receive media coverage during the drama, which can be drawn out, but also after it is over. Even a failed attempt to take hostages or to negotiate a concession will receive a good deal of news coverage. By contrast, a massive bombing is over in seconds and receives coverage only in its aftermath. Hostage taking may yield concessions that augment the terrorists' prestige, cause, recruitment, and resources. Other kinds of terrorist events seldom result in a concession. If the media are properly exploited by the terrorists, hostage events can yield a great deal of publicity for the terrorist cause. During the hijacking of TWA flight 847, the terrorists used the media on several occasions to make their grievances and concerns known. As explained in Chapter 2, the Popular Front for the Liberation of Palestine (PFLP) takeover of an El Al flight on 22 July 1968 resulted in the Israelis having to recognize and negotiate with the Palestinians. The drama of hostage events may be more efficient than most terrorist events in creating an atmosphere of fear, where the public

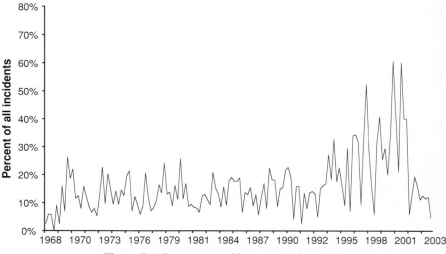

Figure 7.1. Percentage of hostage-taking missions.

feels more vulnerable than the true underlying probabilities warrant. The need for screening of the flying public is a constant reminder of these risks.

Figure 7.1 depicts the quarterly percentage of hostage-taking missions for 1968–2003, based on ITERATE data. As mentioned earlier, the overall mean is 14.2% of all events. From July 1968 until 1970, the percentage of hostage incidents increased greatly owing to the success of the PFLP hijacking of the El Al flight. Thereafter, the percentage of hostage-taking events displays a cycle in which a successful event yields an upturn in the percentage owing to a demonstration effect, followed by a downturn as terrorists either experience a failure or have to accumulate resources for future events (Sandler and Enders, 2004). From 1992 until the end of 2000, hostage-taking events display a heightened presence and greater variability. After 9/11, the number of hostage incidents dropped precipitously in percentage terms (see Chapter 8 and Enders and Sandler, 2005a). The kidnapping of foreigners in Iraq in 2004 should increase this percentage greatly.

PAST INCIDENTS

In Table 7.1, we display some key hostage-taking incidents prior to 1986, beginning with the PFLP hijacking of the El Al flight in July 1968. For each of the nine incidents listed, we provide the incident date, the terrorists responsible, the incident's nature, and its outcome. These hostage incidents are chosen because they are watershed events; the list is, however, highly selective and ignores many other watershed incidents. The July 1968 incident demonstrated to other terrorists worldwide the publicity value of the hijacking of an international flight and resulted in numerous copycat events. Because of this hijacking, terrorists realized the benefit of bringing their struggle to the world stage through transnational terrorism. As such, this one event gave rise to the modern era of transnational terrorism, where many local struggles motivate terrorist events in distant venues (see Chapter 2). The August 1969 hijacking, also by PFLP, showed that a nation could aid and abet the terrorists during the incident. In particular, Syria exploited the incident and engineered a prisoner exchange involving itself, Israel, and Egypt. This exchange underscored the idea that even the staunchest supporters of the no-negotiation policy may make an exception and negotiate if the cost of holding firm is too high. Such deals mean that terrorists will be less inclined to believe a government's stated policy never to concede to the demands of terrorists.

The 1972 Munich Olympics incident, where nine Israeli athletes were taken hostage, represents the first true terrorist "spectacular" that captured the attention of the world's viewing audience. The drama was especially poignant because satellite technology meant that it could be broadcast live to the global community. The Munich Olympics etched transnational terrorism in everyone's mind; the world lost a good deal of innocence with this event. Even though the terrorists failed to secure any of their demands, this incident led to many recruits for the Palestinian cause (Hoffman, 1998). It also motivated governments to improve their commando forces to manage such crises.

The infamous Maalot incident of 15 May 1974, where ninety schoolchildren were taken hostage, is an instance in which Israeli Premier Golda Meir appeared willing to negotiate with terrorists. Apparently, the government agreed to swap the requested prisoners held in Israeli jails for the children. Kozo Okamoto, the sole surviving Japanese Red Army terrorist from the Lod Airport massacre (30 May 1972), was among the prisoners to be exchanged (Mickolus, 1980). The prisoners had been taken out of their Israeli cells and were on a bus on their way to the exchange when the Israeli commandos sensed something wrong and stormed the school. Twenty-one children died in the raid. This incident again illustrates that if the "right" hostages are captured, negotiations may ensue. The Maalot takeover has many parallels with the Beslan school incident three decades later.

Table 7.1. *Select Key Hostage-Taking Incidents Prior to 1986*

Date	Terrorists	Incident	Outcome
22 July 1968	Popular Front for Liberation of Palestine (PFLP)	Hijacking of El Al Boeing 707 en route from Rome to Tel Aviv. Plane flown to Algiers.	Negotiated settlement: ransom paid by France; Israel released some prisoners. Algeria aided the hijackers in Algiers.
29 Aug. 1969	PFLP	TWA flight 840 with 113 people aboard was hijacked after leaving Rome. Plane flown to Damascus, Syria.	After letting passengers and crew off of the plane, the terrorists blew up the cockpit. Two Israeli passengers held by Syria. On 5 Dec. they were released in a prisoner exchange involving Syria, Israel, and Egypt.
5 Sept. 1972	Black September	Seizure of nine Israeli athletes at the Munich Olympics.	All hostages killed when the West German police shot at the terrorists at Fürstenfeldbruck Military Airport as preparations were being made to fly the terrorists and hostages to Egypt.
15 May 1974	Democratic Front for Liberation of Palestine	Seizure of ninety schoolchildren and some adults at a school in Maalot, Israel.	Negotiated deal arranged but never consummated when Israeli commandos stormed the school. Twenty-one children died.
21 Dec. 1975	PFLP	Seizure of seventy hostages including eleven Organization of Petroleum Exporting Countries (OPEC) ministers in Vienna.	Ransom paid and ministers released.

166

Date	Group	Incident	Outcome
27 June 1976	PFLP	Hijacking of Air France flight 139 with 257 people aboard, en route from Athens to Paris. Flight originated in Tel Aviv.	Hostage-freeing mission at Entebbe Airport, Uganda. Israeli commandos stormed the airport in Operation Thunderbolt. All terrorists killed, along with a few hostages. Mission was a success.
23 Aug. 1976	Three hijackers	Hijacking of EgyptAir flight with ninety-six people aboard, en route from Cairo to Luxor.	Egypt mounted a successful commando raid in which all hostages were released unharmed.
4 Nov. 1979	500 radical Moslem students	Seizure of over 100 hostages at the US embassy in Tehran, Iran.	Ended after 444 days with the release of the remaining hostages. A US rescue mission was aborted following a helicopter crash. Iran aided the terrorists.
14 June 1985	Lebanese and Amal terrorists	Hijacking of TWA flight 847 with 153 people aboard, en route from Athens to Rome. Plane diverted to Beirut and then to Algiers. From Algiers, it went back to Beirut. The plane was flown back to Algiers before returning for a third time to Beirut. During the incident, one hostage was killed and dumped on the tarmac. Also, hostages were released sequentially.	A negotiated settlement was reached between the United States, Syria, and Israel on 30 June. The United States released a statement guaranteeing Lebanon sovereignty. Israel released 735 Lebanese prisoners some time after the incident.

Sources: For incidents prior to 1980, the source is Mickolus (1980). For TWA flight 847, the source is Mickolus, Sandler, and Murdock (1989).

Another important hostage-taking event was the seizure of eleven Organization of Petroleum Exporting Countries (OPEC) ministers in Vienna on 21 December 1975. The PFLP terrorists were led by Illich Ramirez Sanchez ("Carlos"), who was involved in many high-profile terrorist attacks in the 1970s and 1980s. A large ransom – reputed to be $5 million – was paid to the terrorists (Mickolus, 1980, pp. 570–3). This incident sent two disturbing messages: almost anyone could be taken hostage, and capturing high-value hostages led to media coverage and money for future operations.

In a much less successful event, the PFLP hijacked Air France flight 139, with 257 people aboard, on 27 June 1976. This event is noteworthy because Israeli commandos eventually freed the hostages at the Entebbe Airport in Uganda. The rescue mission, known as Operation Thunderbolt, required the Israeli commandos to fly from Israel to Uganda in a troop-transport plane that landed on the darkened runway. In a complex and dangerous mission, the commandos managed to kill all of the terrorists and many of the Ugandan troops who had been providing cover for the terrorists at the Entebbe Airport. This incident indicated that a government could execute a successful hostage rescue in a distant venue. Operation Thunderbolt resulted in little loss of life to the hostages. Another daring rescue characterized Egyptian efforts to free 103 hostages on an Egyptair flight while it was on the ground for refueling in Luxor before it was to fly to Benghazi, Libya (Mickolus, 1980, pp. 639–40). The commandos gained access to the plane disguised as mechanics – a ploy that would be copied in other rescue missions. Media reports of this tactic eventually rendered it useless over time. In the Egyptian operation, the hostages were freed with little in the way of injuries.

Another watershed event was the seizure of the US embassy in Tehran, Iran, on 4 November 1979 by 500 radical Moslem students. Although the takeover appeared to be spontaneous and not orchestrated by the Iranian government, the latter quickly stepped in to protect the students and began negotiations with the United States on ending the barricade mission.[4] At first, the United States used economic, diplomatic, and legal channels in an attempt to end the crisis. Thus, President Carter froze Iranian assets, expelled Iranian diplomats, and ended US purchases of Iranian oil. The US government also sought international condemnation of the embassy takeover. On 7 April 1980, the United States broke off diplomatic relations with Iran and began an economic embargo that banned all exports except food and medicine to Iran. On 24 April 1980,

---

[4] The facts in this paragraph come from Mickolus (1980, pp. 880–5).

the United States launched a rescue mission, which had to be aborted when a helicopter collided with a transport plane in the Iranian desert, some distance from Tehran. The remaining hostages were finally released after 444 days of captivity on the Inauguration Day of President Reagan. This incident illustrated not only state sponsorship, but also the difficulty of a hostage rescue in a distant venue. Operation Thunderbolt is not easy to copy. Following this embassy takeover, there was a rise in fundamentalist and state-sponsored terrorism. This incident also highlighted that a hostage incident, when perceived as poorly handled, could lose an elected leader his or her office. Thus, high-profile terrorist incidents may have significant political repercussions even when concessions are not granted.

The final watershed event in Table 7.1 is the one with which the chapter began – the hijacking of TWA flight 847. The incident is noteworthy because of the media attention that it received and the concessions made by the United States and Israel to the terrorists' demands. During this hijacking, the terrorists operated not only with impunity but also with the help of the Amal militia in Beirut and supporters in Algiers. After this incident, there were six additional hijackings in 1985 and another five in 1986; clearly, a successful hijacking stimulates future incidents.

These incidents illustrate a number of lessons:

- Palestinian terrorists were the first to exploit hostage taking for political advantage.
- A successful hostage mission spawns additional incidents.
- Some watershed hostage incidents can affect the nature of terrorism.
- Governments have not been consistent in adhering to a no-negotiation policy, especially if high-value hostages are secured.
- Successful hostage missions push governments to develop effective defensive and crisis-management techniques. Such techniques motivate terrorists to devise effective countermeasures.
- In some major incidents, state sponsorship has lengthened the incident and provided cover for the terrorists.
- Hostage incidents can have large payoffs or large losses for the terrorists.

These messages also characterize key hostage incidents in the 1990s and beyond. For example, the hijackings on 9/11 illustrate that hostage missions can alter the future of transnational terrorism: passengers are now less apt to be passive, and some governments are prepared to shoot down a hijacked plane. The hijacking of Indian Airline flight 814 on 24 December 1999 shows that a government may still protect the terrorists during their mission. This flight was hijacked by five members of Harkul ul-Mujahideen, an Islamic group opposed to Indian rule in Kashmir.[5] The plane was commandeered after it left Kathmandu International Airport with 186 people aboard. After stops in Amritsar (India), Lahore (Pakistan), and Dubai, the plane landed in Kandahar, Afghanistan, where it remained, surrounded by Taliban militia, until a negotiated deal with the Indian government on 30 December 1999. The terrorists gained the release of a comrade jailed in India and were allowed safe passage to Pakistani-controlled Kashmir. The Taliban government of Afghanistan did nothing to end the incident and permitted the hijackers to escape. Moreover, by surrounding the plane in Kandahar, the Taliban made a rescue mission impossible.

Kidnappings

Kidnapping has been, and remains, an important terrorist tactic. The potential political consequences of kidnapping are aptly illustrated by a domestic terrorist event: the kidnapping of former premier Aldo Moro on 16 March 1978 by twelve members of the Italian Red Brigade (Mickolus, 1980, pp. 780–2). At the time of his abduction, Moro was the president of the ruling Christian Democrats, and it was anticipated that he would be elected to lead Italy in the next election. At 8:15 A.M., the terrorists ambushed Moro's car and the accompanying police car – in the ensuing mayhem, 710 shots were fired and 5 policemen were killed. An unharmed Moro was taken hostage and driven away. On 6 May 1978, his bullet-riddled body was discovered in the trunk of a car parked in central Rome, not far from the headquarters of the Christian Democrats. This kidnapping determined the leadership of the Italian government and enraged the authorities, who eventually brought the kidnappers to justice.

More generally, terrorists rely on kidnappings to generate ransoms to finance operations. This was true of the left-wing European terrorists during the late 1970s and 1980s. In Latin America, unprotected foreign businessmen and dependents make inviting targets for today's ransom-hungry leftist terrorists. In some cases, kidnappers demand the release of an imprisoned comrade or the publication of a political statement.

At times, kidnapping campaigns have been used to gain political concessions. Islamic fundamentalists – Hezbollah and Islamic Jihad – relied on kidnappings in Beirut during 1982–1992 to obtain ransoms and political concessions. Table 7.2 lists some of the most noteworthy hostages

---

[5] The description of this incident derives from Silke (2001).

captured during this period, along with the nationality, position, abduction date, and final status of each. A number of insights can be gleaned from the table. First, Westerners were a desired target. Second, the terrorists went for soft targets: academics, journalists, and businessmen were favored. Third, hostage releases were often followed by the taking of more hostages. For example, the release of Rev. Benjamin Weir, Rev. Lawrence Jenco, and David Jacobsen was followed by the capture of Robert Polhill, Allan Steen, and Jesse Turner. Thus, three American academic hostages replaced the three Americans who had been released. This replacement was highly publicized when it became known that the Reagan administration had traded arms for hostages to obtain the release of Weir, Jenco, and Jacobsen (Islam and Shahin, 1989; Mickolus, Sandler, and Murdock, 1989, vol. 2). A fourth American hostage – William Buckley – had been murdered by the terrorists before the trade could be made. The action of the Reagan administration became known as "Irangate" and again illustrated that governments may go against their stated no-negotiation policy to gain release of a valued hostage. Apparently, Buckley's status as a Central Intelligence Agency (CIA) officer, stationed at the US embassy in Beirut, first motivated the Reagan administration to negotiate with the hostage takers. Once the terrorists realized that gains could be made, they simply replenished their supply of hostages upon negotiated releases.

Since April 2004, a new and even more ominous kidnapping campaign has emerged in Iraq, undertaken by radical Islamic fundamentalists as a means to pressure foreign governments and nongovernmental organizations (NGOs) to pull their people out of Iraq. Table 7.3 lists some select hostages captured in this campaign during 2004. These hostage-taking incidents began shortly after the abuse of prisoners by US service personnel at Abu Ghraib became known. The situation took an especially grisly and repulsive turn when the beheading of Nicholas Berg was video recorded and posted on the internet. Terrorists again exploited modern technology to heighten the public's anxiety. A group called Tawhid and Jihad, headed by Abu Masab al-Zarqawi, claimed responsibility for Berg's abduction and murder. Credit for subsequent kidnappings has been claimed by various groups, including Tawhid and Jihad, Holders of the Black Banners, Islamic Army in Iraq, Ansar al-Sunna Army, and the Green Brigade of the Prophet (Lexis Nexis, 2004). Favored hostages have included security guards, construction workers, truck drivers, aid workers, and journalists. In some cases, governments have caved in to demands – for example, the Philippine government withdrew its troops and secured the release of Angelo de la Cruz, a truck driver threatened with beheading.

Table 7.2. *Select Hostages Captured during the 1982–1992 Lebanon Hostage Crisis*

Hostage	Nationality/Position	Capture Date	Final Status[a]
David Dodge	American/acting president of American University of Beirut (AUB)	19 July 1982	Released 21 July 1983
William Buckley	American/CIA officer	16 March 1984	Murdered
Rev. Benjamin Weir	American/Presbyterian minister	8 May 1984	Released 14 Sept. 1985
Peter Kilburn	American/librarian, AUB	3 Dec. 1984	Murdered 17 April 1986
Rev. Lawrence Jenco	American/Catholic Relief Services	8 Jan. 1985	Released 26 July 1986
Terry Anderson	American/Associated Press, Middle East bureau chief	16 March 1985	Released 4 Dec. 1991
Marcel Fontaine	French/diplomat	22 March 1985	Released May 1988
Marcel Carton	French/diplomat	22 March 1985	Released May 1988
Alec Collett	British/journalist working with UN Relief and Works Agency	26 March 1985	Murdered April 1986
Jean-Paul Kauffman	French/journalist	22 May 1985	Released May 1988
Michael Seurat	French/researcher, French Center for Studies of Contemporary Middle East	22 May 1985	Murdered 6 March 1986
David Jacobsen	American/directed Medical School, AUB	28 May 1985	Released 2 Nov. 1986
Thomas Sutherland	American/dean, AUB	9 Jan. 1985	Released 18 Nov. 1991
Albert Molinari	Italian/businessman	11 Sept. 1985	Presumed murdered

172

Name	Description	Date	Status
Do Chae-sung	South Korean/diplomat	31 Jan. 1986	Released 31 Oct. 1987
Jean-Louis Normandin	French/TV journalist	8 March 1986	Released 27 Nov. 1987
Brian Keenan	Irish/educator, AUB	11 April 1986	Released 24 Aug. 1990
John McCarthy	British/TV reporter	17 April 1986	Released 8 Aug. 1991
Frank Reed	American/director of Lebanese International School	9 Sept. 1986	Released 30 April 1990
Joseph Cicippio	American/comptroller, AUB	12 Sept. 1986	Released 2 Dec. 1991
Edward Tracy	American/writer	21 Oct. 1986	Released 11 Aug. 1991
Roger Augue	French/photojournalist	13 Jan. 1987	Released 27 Nov. 1987
Rudolf Cordes	West German/businessman	17 Jan. 1987	Released 7 Sept. 1988
Terry Waite	British/Church of England, envoy	20 Jan. 1987	Released 18 Nov. 1991
Alfred Schmidt	West German/engineer	21 Jan. 1987	Released Sept. 1987
Robert Polhill	American/educator, Beirut University College (BUC)	24 Jan. 1987	Released 28 April 1990
Allan Steen	American/educator, BUC	24 Jan. 1987	Released 3 Dec. 1991
Jesse Turner	American/educator, BUC	24 Jan. 1987	Released 22 Oct. 1991
Mithileshwar Singh	Indian with US resident status/educator, BUC	24 Jan. 1987	Released Oct. 1988
Charles Glass	American/journalist	17 June 1987	Escaped 18 Aug. 1987
Ralph Schray	West German/businessman	27 Jan. 1988	Released March 1988
Lt. Col William Richard Higgins	American/Marine Corps	17 Feb. 1988	Murdered

[a] Exact dates are given when known.

Source: US Department of State (1987–1992) and Mickolus, Sandler, and Murdock (1989)

Table 7.3. *Select Hostages Captured during 2004 in Iraq*

Hostage	Nationality/Occupation	Capture Date	Final Status
Eight hostages	South Korean/ missionaries	8 April 2004	Released 9 April 2004
Nicholas Berg	American/businessman	9 April 2004	Murdered 8 May 2004
Keith Mopan	American/soldier	9 April 2004	Murdered 28 June 2004
Thomas Hamil	American/truck driver	9 April 2004	Escaped 2 May 2004
Elmer Krause	American/soldier	9 April 2004	Murdered 23 April 2004
Seven hostages	Chinese/construction workers	11 April 2004	Released 12 April 2004
Fabrizio Quattrocchi	Italian/security guard	12 April 2004	Murdered 14 April 2004
Salvatore Stefio	Italian/security guard	12 April 2004	Released 8 June 2004
Umberto Cupertino	Italian/security guard	12 April 2004	Released 8 June 2004
Maurizio Agliana	Italian/security guard	12 April 2004	Released 8 June 2004
Hussein Ali Alyan	Lebanese/construction worker	10 June 2004	Murdered 12 June 2004
Sun-Il Kim	South Korean/ translator	17 June 2004	Murdered 22 June 2004
Georgi Lazov	Bulgarian/truck driver	27 June 2004	Murdered 15 July 2004
Ivaylo Kepov	Bulgarian/truck driver	27 June 2004	Murdered 22 July 2004
Angelo de la Cruz	Filipino/truck driver	7 July 2004	Released 20 July 2004
Abdurrahman Demir	Turkish/truck driver	31 July 2004	Released 4 Aug. 2004
Sait Unurlu	Turkish/truck driver	31 July 2004	Released 4 Aug. 2004
Durmas Kumdereli	Turkish/truck driver	14 Aug. 2004	Murdered 17 Aug. 2004
Mustafa Koksal	Turkish/truck driver	14 Aug. 2004	Released 18 Aug. 2004
Anzo Baldoni	Italian/journalist	20 Aug. 2004	Murdered 27 Aug. 2004
Scott Taylor	Canadian/journalist	7 Sept. 2004	Released 11 Sept. 2004
Jack Hensley	American/civil engineer	16 Sept. 2004	Murdered 21 Sept. 2004
Eugene Armstrong	American/civil engineer	16 Sept. 2004	Murdered 20 Sept. 2004
Kenneth Bigley	British/civil engineer	16 Sept. 2004	Murdered 8 Oct. 2004

Source: Lexis Nexis (2004) at [http://web.lexis-nexis.com/universe].

Such concessions imply negative externalities on other governments as terrorists reap rewards for their actions and are encouraged to take more hostages from other countries.[6] The table clearly shows that the release of hostages is quickly followed by the capture of new hostages – for example, the release of de la Cruz on 20 July was followed by the abduction of two Turkish truck drivers on 31 July. Their later release on 4 August, after their company withdrew employees, was followed by the kidnapping of two more Turkish truck drivers on 14 August. Unless nations devise a way to keep from conceding to kidnappers' demands, the campaign will continue to increase in scope. This required international coordination is extremely difficult to achieve, thereby bolstering the terrorists' efforts as nations act independently (see Chapter 6).

NON-GAME-THEORETIC ANALYSIS OF HOSTAGE TAKING

To date, there have been three analytical non-game-theoretic analyses of hostage taking – two have been theoretical and one has been empirical in nature. All three have used an expected utility approach, where the likelihood of each possible outcome (that is, state of the world) is determined and then multiplied by the associated value to give an expected value of the outcome. The sum of these expected values over all possible states is the associated *expected utility*, *EU*. In Chapter 5, we found the expected utility of a skyjacking by computing

$$EU^{SKY} = \pi U^S + (1 - \pi) U^F, \tag{1}$$

where U^S is the gain from a successful hijacking; U^F is the payoff from a failed hijacking; π is the probability of success; and $(1 - \pi)$ is the probability of failure. Probabilities must sum to one so that all possible outcomes are included. The analysis can be expanded by allowing for more states of the world. In addition, we can compare the expected utility of one risky choice to that of another in order to ascertain the best by picking the choice with the greatest expected utility. This decision can be made even more interesting by allowing the payoffs *or* the probabilities to depend on decision variables or policy parameters. In such cases, the choice of the government – say, to take punitive action against the captured hostage takers – may influence the number of hostages taken.

---

[6] A negative externality results because one country's action creates costs for another country, not party to the transaction.

Islam and Shahin (1989) constructed an expected utility model to conceptualize how a government's past behavior to negotiate may influence terrorists' future hostage taking. Three states of the world characterize their situation from the hostage takers' viewpoint: the targeted government takes no actions, W, with probability p; the targeted government concedes a gain, G, to the terrorists with probability q; or the targeted government takes a punitive action, L, with probability $1 - p - q$. The expected gain, EU^H, to the terrorists is then

$$EU^H = pW(n, m) + qG(n, m) + (1 - p - q) L(n), \qquad (2)$$

where n is the number of hostages, and m is the media manipulation by the hostage takers. The net gain to the hostage takers is the difference between EU^H and the associated cost of hostage taking. Under various assumptions on the W and G relationships, the authors analyzed whether an increase in the likelihood of negotiation by the government, q, would increase hostage taking.[7] Alternative cases were identified.

Such analytical models have not been part of the standard terrorism literature. We agree with a recent article by Silke (2001) that such models could have a real role to play in shaping government policy if the model were appropriately formulated. Models allow a researcher to simplify a complex reality in order to gain insights not apparent without such simplification. The trick is to simplify, while maintaining key ingredients so that the skeleton relationship provides useful insights. The trouble with the nongame analyses of hostage taking is that the interplay between the adversaries is missing. Thus, the government's likelihood of punitive action depends on the hostage takers' choice of n, and vice versa. Non-game-theoretic models ignore such essential interactions.

This same criticism applies to the other two non-game-theoretic models of hostage taking by Shahin and Islam (1992) and Landes (1978). In the former, the authors showed that in some cases a policy mix of penalties and rewards to hostage takers leads to a superior result when compared to just punishment *or* reward. Reward involves a positive payoff to terrorists who release their hostages and then engage in legal activities. In a true interactive framework, hostage takers will view rewards as an inducement for grabbing more hostages – a frequent outcome, as shown in Tables 7.2 and 7.3. Shahin and Islam tried to eliminate this likely outcome by assuming

---

[7] Islam and Shahin (1989) used the first-order conditions of the objective function in equation (2) to compute comparative-static changes such as $\partial n / \partial q$ – that is, the change in the optimal number of hostages for a change in a government's likelihood to concede.

that the reward is used sparingly and appears unanticipated. This assumption is, however, inconsistent with the way expectations are formed – that is, past concessions condition would-be hostage takers to anticipate a greater likelihood of future concessions (Sandler, Tschirhart, and Cauley, 1983). Even if the original hostage takers "go straight" because of the reward, the reward sends a signal to other potential hostage takers that such actions pay. By assuming a response *not in keeping* with anticipated actions of adversaries, the authors greatly limited the usefulness of their model. The strategic interactions of adversaries must be part of a hostage-taking analysis. In the Shahin-Islam framework, there were really three active participants – the hostage takers, the government, and the media – that should make choices in an interactive framework. To simplify, the modeler may have the government control the media's decision.

The Landes (1978) article also suffers from the lack of a strategic framework, because the only choice modeled is that of the skyjacker who faces three states of the world: a successful hijacking and freedom in another country; apprehension and no conviction; and apprehension and conviction. Once again, a true interactive scenario between the hijacker and the government is not analyzed. This is, however, less of a concern for the Landes study because his main goal was to ascertain the *empirical* impact of government actions on the number of hijackings or the time interval between hijackings. If government policies are effective deterrents, then the number of hijackings should fall and/or the time interval between hijackings should lengthen (also see our remarks in Chapter 5). Using data on US hijackings from 1961 to 1976, Landes (1978, p. 12) found that an increase in the probability of apprehension had a negative and highly significant influence on the number of hijackings, a reduction of 1.1 to 2.2 hijackings per quarter. Other important deterrents included a higher probability of conviction and longer prison sentences. Landes also found that a greater probability of apprehension, a greater likelihood of conviction, and longer prison sentences also lengthened the time interval between successive hijackings. A greater chance of being killed during the hijacking also deterred hijackings. Finally, increases in unemployment made for more frequent hijackings, a finding consistent with fewer opportunities in the host country.

As mentioned in Chapter 5, Landes's (1978) evaluation of metal detectors failed to account for the motivation of terrorists to substitute from the now more costly skyjackings into less costly kidnappings and other kinds of attacks. Enders and Sandler (1993) uncovered clear evidence of such substitutions following actions by the government to make skyjackings less successful through the installation of metal detectors. This shortcoming of Landes's (1978) important study is a consequence of his failure to account for strategic interaction among adversaries.

GAME THEORY AND HOSTAGE TAKING

To date, there have been four game-theoretic analyses of hostage-taking events by Atkinson, Sandler, and Tschirhart (1987), Lapan and Sandler (1988), Sandler, Tschirhart, and Cauley (1983), and Selten (1988). We focus our remarks on the Lapan and Sandler study, which investigated the practicality of a policy that commits governments never to negotiate with hostage takers. The conventional wisdom hinges on the notion that if terrorists know ahead of time that they have nothing to gain, then they will never abduct hostages. As we show, the success of this policy depends on some unstated assumptions that may not always hold in practice. Our earlier examination of real-world incidents identified cases where governments reneged on their stated no-concession policy. We explain the pitfalls of this policy and what can be done to keep governments true to their pledge.

The underlying game tree is displayed in Figure 7.2, where the government goes first and chooses a level of deterrence that determines the likelihood of a logistical failure by the terrorists – that is, the probability, θ, that the terrorists will fail to secure their intended hostage(s). Given their perceived likelihood of logistical success or failure and also their perceived likelihood of negotiated success or failure, the terrorists decide whether or not to take hostages. If there is no hostage incident, the game ends. If the terrorists attempt to take hostages, then either the terrorists fail and the game ends, or they succeed and secure hostages. In the latter case, the government must then decide whether or not to capitulate to the terrorists' demands. Terrorists perceive the capitulation probability to be p.

For each of the four possible endpoints of the game, the government's payoff is listed on top and the terrorists' payoff is underneath. In every contingency, the government must cover deterrence cost, which is like an insurance premium that must be paid regardless of the outcome. If the terrorists attempt an incident but fail, then the cost to the government is $D(\theta)$ plus a. The latter represents any expense incurred from putting down the incident – for example, expenditures to stop the incident in the planning stage. When an incident succeeds, the government incurs an additional expense of h if they capitulate and an expense of n if they do not capitulate. The relative values of h and n depend, in part, on the

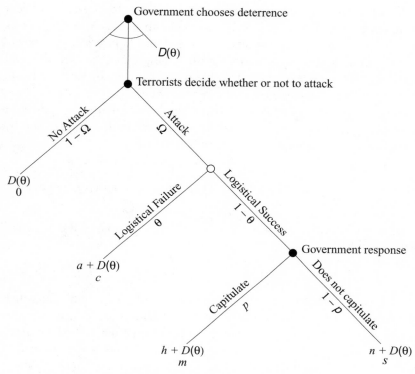

Figure 7.2. Game theory for hostage event.

value of the hostage(s) taken. The government is motivated to choose D to minimize its cost. From the terrorists' viewpoint, they receive nothing if they do not attack. A failed attack gives them c. If they abduct hostages, then they get m for a successful negotiation and s for a failed negotiation. Obviously, the payoffs are ordered as follows: $m > s > c$. Moreover, c is typically negative, while s may be positive or negative depending on how the terrorists value publicity for their cause. Media attention may, at times, provide a net positive benefit for the cause even if negotiations are unsuccessful. This was true for the Palestinian cause following the 1972 Munich Olympics incident, when recruitment increased despite the terrorists' failure to obtain any concessions.

Given the game in Figure 7.2, the terrorists will take hostages provided that they perceive there to be an expected positive benefit. This occurs if the following inequality holds:

$$(1 - \theta) \times [pm + (1 - p)s] + c\theta > 0. \tag{3}$$

In (3), the expected gain from a logistical success exceeds the expected cost from a logistical failure. The former is made up of the expected payoffs from either a negotiated success or a negotiated failure.[8] From (3), the likelihood of an attack increases as either the probability of a logistical success, $(1 - \theta)$, or the perceived likelihood of government capitulation, p, rises, since $m > s$. An increase in the level of concessions, m, or a decrease in the consequences of a logistical failure, c, also augments the chances of a terrorist action by raising the left-hand side of the inequality, thereby increasing the chances that it will be positive.

Conventional Wisdom about not Conceding to Terrorists' Demands

Suppose that the government pledges never to negotiate *and* its pledge is believed by the terrorists, so that $p = 0$. In this scenario, the terrorists will only take hostages when

$$(1 - \theta)s + c\theta > 0. \tag{4}$$

If, moreover, the terrorists gain nothing from a failed negotiation, in which the government does not concede, then $s < 0$. Because c is also negative, the terrorists will perceive no gain from hostage taking and refrain from taking hostages. When, alternatively, deterrence makes $\theta = 1$, so that logistical failure is a certainty, no attacks ensue provided that $c < 0$. These are the implicit assumptions consistent with the conventional wisdom that hostage taking stops with a pledge by government never to capitulate.

If, however, the government's pledge is not believed by the terrorists, then $p > 0$ and the relevant inequality is (3), which exceeds the left-hand side of (4) by $(1 - \theta)(pm - ps)$. When the expected payoff from a successful negotiation, $(1 - \theta)pm$, is large, the government's pledge is not a sufficient deterrent. Next, suppose that the terrorists view a failed negotiation or even a logistical failure as having a positive payoff, so that $s > c > 0$. The latter may hold when a fanatical terrorist group considers self-sacrifice – martyrdom or imprisonment – to be a positive payoff. In this scenario, inequality (4) holds, and hostages are abducted despite the government's pledge *even when it is fully credible*.

Because this is an interactive framework, we must next examine what the government is going to do in those cases when the terrorists are not

---

[8] In Figure 7.2, Ω corresponds to $\int_0^{c*} f(c)dc$, where $f(c)$ is the probability density for c, which reflects the unknown resolve of the terrorists, where
$$c* = [(1 - \theta)/\theta] \times [pm + (1 - p)s] > -c.$$

deterred from capturing hostages. First, suppose that the costs of capitulation, h, or of not capitulating, n, are known with certainty and that $h > n$. In this scenario, the government will stick by its pledge because it is more costly to do otherwise. If, however, n or h is not known beforehand because the identity of the hostage(s) is not known, then the outcome may be different. When the revealed value of n exceeds h, the government will renege on its pledge. Thus, the right hostage(s) (for example, a CIA agent, schoolchildren, soldiers, or a member of parliament) may induce the government to give in to the terrorists. The terrorists' task is to abduct hostages that make the government's pledge too costly to maintain.

The game representation can be made more realistic by allowing for multiple periods and reputation costs. A government concession to hostage takers in one period makes terrorists raise their expectations about future concessions. As the perceived p increases for future periods,[9] more hostages will be taken, so that there is an added cost to conceding in any period. This cost is denoted by R for loss of reputation, and results in the capitulation cost to the government becoming $h + R$. Even when the government's reputation cost is included, conceding is not eliminated as a possible outcome unless $h + R$ exceeds n for all its possible realizations. Such a scenario may be achieved through the institution of rules that do not allow the government to have any negotiating discretion. Only when these rules impose sufficiently severe punishments on conceding to terrorists' demands will the government not go back on its word. The Irangate hearings were intended to keep future administrations from making covert deals.

In summary, the never-concede policy hinges on at least five implicit assumptions: (i) the government's deterrence is sufficient to stop all attacks; (ii) the government's pledge is fully credible to all potential hostage takers; (iii) the terrorists' gain from hostage taking derives only from fulfillment of their demands; (iv) there is no uncertainty concerning the costs to government from having hostages abducted; and (v) the government's costs from making concessions always exceed those of holding firm. Our analysis clearly demonstrates that a game-theoretic framework is required to understand why such pledges do not necessarily work. The strategic interaction between adversaries must be taken into account.

---

[9] The first analysis of this dependency of p on past concessions is in Sandler, Tschirhart, and Cauley (1983).

EMPIRICAL TESTS OF BARGAINING IN HOSTAGE INCIDENTS

Two research papers applied the theory of bargaining to the study of hostage-taking events. In particular, these papers tailored the Cross (1969, 1977) theory of bargaining to a scenario in which the terrorists (government officials) are viewed as maximizing the present value of their perceived net benefits from negotiations over hostages. A bargaining framework is a game-theoretic framework in which strategic interactions among agents are part of the analysis. The *duration* of the incident is an essential consideration, because the longer one must wait for the payoff, the smaller will be the present value of the payoff. Each party perceives this duration to equal the difference between current demands and concessions divided by the concession rate of the opponent. In choosing demands (concessions) in each period, the terrorists (officials) can trade off large values of demands (concessions) at the expense of a longer incident with its concomitant greater costs and reduced present value of an eventual payoff. An incident concludes with a settlement when demands match concessions.

In their analysis, Atkinson, Sandler, and Tschirhart (1987) tested three hypotheses that emerged from the Cross model:

(i) Increases (decreases) in bargaining costs to the terrorists induce them to decrease (increase) their demands owing to the opportunity costs of waiting. Similarly, increases (decreases) in bargaining costs to the government cause it to raise (reduce) concessions.

(ii) Increases (decreases) in bargaining costs to either side will shorten (lengthen) the duration of the incident.

(iii) Bluffing will diminish a party's payoff, since exaggerated demands lead to a faster concession rate, which induces the opponent to hold firm.

Greater terrorist demands are anticipated to make for greater payoffs and longer incidents. Bluffing can show up in the form of allowing a deadline to pass uneventfully – for example, a threat to kill a hostage that is not executed. These authors hypothesized that such bluffs will reduce the final ransom and will shorten the incident by signaling a lack of terrorist resolve. The number of hostage nationalities involved in an incident should, however, increase the cost to the government, which then results in greater concessions. Actions by the terrorists to sequentially release hostages indicate a willingness of both parties to negotiate, and this should lead to greater ransoms being paid and a longer incident. The incident's duration is anticipated to be long if it is a kidnapping (owing to its unknown location) or involves US hostages. In addition, the larger the final payment, the longer the incident. Finally, the greater the number of wounded terrorists in the incident, the shorter the incident, because such injuries raise the terrorists' cost of holding firm.

Atkinson, Sandler, and Tschirhart (1987) ran two regressions to ascertain the importance of some of these bargaining variables from ITER-ATE data. In particular, they examined 122 hostage incidents from 1968 to 1977. First, they made ransom paid the dependent variable and determined the significant influences on this variable. Second, they presented a "time-to-failure" investigation, where the duration of the hostage incident in hours is the dependent variable. The significant determinants on incident duration were tested for numerous independent variables. In the top half of Table 7.4, the significant variables are indicated for ransom paid and for duration. The authors' priors are largely confirmed by the empirical results. For example, bluffing (e.g., allowing a deadline to pass uneventfully) reduced ransoms received. Sequential release of hostages, a larger number of hostage nationalities, and greater ransom demands resulted in larger ransom payments. The influences on the duration of the incident are also confirmed in many cases – for example, wounded terrorists reduced the incident's duration, while the presence of US hostages increased the incident's length.

In a related study, Sandler and Scott (1987) relied on both a choice-theoretic model of terrorism and Cross's theory of bargaining to identify the influences on logistical and negotiated success. These authors related the probability of a logistical success to various variables. For example, terrorist resources were viewed as a positive determinant of such success. Thus, the number of terrorists in the attack force and the type of weapons used (that is, high-powered weapons or not) should influence the terrorists' ability to accomplish the mission as planned. The number of nationalities in the attack force served as a proxy for terrorist resources, since terrorist squads with more nationalities might draw support from more sources. Kidnappings were thought to be more successful owing to their relatively uncomplicated nature and unknown locations compared to other hostage events. The killing of hostages or innocent bystanders was anticipated to decrease the likelihood of logistical success. Finally, the number of hostages was thought to be a positive influence on success. When terrorists attempt to capture a large number of hostages, logistical success may be achieved even though some of the intended hostages escape. In the case of a large hostage grab, authorities might be more

Table 7.4. *Significant Determinants of Various Aspects of Hostage Incidents*

Ransom paid[a]

Significant variables	Influence
Terrorists allowed sequential release of hostages	Greater ransom
Ransom demanded	Greater ransom
Number of nationalities of the hostages	Greater ransom
Terrorists allowed a deadline to pass uneventfully	Smaller ransom

Duration of incident[a]

Significant variables	Influence
Terrorists allowed sequential release of hostages	Greater duration
Kidnapping incident	Greater duration
Ransom demanded	Greater duration
Ransom paid	Greater duration
US hostage	Greater duration
Number of terrorists wounded	Smaller duration

Logistical success[b]

Significant variables	Influence
Number of terrorists in attack force	+0.3%
Number of dead (square root)	−7%
Number of terrorist nationalities	2–3%
Number of hostages (square root)	0.1%
Kidnapping incident	17–18%

Negotiated success[b]

Significant variables	Influence
Number of dead (square root)	−(19–21)%
Number of terrorist nationalities	1%
Kidnapping incident	8–12%
Two or more demands	23–26%

[a] Results are from Atkinson, Sandler, and Tschirhart (1987), which examined 122 hostage-taking incidents during 1968–1977.
[b] Results are from Sandler and Scott (1987), which examined 549 hostage-taking incidents during 1968–1984.

reluctant to intervene due to the presence of many innocent people. The authors used the square root of the number of dead and the square root of the number of hostages owing to diminishing returns as numbers are increased.

Sandler and Scott (1987) relied on Cross's model of bargaining for their hypothesized influences on negotiated success. If the terrorists make two or more demands, then this should increase their chances for a negotiated success, because there is a large set of possible deals that can be struck – that is, the negotiation set is larger. By allowing deadlines to pass uneventfully, bluffing was anticipated to reduce the likelihood of negotiated success. Since governments do not want to be viewed as giving in to murderers, the killing of hostages or others should decrease the probability of a negotiated success. Kidnappings should be more successful in terms of negotiations than other kinds of hostage events. Terrorist resource variables were hypothesized to bolster the likelihood of successful negotiations.

To ascertain the influences on successful negotiations, Sandler and Scott (1987) investigated 549 hostage-taking incidents during the 1968–1984 period. The data was provided by the US government and included over four times the number of hostage events as the Atkinson, Sandler, and Tschirhart (1987) study. Sandler and Scott's results are indicated in the bottom half of Table 7.4, where the influences of significant variables are indicated in terms of their marginal influence on the probability of a logistical or a negotiated success. For example, a kidnapping incident increased the likelihood of logistical success by 17 to 18% over other types of hostage missions. As the number of terrorist nationalities in the attack squad increased by one, the probability of a logistical success increased by 2 to 3%. During the operation, deaths reduced the logistical success at the margin by 7%. For negotiations, deaths decreased the marginal probability of success by 19 to 21%. Kidnappings, two or more demands, and the number of terrorist nationalities bolstered the marginal probability of successful negotiations by 8 to 12%, 23 to 26%, and 1%, respectively. Not all of the authors' hypotheses held. For example, bluffing did not have the anticipated negative impact on the probability of a negotiated success. Moreover, the presence of a US hostage did not significantly affect the probability of either logistical or negotiated success – the latter reflects a general adherence to a no-negotiation policy.

In a recent paper, Silke (2001) criticized these studies as coming to different conclusions. Moreover, Silke applied the hypotheses of the bargaining model to three hostage events – the hijacking of Air France flight 8969 on 24 December 1995; the barricade siege of the Japanese embassy in Lima, Peru, on 17 December 1996; and the hijacking of Indian Airlines flight 814 on 24 December 1999 – with diverse outcomes. In evaluating the two studies from 1987, one must remember that different things were being tested. That is, Atkinson, Sandler, and Tschirhart (1987) examined the significant influences on the *duration* of a hostage incident, while Sandler and Scott (1987) studied the significant influences on a *logistical* success. These variables relate to different phases of a hostage incident: logistical success concerns the period when the hostages are initially being abducted, while the duration involves the period *after* the hostages are secured. There is no reason for these influences to be the same. Even the negotiation variable – ransom paid and the probability of a negotiated success – differs between the two studies. A negotiated success may not imply that a ransom is paid, because the negotiation may involve a prisoner release, a media statement, or an escape to a safe haven. A paid ransom, however, implies a negotiated success. Also, the samples for these two studies were vastly different, and this is expected to influence the variables.

Silke's (2001) dismissal of bargaining models because of their failure to give consistent predictions for three *specific* hostage incidents indicates a fundamental flaw in reasoning that one sees in some criticisms of quantitative studies. A theory is *not* intended to explain every case; instead, it is meant to explain a large portion of instances. The ability to find select hostage missions that do not abide by a theoretical prediction does not refute a theory. If, however, the empirical analysis of a sufficiently large sample does not conform to the theory, then there is ample reason to develop a new theory.

CONCLUDING REMARKS

Although hostage-taking missions involve a relatively small portion of terrorist attacks, these operations have had a disproportionately large influence and have included some of the most noteworthy terrorist incidents of the last four decades. Despite pledges never to concede to terrorist demands, governments have not always honored such declared commitments, particularly when highly valued hostages are abducted. We have applied game theory to explain such policy inconsistencies. Because past concessions by countries influence terrorists' perceptions of how other governments may behave, there is an interdependence among governments' negotiations that must receive greater recognition. Hostage incidents involve a strategic interdependence between terrorists and the target government that can only be understood using game theory. Moreover, the strategic interdependence among targeted governments involves game-theoretic notions, as does the bargaining process between terrorists and officials once hostages are taken.

There are numerous future directions. First, there is a need to build better bargaining models to represent negotiations in hostage-taking events. Differences in negotiations between domestic and transnational incidents have not been adequately explored. We would anticipate that pledges not to concede are more apt to be upheld in domestic than in transnational incidents, because the consequences of being inconsistent (that is, of conceding to demands) in a domestic incident are borne solely at home and are not shared with all countries. Second, there is a need to construct multistage and multiperiod models of negotiations that better account for the importance of reputation on the part of adversaries. Third, data sets are needed that are richer in terms of observations on the actions of governments during negotiations. We typically know more about the responses of terrorists than about those of government officials. Unless we have the latter observations, we cannot develop the best practice for the field during hostage crises. Fourth, there is much more data on hostage incidents now than when the two bargaining studies were done in 1987; thus, new empirical investigations on bargaining variables and hostage-taking missions are required.

EIGHT

After 9/11

In February 1998, Osama bin Ladin and Ayman al Zawahiri published a signed statement declaring a *fatwa* against the United States. Bin Laden, al Zawahiri, and the other signatories to the statement called for retribution against the Unites States for its having "declared war against God."[1] The statement went on to claim that it was the individual duty of every Muslim to murder any American anywhere on earth. Three months later, in an interview on ABC-TV, bin Laden stated: "We believe that the worst thieves in the world today and the worst terrorists are the Americans. Nothing could stop you except perhaps retaliation in kind. We do not have to differentiate between military and civilian." As we now know, the *fatwa* resulted in an unprecedented 9/11 attack against the United States.

As we discuss in subsequent chapters, the tragedy of 9/11 was a defining moment for the United States, other Western nations, and the Islamic nations in many profound ways. Chapter 9 focuses on the economic costs of terrorism, including the direct and indirect costs of 9/11. Chapter 10 evaluates homeland security, and Chapter 11 speculates on the future of terrorism. In this chapter, we report the results of two studies that quantify the ways in which 9/11 has changed the types and locations of terrorist incidents.

[1] All quotations in this paragraph use the translations from the National Commission on Terrorist Attacks upon the United States (2004, p. 47), *The 9/11 Commission Report.*

THE COMPETING FORCES: REDUCED STRENGTH
VERSUS ENHANCED SENSITIVITY

As a result of the US-led war on terror, about two-thirds of al-Qaida leaders have been either killed or captured. Even though there is a large supply of volunteers willing to assume leadership positions, such attrition should severely limit the amount of entrepreneurship that al-Qaida's highest echelon can display. The rank-and-file membership has also been reduced, as 3,400 al-Qaida suspects have been arrested worldwide since 9/11 and many of its operatives were lost during the Afghan war in 2001 (Gerges and Isham, 2003). Additionally, the White House (2003) reported that more than $200 million of the al-Qaida network's assets has been frozen following 9/11. These manpower, leadership, and financial losses should limit the network's ability to engage in logistically complex modes of attack such as hostage taking.

At the same time, 9/11 has sensitized the public in such a way that future terrorist actions are likely to have enhanced effects on the electorate's psyche. Graham (2001) indicated that stress-related illnesses are more likely to result from events caused by deliberate violence than from natural disasters. Had the World Trade Center been destroyed by an off-course airplane approaching New York's LaGuardia Airport, the amount of post-traumatic stress disorder would have been markedly reduced. Graham also noted that the fear of the unknown often has profound psychological consequences on individuals already having problems struggling with the problems of daily life. When people are afraid of something specific, they can find ways to avoid the source of their anxiety. For some, a generalized fear of a future attack at some unspecified place and date can be debilitating.

In November 2001, Gallagher (2003) surveyed the directors of eighty-two university and college testing centers. The intent of the survey was to determine how college students had been affected by 9/11. Eighty-eight percent of the counseling centers reported a considerable increase in their caseloads after 9/11, which averaged 21% for schools located on the Eastern seaboard and 15% for schools elsewhere. Both numbers are underestimates, since more than two-thirds of the respondents reported that the increase in caseloads was so sudden that many students had to be placed on a waiting list before seeing a counselor. Respondents also indicated that their student-clients directly linked their problems to 9/11. Students suffered from nightmares, depression, sleeplessness, anxiety attacks, and an inability to focus on their studies. Notably, the attacks themselves did not cause the psychological problems; rather, the students' problems resulted from the general climate of "fear and vulnerability that followed 9/11." Perhaps the most worrisome part of the survey is that the majority of center directors believed that the problems experienced by these students can be quite long-lived.

In another study, Wolinsky and colleagues (2003) surveyed 291 older adults who participated in an ongoing longitudinal study regarding coronary artery disease. Since the original study had started prior to 9/11, they were able to measure pre- and post-9/11 attitudes about personal stress, mental health, and a sense of self-control. The study is also interesting because social gerontologists believe that older adults are most vulnerable to stress-related disorders. Each patient was interviewed three times before and three times after 9/11. The study's participants reported a reduced sense of control over their personal lives that was heightened among higher-income individuals and those reporting greater religiosity.

Although the terrorists' ability to conduct attacks may have been weakened, any given attack is now likely to produce a greater feeling of fear and insecurity than during the pre-9/11 period. One further unknown is the "recruitment" factor. Faria and Arce (2005) argued that each terrorist success makes it easier for groups such as al-Qaida to recruit new members. To the extent that recruitment has been enhanced by 9/11 and the recent events in Iraq, the composition of terrorist groups will have shifted from older and experienced members to new recruits. The ways in which terrorists respond to these simultaneous changes by altering the number, targets, locations, and types of attacks is clearly an empirical issue.

CHANGES IN THE NUMBER AND TYPES OF ATTACK MODES

As a consequence of the reduction in its leadership and resource base, the al-Qaida network can be expected to turn to logistically simple, but deadly, bombings. Such bombings can also be more attractive than assassinations or hostage takings, which can be logistically complex and yield just a few victims. Given the events following 9/11 and the preferences of many of today's terrorist groups for carnage, we anticipate a smaller reliance on hostage-taking events and assassinations and a greater reliance on deadly bombings.

There is evidence of a shift in the composition of events, such that bombings have increased and logistically complex incidents have declined. The US Department of State (1997, 2004) data indicates that the total number of significant anti-US transnational terrorist attacks rose from seventy-three in 1996 to eighty-two in 2003. The number of bombings plus firebombings increased by sixteen events from fifty-five to seventy one, while the number of kidnappings declined by four events from six to two. In Enders and Sandler (2005a), we wanted to determine whether these changes are statistically significant, whether they pertain to other classifications of incident types, and whether they are specifically related to 9/11. We extracted eight primary time series from ITERATE to determine how the number of attacks and the attack modes have changed since 9/11.[2] The ALL series includes quarterly totals of *all* types of transnational terrorist incidents; the most important component of this quarterly series is BOMBINGS, accounting on average for over half of all annual terrorist attacks. The BOMBINGS series combines seven types of events: explosive bombings, letter bombings, incendiary bombings, missile attacks, car bombings, suicide car bombings, and mortar and grenade attacks. The HOSTAGE series includes quarterly totals of kidnappings, skyjackings, nonaerial hijackings, and barricade and hostage-taking missions, whereas the assassinations series consists of politically motivated murders. Two additional primary series are: (i) the quarterly DEATH series, recording the number of terrorist incidents where one or more individuals (including terrorists) died; and (ii) the more-inclusive CAS series, recording the quarterly total number of incidents where one or more individuals were injured or killed. We further broke down the bombing series by identifying the quarterly number of bombings with one or more deaths and the number of bombings with one or more casualties.

To test for a structural break at 9/11, we estimated an intervention model of the form discussed in Chapter 3. Consider the simplified intervention model

$$y_t = a_0 + a_1 y_{t-1} + \alpha_1 D_P + \alpha_2 D_L + \varepsilon_t, \tag{1}$$

where y_t is the series of interest, and D_P and D_L are dummy variables representing 9/11. In equation (1), D_P is a dummy variable such that $D_P = 1$ if $t = 2001{:}Q3$ (third quarter of 2001) and $D_P = 0$ otherwise. This type of *pulse* variable is appropriate if the 9/11 attacks induced an immediate change in the series lasting for a single quarter. The magnitude of α_1 indicates the initial effect of 9/11 on y_t, and the rate of decay or residual effect in subsequent quarters is determined by the magnitude of a_1. To allow for the possibility that 9/11 had a permanent effect on the level of the time series of terrorist events of a particular type, the second dummy variable in

---

[2] The series were described in detail in Chapter 3.

equation (1) is such that $D_L = 0$ prior to 9/11 and $D_L = 1$ for 2001:Q3 and thereafter. The impact effect of the *level* dummy variable on the time series is given by α_2. We began by estimating the ALL series with both *pulse* and *level* breaks. The key features of the estimated equation were such that the estimated coefficients for the *level* and *pulse* variables are both negative. This might seem to imply that both series fell as a result of 9/11; however, as you can see from Figure 3.2, the ALL series actually began its downward movement prior to 9/11. Even though the ALL series seems to decline around 9/11, the issue is whether these coefficients are spurious. The *level* and *pulse* variables are not statistically significant; hence, there are no statistically significant short-run or long-run effects in the behavior of the ALL series resulting from 9/11. The fact that the coefficients are negative might just be a fluke. Since bombings (also shown in Figure 3.2) comprise the majority of incidents, it is not surprising that we found similar results for the bombing series. In particular, bombings are also quite persistent, but the total number of bombings was not affected by 9/11.

When we examined the other series, none of the pulse dummy variables were significant at conventional levels. The level-shift dummy was significant only for the HOSTAGE series. The short-run effect is such that HOSTAGE incidents are estimated to fall by about six incidents in 2001:Q3. Given the persistence in the series, a low number of incidents is expected to be followed by other low-incident periods. We calculated the long-run effect to be a decline of approximately nine incidents per quarter. However, even this finding is problematic, because a careful inspection of the HOSTAGE series (see Figure 3.3) shows that the sharp drop in hostage incidents actually started in 1999.

We also examined how the composition of the ALL series changed over time. Specifically, we estimated an intervention model in the form of equation (1) for the ratio of each incident type to ALL. The *pulse* dummy variable is statistically significant for incidents with a death as a proportion of all incidents (P_DEATH) and for incidents with a casualty (that is, death or injury) as a proportion of all incidents (P_CAS). Immediately following 9/11, the proportion of incidents with deaths rose by 54 percentage points and the proportion of incidents with casualties rose by 48 percentage points. The level dummy variables were, however, not significant at conventional levels; hence, the jumps in the P_DEATH and P_CAS were not permanent.

The *level* dummy variable was, however, highly significant for the proportion of hostage incidents (P_HOSTAGE) and the proportion of deadly incidents due to bombings (P_DEATH_B). The proportion of hostage takings was approximately 13% of all incidents prior to 9/11. As a result of 9/11, the short-run change in the P_HOSTAGE series was estimated to fall to just 4% of all incidents. In the longer run, the proportion of hostage incidents was near zero. We also found evidence of a significant 16 percentage point decline in assassinations as a proportion of all incidents. In contrast, the P_DEATH_B series rose by 20 percentage points.

Our conclusion is that the US-led offensive against al-Qaida and its network has taken a toll on al-Qaida's leadership and finances by compromising al-Qaida's ability to direct complex operations. The ALL, DEATH, and CAS series have *not changed following 9/11*. The main influence of 9/11 has been on the composition of the ALL series. In particular, hostage-taking incidents have fallen after 9/11 as terrorists, bent on carnage, have substituted into deadly bombings. As a consequence, the proportion of deadly incidents due to bombings has increased as the proportion of hostage-taking and assassination attacks have decreased. The net result is that al-Qaida has substituted away from logistically complex attacks (for example, hostage takings and assassinations) to logistically simpler bombings.[3]

DISTRIBUTION OF TERRORIST INCIDENTS BY COUNTRY

Post-9/11 actions to augment security in wealthy nations may have unintended negative consequences by inducing terrorists to stage their attacks in countries less able to afford widespread defensive measures. Thus, the new emphasis on homeland security in the United States and throughout the European Union (EU) may merely displace terrorist attacks to softer venues, where people and property from prime-target countries are attacked abroad (Enders and Sandler, 1993, 1995; Sandler and Enders, 2004). The point is that rational terrorists weigh the costs, risks, and benefits when choosing the venue for an attack. As a result, attacks may be displaced from high-income countries (HICs) to low-income countries (LICs) as some HICs deploy enhanced security measures that make attacks more difficult and costly for terrorists to accomplish.

Geographic transference will occur as attack venues shift across regions (e.g., from Europe to the Middle East or Asia). A geographical shift may also be motivated by the ability of the terrorists to blend in and establish a support system, especially for religious fundamentalist terrorists. If

---

[3] We also utilized a number of other methods, including one that allows us to search for the most likely break dates.

terrorists attack foreign interests nearer to home, then they do not have to cross borders that are more guarded in some regions after 9/11. In the 1980s, there was a significant "spillover" of Middle Eastern terrorism throughout Europe – for example, there were forty-three terrorist incidents of Middle Eastern origin in Europe in 1987 (US Department of State, 1988, pp. 16, 18). Given the increased scrutiny given to Middle Easterners in Europe following 9/11, it is anticipated that more incidents will be staged in the Middle East.

In Enders and Sandler (2005b), we used intervention analysis to determine whether terrorists have shifted their venues based on the target countries' income and/or regional location in response to 9/11. To accomplish this task, we partitioned countries into income categories based on the World Bank's classification of countries into low, middle (MIC), and high per capita income countries.[4] In constructing our time series, we take account of the fact that individual nations may switch among the three income groups. As a result of economic growth, the number of nations included in the HIC group has generally increased, thereby working against a possible transnational terrorism substitution from HICs to LICs. For instance, Algeria and Mexico moved from the LIC group to the MIC group, and Israel, Portugal, and Spain switched from the MIC group to the HIC group owing to high per capita income growth. In the late 1980s, Poland moved in the opposite direction, from the class of MIC to LIC, when it was a transition economy, but it returned to the MIC group in the mid-1990s.

We focused our analysis on four different time series of transnational terrorist events: all incidents, incidents with casualties, incidents with a US target, and casualty incidents with a US target. A useful way to simplify the long-run movements in these time series is to examine the proportion of incidents staged in the LIC group. Figure 8.1 presents the proportion of each incident type (measured on the vertical axis) occurring in this income class.[5] In Figure 8.1, panels 1–3 indicate a clear upward trend in

---

[4] The groupings are described in detail in each issue of the World Bank's (various years) *World Development Report*. For 2000, LICs had per capita Gross National Income (GNI) of $755 or less; MICs had per capita GNI greater than $756 and less than or equal to $9,265; and HICs had per capita GNI in excess of $9,265. Country codes from ITERATE for location start of incidents allow us to associate a terrorist event's location with the country's income classification. When matching countries to terrorist attacks and income classes, we also had to adjust for changes in the political maps of Eastern Europe, Africa, and elsewhere over the entire sample period.

[5] Because the proportions can be quite erratic, we smoothed each series using a one-period lead and lag.

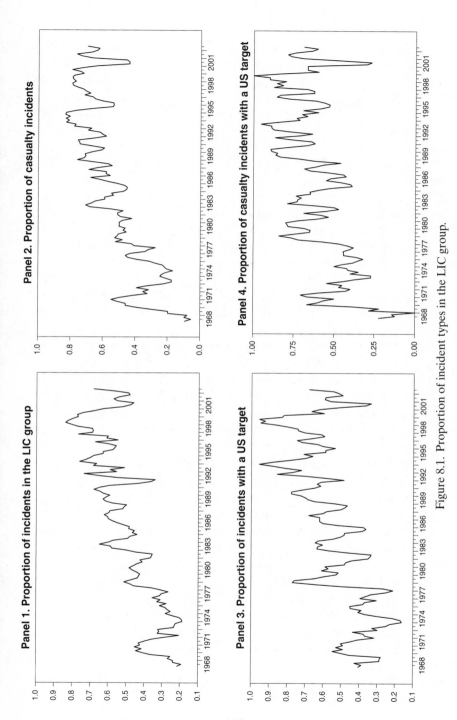

Figure 8.1. Proportion of incident types in the LIC group.

195

the proportion of all incidents, casualty incidents, and incidents with a US target taking place in the LIC group. Although there are now more casualty incidents with a US target in LICs compared to earlier periods, there is no clear upward trend for this series since 1979 (see panel 4). An interesting feature of the four series is that each experienced a sharp decline around 1999 and a sharp rise following 9/11. The magnitude of the rebound is, however, smaller than the 1999 decline; thus, the proportion of terrorist incidents in LICs is greater in the late 1990s than after 9/11.

Table 8.1 reports two descriptive statistics – quarterly mean and variance – for the four quarterly time series for several essential time periods. For example, the mean number of ALL incidents is 66.4 per quarter from 1992:Q2 through 2001:Q2. In Table 8.1, the variance indicates how volatile the series is. The start of this period roughly corresponds to the decline in the number of incidents resulting from the collapse of the Soviet Union. Over the same time period, the quarterly means for the LIC, MIC, and HIC groups are 42.9, 5.7, and 17.8 incidents, respectively. We also list two descriptive statistics for each of the four time series in the nine quarters prior to 9/11 and the nine quarters following 9/11. Table 8.1 also reports the proportion of terrorist incidents occurring in LICs. Prior to 9/11, 74.3% of these incidents took place in LICs, while following 9/11, only 57.0% occurred in LICs. There appear to be only modest differences in the pre-9/11 and post-9/11 series for all terrorist events. The mean of the worldwide ALL incident series rises from 42.3 to 46.6 incidents per quarter following 9/11; thus, the overall level of terrorism rises by 10%. There is an interesting and unexpected change in the composition of incidents by income categories. After 9/11, the mean number of incidents in LICs falls by 6.8 per quarter, while this mean in HICs rises by 7.3 per quarter. A more pronounced increase characterizes incidents with casualties, where the world's mean rises from 12.9 incidents per quarter before 9/11 to 20.6 incidents per quarter after 9/11. Although the overall level of terrorism increases, the proportion of incidents with casualties in the LICs falls from 72.2% to 67.9%. There is a 44% increase worldwide in the mean number of incidents with a US target (24.1/16.7 = 1.44) following 9/11, and a more than threefold increase in the mean number of casualty incidents with a US target (2.6 versus 9.4 incidents per quarter) following 9/11. Because these incidents are not occurring in the United States, Americans may be safer at home but not abroad in the aftermath of 9/11 and its security increases. About half of this increase – 4.8 incidents per quarter – occurred in LICs.

Table 8.1. *Summary Statistics of the Various Incident Types by Income Group*

Series[a]	Start	End	Mean	Variance	Mean	Variance
			ALL Incident Types		*Incidents with Casualties*	
WORLD	1992:Q2	2001:Q2	66.4	44.0	22.7	14.3
	1999:Q2	2001:Q2	42.3	22.2	12.9	7.3
	2001:Q4	2003:Q4	46.6	29.4	20.6	12.8
LICs	1992:Q2	2001:Q2	42.9	24.7	16.5	11.3
	1999:Q2	2001:Q2	33.1	20.4	9.9	6.8
	2001:Q4	2003:Q4	26.3	16.8	14.0	9.5
MICs	1992:Q2	2001:Q2	5.7	3.9	2.3	2.2
	1999:Q2	2001:Q2	3.7	1.1	1.8	1.5
	2001:Q4	2003:Q4	7.3	8.7	2.8	3.0
HICs	1992:Q2	2001:Q2	17.8	28.7	4.0	4.6
	1999:Q2	2001:Q2	5.6	2.3	1.2	1.1
	2001:Q4	2003:Q4	12.9	8.1	3.8	2.0
LICs/	1992:Q2	2001:Q2	67.5%	0.145	71.8%	0.122
WORLD	1999:Q2	2001:Q2	74.3%	0.095	72.2%	0.134
	2001:Q4	2003:Q4	57.0%	0.117	67.9%	0.112
			Incident with a US Target		*Casualty Incidents with a US Target*	
WORLD	1992:Q2	2001:Q2	16.2	10.4	3.9	3.3
	1999:Q2	2001:Q2	16.7	12.9	2.6	1.2
	2001:Q4	2003:Q4	24.1	17.1	9.4	6.5
LICs	1992:Q2	2001:Q2	12.3	9.6	2.9	3.0
	1999:Q2	2001:Q2	13.9	12.8	1.9	1.3
	2001:Q4	2003:Q4	13.6	9.4	6.7	4.7
MICs	1992:Q2	2001:Q2	1.6	1.9	0.4	0.7
	1999:Q2	2001:Q2	1.0	0.9	0.4	0.5
	2001:Q4	2003:Q4	4.3	5.4	1.0	1.9
HICs	1992:Q2	2001:Q2	2.3	2.2	0.6	0.8
	1999:Q2	2001:Q2	1.8	2.5	0.2	0.4
	2001:Q4	2003:Q4	6.2	4.9	1.8	1.2
LICs/	1992:Q2	2001:Q2	73.6%	0.183	71.6%	0.243
WORLD	1999:Q2	2001:Q2	78.7%	0.210	69.8%	0.209
	2001:Q4	2003:Q4	57.1%	0.133	71.1%	0.119

[a] LICs denotes low-income countries; MICs indicates middle-income countries; HICs denotes high-income countries.

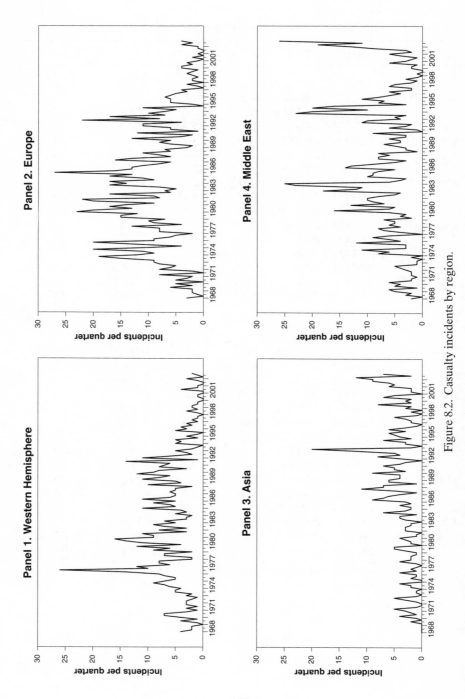

Figure 8.2. Casualty incidents by region.

198

THE DISTRIBUTION OF TERRORISM ACROSS REGIONS

For geographical groupings, we apply the six regional classifications given in the US Department of State (2003) *Patterns of Global Terrorism.* These regions are the Western Hemisphere (North, Central, and South America), Africa (excluding North Africa), Asia (South and East Asia, Australia, and New Zealand), Eurasia (Central Asia, Russia, and the Ukraine), Europe (Western and Eastern Europe), and the Middle East (including North Africa). This partition of countries puts most of the Islamic population into the Middle East, Eurasia, and Asia. This geographical division *does not correlate* with the income taxonomy, so that geography is likely to display different substitution possibilities before and after 9/11.

Figure 8.2 depicts the casualty series for four of the major geographical regions. The most striking feature is the sharp upward trend in these terrorist incidents in the Middle East starting in 2000, with a pronounced increase following 9/11. Much smaller increases characterize the other regions. In Asia (panel 3), the increase in terrorist incidents after 9/11 is followed by a decrease.

Table 8.2 reports two descriptive statistics for three periods for the four incident series and the six geographical regions. We focus our remarks on the ALL incident series. For the 1992:Q2–2001:Q2 period, Europe's mean of 19.27 incidents per quarter exceeds that of the other regions. The quarterly mean number of terrorist incidents in the Western Hemisphere (11.84), Africa (10.05), the Middle East (12.92), and Asia (9.76) are all quite similar; there are, however, some contrasting regional changes for the two time intervals surrounding 9/11. In the nine pre-9/11 quarters, the Western Hemisphere and Africa experienced an average of 12.33 and 9.44 incidents per quarter, respectively; in the nine post-9/11 quarters, the Western Hemisphere and Africa experienced an average of 5.33 and 2.44 incidents per quarter, respectively. These are rather drastic declines. In sharp contrast, the Middle East and Asia had incident means that rose very sharply from 4.78 and 7.78 to 15.00 and 13.00 incidents per quarter, respectively, for the same comparison intervals. The mean number of European incidents showed a more modest rise, from 6.33 to 10.78 incidents per quarter.

In the casualty series, the Middle East displayed the largest change on either side of 9/11 – a rise of almost 8.5 incidents per quarter. By contrast, Africa's casualty series fell by 2.78 incidents per quarter. For incidents with a US target, the Western Hemisphere experienced a reduction of

Table 8.2. *Summary Statistics of the Various Incident Types by Region*

Series	Start	End	Mean	Variance	Mean	Variance
			ALL Incident Types		*Incidents with Casualties*	
West. Hem.	1992:Q2	2001:Q2	11.84	8.41	1.97	1.71
	1999:Q2	2001:Q2	12.33	12.19	0.67	0.71
	2001:Q4	2003:Q4	5.33	4.80	1.00	1.00
Europe	1992:Q2	2001:Q2	19.27	27.57	4.81	4.69
	1999:Q2	2001:Q2	6.33	2.60	2.22	1.39
	2001:Q4	2003:Q4	10.78	9.19	1.44	1.59
Eurasia	1992:Q2	2001:Q2	3.00	2.17	1.51	1.82
	1999:Q2	2001:Q2	2.33	2.00	0.56	1.01
	2001:Q4	2003:Q4	1.00	0.71	0.44	0.73
Africa	1992:Q2	2001:Q2	10.05	9.46	4.78	5.31
	1999:Q2	2001:Q2	9.44	6.42	4.22	3.73
	2001:Q4	2003:Q4	2.44	2.46	1.44	2.30
Mid. East	1992:Q2	2001:Q2	12.92	9.84	5.84	5.86
	1999:Q2	2001:Q2	4.78	3.99	1.89	1.83
	2001:Q4	2003:Q4	15.00	9.95	10.33	8.00
Asia	1992:Q2	2001:Q2	9.76	8.48	3.86	3.81
	1999:Q2	2001:Q2	7.78	6.22	3.44	2.65
	2001:Q4	2003:Q4	13.00	10.91	6.44	3.28
			Incident with a US Target		*Casualty Incidents with a US Target*	
West. Hem.	1992:Q2	2001:Q2	6.30	6.90	0.76	1.04
	1999:Q2	2001:Q2	9.22	10.91	0.44	0.53
	2001:Q4	2003:Q4	3.33	3.46	0.78	0.83
Europe	1992:Q2	2001:Q2	1.59	1.26	0.35	0.48
	1999:Q2	2001:Q2	1.78	1.48	0.44	0.53
	2001:Q4	2003:Q4	4.67	5.00	0.22	0.44
Eurasia	1992:Q2	2001:Q2	0.49	0.65	0.16	0.44
	1999:Q2	2001:Q2	0.67	0.71	0.22	0.67
	2001:Q4	2003:Q4	0.44	0.73	0.22	0.67
Africa	1992:Q2	2001:Q2	2.68	3.58	1.30	2.82
	1999:Q2	2001:Q2	1.78	1.64	0.44	0.53
	2001:Q4	2003:Q4	1.00	1.00	0.11	0.33
Mid. East	1992:Q2	2001:Q2	2.86	2.35	0.62	0.83
	1999:Q2	2001:Q2	1.33	1.58	0.33	0.50
	2001:Q4	2003:Q4	7.56	4.82	4.78	4.09
Asia	1992:Q2	2001:Q2	2.41	2.58	0.76	1.06
	1999:Q2	2001:Q2	2.00	1.73	0.78	0.97
	2001:Q4	2003:Q4	7.56	8.40	3.11	2.32

5.89 incidents per quarter when the periods on either side of 9/11 are compared. Europe, the Middle East, and Asia, however, attracted more US-targeted events following 9/11. This same pattern held for the Middle East and Asia for casualty incidents with a US target.

CONCLUDING REMARKS

The attacks of 9/11 and the associated copycat anthrax attacks created a heightened state of anxiety among citizens desperately looking for security. In a climate of intimidation and fear, each new attack has the potential for enhanced benefits to the terrorists, so there is little reason to suppose that terrorism will decline. At the same time, the 9/11-motivated increases in homeland security in some high-income countries and the terrorists' hunt for soft targets are expected to change the types and locations of terrorist incidents. Our findings suggest that changes in al-Qaida's top leadership positions and finances have induced a substitution away from logistically complex hostage takings and into deadly bombings. With the exception of incidents with US causalities, we do not find a substitution from rich to poor countries. When, however, countries are classified into six regional groups, there is evidence of shifting venues based on geography. For terrorist incidents with a US target, we find a clear transference away from the Western Hemisphere and Africa to the two regions with the largest Islamic populations (that is, the Middle East and Asia). Thus, today's fundamentalist terrorism is shifting to the Middle East and Asia, where large support populations exist and terrorists do not have to transcend fortified borders to attack US and Western interests.

Overall, there appears to be a shift in target countries away from liberal democracies, which once provided a more supportive environment to terrorists, to failed states, which have little control over lawless elements. Upgrades in antiterrorism activities in the liberal democracies are, in part, behind this shift in terrorist venues to regions where terrorists can operate relatively freely. Nations that are not able to check terrorists' behavior because of a lack of political will and weak law-enforcement mechanisms are today's safe havens for terrorist groups.

Augmented homeland security seems to have made Americans safer at home, while placing them at greater risk when abroad. This vulnerability should also apply to the people and property of other countries that have assisted the US agenda in the Middle East. Current US policy is to assist certain LICs in their efforts to fight terrorism. Given the changing post-9/11 pattern of transnational terrorism aimed at US targets, this policy is somewhat misdirected, since soft targets can exist anywhere. Countries such as Saudi Arabia and the Philippines are not LICs, but are located in areas experiencing increasing levels of religious-based terrorism. Government's *ability to track* the shifting patterns of transnational terrorist attacks and the interests targeted is absolutely essential for allocating support to other countries. Future homeland security measures in the United States and elsewhere will continue to alter patterns of terrorism. The decision announced in April 2005 by the Bush administration to discontinue publication of the *Patterns of Global Terrorism* hinders efforts to stay on top of these shifting patterns. Moreover, this discontinuation limits the ability of private interests (for example, businesses and tourists) to assess terrorism risks.

NINE

The Economic Impact of Transnational Terrorism

On 12 October 2000 in Aden, Yemen, a small motorboat full of explosives rammed the USS *Cole* while it was in port for a refueling stop. Seventeen sailors died and another thirty-nine were injured by the explosion, which ripped a forty-foot by forty-foot hole in the ship's side. The USS *Cole* returned to the United States carried aboard a transport ship on 13 December 2000 for repairs that lasted fourteen months. Two years later (6 October 2002), Yemeni terrorists attacked the French tanker *Limburg* while it was readying to receive its cargo of crude oil from an offshore terminal. Although Yemen is ideally located as a major Middle Eastern port because it borders the Red Sea and the Arabian Sea, the combined attacks on the USS *Cole* and the *Limburg* crushed Yemen's shipping industry. A US Department of State Fact Sheet (2002) indicates that a 300% increase in insurance premiums has led to ships routinely bypassing Yemen for competitive facilities in Djibouti and Oman. As a result of a 50% decrease in port activity, Yemen expects to lose $3.8 million per month because of the attacks.

The incidents in Yemen illustrate the direct and indirect costs of terrorism. The direct costs can be calculated by summing the replacement costs of damaged goods, equipment, structures, and inventories. Despite the difficulty of measuring the cost of a human life or the cost of pain and suffering, such calculations are now routine, using either lost earnings or the value of a statistical life. The indirect costs, such as the decline in Yemeni shipping revenues, are more difficult to measure. How much of the actual decline is due to insurance costs rather than to military activities associated with the war in Iraq or to higher oil prices is difficult to gauge. Beyond these lost revenues, Yemen faces increased security costs as it decided to purchase additional patrol boats and helicopters to guard its waters. Calculating the associated cost of any attack is difficult, since, unlike traditional crimes, terrorism is designed to create a general and ongoing atmosphere of intimidation and fear. Terrorists are most successful when they lead the public to expect future attacks. Because the psychological effects of the two Yemeni attacks were mutually reinforcing, they increased the "risk premium" necessary to compensate insurers for the potential damages of future attacks.

These episodes also illustrate one of the essential lessons of this chapter. The effects of terrorism are likely to be greatest in small, nondiversified economies facing sustained terrorist campaigns. When shipping became risky in Yemen, alternative port facilities in nearby countries were found, and the entire Yemen economy suffered. In large market economies, terrorism is more likely to cause a substitution from sectors vulnerable to terrorism into relatively safe areas; prices can quickly reallocate capital and labor to the sectors where they have the greatest marginal product. This reallocation can limit the economic impact of terrorism in diversified market economies.

MEASURING THE IMPACT OF 9/11

The largest terrorist incident in the largest market economy is the unprecedented attack of 9/11. The Bureau of Economic Analysis (BEA) (2001) reports that damage to structures and equipment (including the destruction of the World Trade Center) amounted to $16.2 billion. As a result of work disruptions, layoffs, and a two-day partial work stoppage, wages and salaries of private-sector employees fell by $3.3 billion. This loss was partially offset by wage gains of $0.8 billion by state and local government employees (primarily police and firefighters). Clean-up costs, estimated to be $10 billion, are not included in the BEA measure of direct losses because they are a component of government spending that appears elsewhere in the gross domestic product (GDP) calculations. Moreover, the indirect costs of the attack (such as a reduction in GDP growth) are not included in the BEA totals insofar as they could not be separately identified.

In addition to the loss of physical capital, human capital was destroyed on 9/11. Even though many people have difficulty with the concept of pricing a human life, each of us places an implied value on our life every day. Suppose that you dash across a busy intersection to save two minutes. Also suppose that you value your time at $45/hour but that the maneuver

Table 9.1. *Insured Losses of Other Terrorist and Natural Disasters*

Catastrophe	Insured Loss
1989 Hurricane Hugo	$5 billion
1992 Los Angeles riots	$844 million
1992 Hurricane Andrew	$16.9 billion
1993 World Trade Center bombing	$542 million
1994 Northridge earthquake	$13 billion
1995 Oklahoma City bombing	$127 million

Source: Navarro and Spencer (2001).

exposes you to a 1 in 1,000,000 chance of being in a fatal accident. You thus save $1.50 (= 2 × $45/60) worth of your time against a one-in-a-million chance of being killed, so that the implicit price you place on your life is no more than $1.5 million ($1.50 multiplied by one million). Navarro and Spencer (2001) actually place the value of a human life at $6.67 million; if we use this figure, the economic value of the approximately 3,000 people killed on 9/11 is about $20 billion.[1] Given that US GDP was almost $10 trillion in 2001, the total direct losses of $48.7 billion represent about 0.5% of total annual output.

These cost estimates are in line with reports that the insurance industry lost between $30 billion and $58 billion as a result of 9/11. As shown in Table 9.1, these costs far exceed those of any other insured disaster.[2] Although these direct costs are staggering, they are overshadowed by the indirect costs of 9/11.

Lost Output

The full macroeconomic cost of 9/11 is difficult to measure, since the attacks occurred while the economy was in the midst of a recession that began in March 2001. Navarro and Spencer (2001) estimate the cost of the two-day partial work stoppage and the associated loss of productivity to be $35 billion. Their estimate of the total output loss is $47 billion. The

---

[1] Navarro and Spencer (2001) used the preliminary figure of 6,000 deaths from 9/11. The numbers in the text have been adjusted to account for the more accurate measure of fatalities.

[2] The insurance company losses include compensation of loss of life and property damage. Hence, to avoid "double counting," we should not add these losses to the direct costs of 9/11. Other sources will have different losses associated with these disasters depending on what is included under insured losses.

Bureau of Labor Statistics (2003) reports that at least 145,000 workers were laid off for thirty days or more as a result of the 9/11 attacks. The unemployment rate jumped by almost one percentage point in the quarter following 9/11. As discussed in the next section, there is reasonable evidence to support the view that the overall macroeconomic effects of the attacks were short-lived; nevertheless, certain sectors of the economy, such as the transportation and tourism industries, experienced persistent problems. For example, immediately following 9/11, passenger fares plummeted by $1.5 billion, and the hotel industry suffered losses estimated to be $700 million. Ito and Lee (2004) estimate that the heightened, albeit temporary, fear of flying reduced airline demand by more than 30%, while other factors, such as increased passenger screening and security checks, caused a permanent 7.4% decline in airline demand.

Lost Stock Market Wealth

The difference between stock prices on 10 September 2001 and those prevailing at the end of the first week of trading after the attack can be readily calculated. Navarro and Spencer (2001) report declines in the prices of shares selling on the New York Stock Exchange (NYSE), Nasdaq, and Amex markets of 11.24%, 16.05%, and 8.10%, respectively. The total market value of these declines equals $1.7 trillion! We must, however, be careful to avoid the double-counting of some losses. Because the value of the four planes lost in the 9/11 attacks was $385 million, airline stocks should have declined to reflect this tangible loss of physical capital. Given the estimated loss of structures and equipment of only $14 billion, most of the $1.7 trillion decline reflects shareholder estimates of lost future profits and a higher risk premium. After the economic environment stabilized following 9/11, stock prices regained much of their value. How much of the decline in stock prices was permanent and how much was a temporary reaction to increased market uncertainty remains unclear.

Victim Compensation Fund

To stem a flood of lawsuits arising from potential liability issues, the federal government established the Victim Compensation Fund.[3] The explicit goal of the fund was to provide a no-fault alternative to compensate

---

[3] Information for this section was taken from the website of the Department of Justice (2004).

individuals who were killed or injured as a result of the 9/11 attacks. Individuals were compensated for economic as well as noneconomic losses in order to make the awards commensurate with those obtainable through the court system. Compensation for noneconomic losses, such as pain and suffering, were set at $250,000 for each deceased victim plus an additional $100,000 for the victim's spouse and each dependent. Some individuals received far more than others, because the economic loss to any individual included the present value of the victim's estimated stream of future earnings. The average amount of compensation paid to date to the 7,407 families of those who died on 9/11 is $2,082,128. Individual death compensation amounts ranged from $250,000 to $7.1 million. The fund also settled 2,682 personal injury claims for amounts reflecting the nature of the injury, the long-term prognosis, and the ongoing pain and suffering. To date, awards have ranged from a low of $500 to a high of over $8.6 million. Including the payments received from insurance companies and charities, the payouts to the victims of 9/11 (dead and injured) and their families totaled $38.1 billion. However, the establishment of the fund raised a number of controversial questions: Was it appropriate that families of high-income individuals received more than those of low-income individuals? Should 9/11 victims have been treated differently from victims of other attacks, such as the Oklahoma City bombing? (Families of military personnel killed in the war in Iraq typically receive a death benefit of $250,000, which was significantly raised in 2005.) If another terrorist attack occurs, should a similar victim compensation fund be established?

Long-term Costs

The long-term indirect costs of terrorism clearly include higher expenditures for security. Becker and Murphy (2001) indicate that the cost of additional airport security is $4 per flight segment and that security checks force travelers to utilize an additional half-hour per flight segment, which includes the increased waiting time resulting from missed and rescheduled flights. If the time of a typical air traveler is valued at $20 per hour, then increased airline security costs are $10 billion per year, which is in addition to the Congressional Budget Office (2004) estimate of $20 billion in increased security costs for the year 2002. The CBO further estimates that total nondefense outlays for homeland security (see Chapter 10) will total $144 billion for 2005–2009. These outlays include Project BioShield's multiyear $5.6 billion appropriation to assist in the development of medicines that can counter a potential biological weapons attack.

Moreover, terrorism-induced risk may be viewed as a long-term tax on the economy. Even though it is possible to insure against an attack, terrorism-prone sectors bear the largest share of the costs. Obviously, consumers want to avoid activities exposing them to possible injury or death. Rational investors will substitute out of high-terrorism activities in order to avoid potential losses. As consumers and investors move out of risky activities, there is a long-run reallocation of resources such that terrorism-prone sectors contract and others expand. This makes it difficult to measure the total output or employment loss resulting from terrorism, since one sector's loss may be another's gains. If, for example, a family decides to drive rather than fly to a tourist destination, some of the lost airfares accrue to gasoline companies and roadside motels.

MACROECONOMIC EFFECTS OF TERRORISM

Contrary to the views often expressed in the media, many economists and political scientists hold the view that the US macroeconomy should experience only small effects from terrorism. The justification for this view is that relatively few attacks are staged in the United States and that US economic activities are sufficiently diverse to absorb the impact of an attack by shifting activities to unaffected sectors. According to Robert Shapiro (2004), a former undersecretary of commerce in the Clinton administration, the immediate costs of terrorist acts such as a kidnapping or an assassination are localized, so that terrorism resembles an ordinary crime. Instead of affecting the entire macroeconomy, terrorism causes a substitution from sectors vulnerable to terrorism into relatively safe areas. If airlines become risky, factors of production will quickly leave the airline sector to find gainful employment in now relatively less risky areas. "Modern economies regularly absorb greater losses from bad weather and natural disasters – for example the 1988 heat wave that took the lives of more than 5000 Americans or the 1999 earthquake in Izmit, Turkey, that killed 17,000 – without derailing" (Shapiro, 2004).

A similar argument is made by Becker and Murphy (2001). They compare terrorism to the Kobe earthquake of 1995 that killed over 6,000 people, destroyed over 100,000 buildings, and resulted in estimated total losses exceeding 2% of Japan's GDP. Part of the reason that Kobe rebounded so quickly was that the earthquake did not represent an ongoing threat. By contrast, terrorists try to create long-term fear and intimidation. Nevertheless, Becker and Murphy argue that modern economies can readily adjust to ongoing threats with the same resilience that was shown during the oil price shocks of the 1970s. They note that the precipitous rise in oil prices during the 1970s increased the total cost of oil imports by 1% of GDP. The total ongoing costs of terrorism (that is, security, loss of life, loss of property, and lost GDP growth) are estimated to be in the neighborhood of 0.3% of GDP.

This representation is in stark contrast to small economies in which terrorism is prevalent, such as Colombia, Israel, and the Basque region of Spain. For these areas, terrorism depresses economic growth and development. Protracted terrorism leads to the expectation of future terrorist events. The fear of future violence leads to high-risk premiums in terrorism-prone activities. There are few available avenues for diversifying the risk in small economies.

Some evidence for the view that the US economy quickly rebounded from 9/11 is provided in Figure 9.1. Each of the six panels of the figure shows the time path of an important US economic variable during the period surrounding 9/11. The vertical line in the center of each panel represents the third quarter of 2001 (i.e., 2001:Q3). Panel 1 shows that real GDP had been stagnant throughout the year 2000 and fell slightly in the first and third quarters of 2001. Notice that real GDP began a sustained upward trend beginning in the fourth quarter of 2001. Panel 2 shows that industrial production had been falling for several quarters prior to 9/11. In the beginning of 2002, industrial production reversed direction and began to increase. The strong growth of consumption helped to bolster real GDP and industrial production. As shown in panel 3, the consumption of durables, the most volatile component of total consumption, jumped in the fourth quarter of 2001. Panel 4 shows a somewhat contradictory picture. The unemployment rate was rising prior to 9/11, but jumped dramatically as a result of the attack. However, since the unemployment rate is a lagging indicator of economic activity, what would have happened had 9/11 not occurred remains an unanswered question.

Macroeconomic Policy Responses to a Terrorist Attack

There is an overwhelming consensus that well-orchestrated macroeconomic policymaking cushioned the blow from 9/11. As a result of 9/11, bond market trading was suspended for a day, and stock market trading did not resume until 17 September. The attacks damaged much of physical infrastructure of the markets; the communication and computer systems at the world's largest settlements bank – the Bank of New York – were severely damaged. Most firms in the New York financial district took

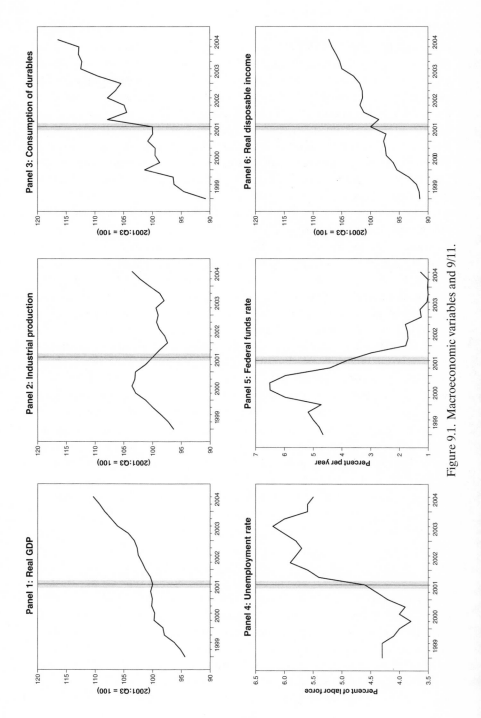

Figure 9.1. Macroeconomic variables and 9/11.

several days to operationalize their backup systems. Risk-averse asset holders did not want to be caught holding financial instruments for which the resale market was severely damaged. In times of uncertainty, investors usually flock to highly liquid assets. With 9/11, the demand for liquidity surged to unprecedented heights. As shown in panel 5 of Figure 9.1, the Federal Reserve reacted to this increased demand by sharply cutting the federal funds rate (the interest rate that banks charge each other for very short-term loans). Liquidity was also increased when the Federal Reserve encouraged banks to borrow at the discount window (the mechanism by which banks directly borrow from the Federal Reserve). Such borrowing, including repurchases, jumped from an average daily level of $24 billion to a total of $61 billion on 12 September.

Fiscal policy played an important role as well. Fortuitously, the first tax cut since 1985 was signed into law in May 2001, months before 9/11. As shown in panel 6 of Figure 9.1, after an initial drop, real disposable income (the after-tax income of households) grew sharply in 2002:Q1. On 14 September, Congress approved a $40 billion supplemental appropriation for emergency spending for such items as search-and-rescue efforts at the four crash sites and tightened security. Not only did this spending provide disaster relief, it also served as a direct stimulus to aggregate demand. Such crisis management played an important role in restoring consumer and business confidence. Although consumer confidence fell by about 20% at the onset of the attacks, this measure of expected economic prospects exceeded its pre-9/11 level by the end of 2001.

STUDIES ON TERRORISM AND THE MACROECONOMY

Due to its extraordinary scale, it is not possible to draw parallels between 9/11 and other terrorist incidents. Moreover, the costs of terrorism borne by the United States are likely to be different from those borne by the global economy, since countries differ in size, confront different terrorism risks, and possess diverse institutional structures. Blomberg, Hess, and Orphanides (2004) provide a formal test of the relationship between terrorism and economic growth using a sample of 177 countries from 1968 to 2000. Of course, a complete set of data for all of the periods is not available for all of the countries; nevertheless, they provide over 4,000 total observations. Consider the following regression equation:

$$\Delta y_i = -1.200 \, \text{COM}_i - 1.358 \, \text{AFRICA}_i - 0.461 \ln y_0$$
$$+ 0.142 \, I/Y_i - 1.587 \, T_i, \tag{1}$$

where Δy_i is country i's per capita average growth rate over the entire sample; COM_i is a dummy variable equal to 1 for a nonoil commodity exporter; AFRICA is a dummy variable equal to 1 for African nation; ln y_0 is the log of the initial value of GDP; I/Y_i is country i's per capita average rate of investment's share of GDP over the entire sample; and T_i denotes the average number years in which there was at least one terrorist event in country i. All variables are statistically significant at the 1% level.

This baseline regression has a number of interesting implications. Nonoil commodity exporters and African nations are associated with low levels of economic growth. On average, the nonoil commodity exporters have growth rates that are 1.2 percentage points less than those of other nations. African nations have growth rates that are 1.358 percentage points lower than those of other countries. The effect of initial GDP on growth is such that high-income countries tend to have lower growth rates than other nations.[4] As expected, large amounts of investment relative to GDP (so that I/Y_i is large) enhance economic growth. For our purposes, the main result is that terrorism is associated with a reduction in economic growth. If a country experiences transnational terrorist incidents on its soil in each year of the sample, per capita growth falls by 1.587 percentage points. Thus, Blomberg, Hess, and Orphanides (BHO) (2004) argue that the costs of terrorism can be sizable for a country experiencing at least one incident per year. Since T_i is the average number of years in which there was at least one terrorist event in country i, a country with multiple incidents across all thirty-three years of the sample period would suffer a 1.587 percentage point reduction in its growth rate. If terrorists struck in one year only, the drop in the growth rate would be 1.587 percentage points divided by 33 (or 0.048).

The BHO results are quite robust to alternative specifications. When they use the per capita number of incidents in a country, rather than the number of years with at least one incident, the results do not change in any meaningful way. Moreover, when the terrorism variable is replaced by a measure of internal conflict, terrorism has a larger effect than the conflict variable.

BHO argue that the negative effect of terrorism on growth is due to a redirection of economic activity away from investment spending and toward government spending; hence, their results seem implausible for

---

[4] The initial value of GDP (y_0) is included because high-income countries tend to grow at lower rates than low-income countries. The initial level of GDP controls for this "convergence" phenomenon.

countries already devoting a substantial share of their resources to anti-terrorism activities, such as Israel, Colombia, and Spain. One possible problem with the BHO model is that the data is purely cross-sectional, such that the regression equation cannot capture the dynamic interrelationship between terrorism and economic growth. Moreover, averaging across countries may not be appropriate. In particular, the specification does not control for the fact that some countries have multiple incidents in a year or for the fact that some incidents can be far more harmful than others. Also, the effects of terrorism in high-terrorism nations may be quite different than the effects in a nation experiencing only one or two events. As was the case in Yemen, the effects of multiple attacks can be mutually reinforcing.

Tavares (2004) uses a data set and a methodology similar to those of BHO. When aggregating across all types of countries and controlling for additional determinants of growth, such as inflation, the degree of trade openness, currency crises, and primary goods exports, Tavares finds that the coefficient on the terrorism variable is negative, but statistically insignificant. Hence, terrorism does not appear to affect a nation's growth rate. However, Tavares (2004) goes on to compare the costs of terrorism in democratic versus nondemocratic countries. For our purposes, the key part of his regression equation is

$$\Delta y_{it} = 0.261 \Delta y_{it-1} - 0.029 T_{it} + 0.121 (T_{it} \times R_{it})$$
$$+ \text{ other explanatory variables}, \tag{2}$$

where Δy_{it} is country i's rate of growth of per capita GDP in year t; Δy_{it-1} is country i's rate of growth of per capita GDP in year $t - 1$; T_{it} is the number of terrorist incidents in country i during year t; and R_{it} is a measure of political rights in country i such that increases in R_{it} imply increased levels of political freedom.

Notice that equation (2) is a dynamic specification for which current-period growth is affected by growth in the previous period. In contrast to Tavares's original specification, which ignored political rights, all of the coefficients reported in equation (2) are statistically significant. The coefficient on T_{it} means that a single terrorist incident in country i in year t reduces its annual growth rate for that year by 0.029 percentage points. Since the model is dynamic, this growth effect is persistent. Nevertheless, the results are not that different from those of BHO, because the cost of a typical terrorist attack is found to be quantitatively small. The interesting result concerns the positive coefficient on the interaction term $T_{it} \times R_{it}$, for which the effect of a typical terrorist attack decreases as the level of political freedom increases. The implication is that democracies are better able to withstand attacks than countries with other types of governmental structures having less flexible institutions. Yet another interpretation is that democracies are better able to withstand terrorist attacks because they are most likely to rely on markets to allocate resources.

Case Studies

Instead of pooling countries with different institutional structures and levels of terrorism, we believe that it is preferable to examine the effects of terrorism on a case-by-case basis. Eckstein and Tsiddon (2004) use the vector autoregression (VAR) methodology introduced in Chapter 5 to study the effects of terrorism on the macroeconomy of Israel. They use quarterly data from 1980 through 2003 to analyze the effects of terrorism on real GDP, investment, exports, and consumption of non-durables. Their measure of terrorism is a weighted average of the number of Israeli fatalities, injuries, and noncasuality incidents. Interestingly, they find that the initial impact of terrorism on economic activity lasts for as little as a single quarter. Moreover, the effect on exports and investment is three times larger than that on nondurable consumption and GDP; thus, the sectoral effects of terrorism are much larger than the overall effect.

Next, Eckstein and Tsiddon use their VAR estimates to calculate the counterfactual time paths of the four macroeconomic variables under the assumption that all terrorism ceased at the end of 2003:Q4. In this counterfactual experiment, real per capita GDP is forecast to grow 2.5% from the beginning of 2003:Q4 to 2005:Q3. If, however, terrorism holds steady, then the estimated VAR predicts a zero rate of growth of real per capita GDP. Thus, continued terrorism would cost Israel all of its real per capita GDP growth. Finally, if terrorism in Israel were to continue its upward trend, real per capita GDP would decline by about 2%. The figures for investment are even more dramatic, since, in this third scenario, investment would fall by 10% annually.

In another set of experiments, Eckstein and Tsiddon estimate the costs of the *intifada*. They use their data to estimate the VAR through 2000:Q3 (the beginning of the *intifada*) and forecast real GDP for the quarters 2000:Q4 through 2003:Q4. Forecasts are conducted assuming no subsequent terrorism and terrorism at the levels that actually prevailed over the 2000:Q4 through 2003:Q4 period. The difference in the forecasts is such that the terrorism cost of the *intifada* was about $1,000 per capita by the end of 2001, $1,700 per capita by the end of 2002, and $2,500 per capita by the end of 2003. By comparison, per capita GDP in Israel was just under $18,000 in 2003.

Abadie and Gardeazabal (2003) focus on the macroeconomic cost of terrorism in the Basque region of Spain. They note that the Basque country was the third richest region of Spain prior to any terrorist conflict. With the onset of Basque terrorism in the early 1970s, the region dropped to sixth place in terms of per capita GDP. After more than thirty years, other factors might be responsible for the decline in the relative position of the Basque region. After controlling for these factors, Abadie and Gardeazabal estimate a 10% loss in per capita GDP due to terrorism. For example, per capita GDP in the Basque region was approximately $10,000 in real US dollars in 1997, but had terrorism ceased, it would have been about $11,000.

As further evidence of the costs of terrorism, Abadie and Gardeazabal are able to construct two different portfolios of common stock. The portfolio consisting of companies with sizable business dealings in the Basque region was found to increase by 10.14% when a credible cease-fire was announced by the Euskadi ta Askatasuna (ETA) in late 1998. The same portfolio fell by 11.21% when the cease-fire collapsed fourteen months later. The non-Basque portfolio did not experience any noticeable movement corresponding to the cease-fire announcements.

MICROECONOMIC EFFECTS OF TERRORISM AND TRANSFER FUNCTION ANALYSIS

In July 1996, at the height of the Spanish tourist season, an ETA bomb exploded at Reus Airport in Tarragona, injuring twenty British vacationers. As might be expected, the number of tourists visiting Spain sharply declined for many months after the bombing. Transfer function analysis is especially well suited to estimating the short-term and long-term effects of such an attack. A transfer function augments the type of dynamic model discussed in Chapter 3 with an explanatory or "independent" variable.[5]

---

[5] If x_t is a pulse or a level-shift dummy variable, equation (3) is nothing more than the intervention model discussed in Chapter 3. You might want to refresh your memory by rereading the sections on intervention analysis in Chapter 3 and on VAR analysis in Chapter 5. Further details of the properties of transfer functions can be found in Enders (2004).

A very simple transfer function for the effect of terrorism on Spanish tourism might be

$$y_t = a_0 + b_1 y_{t-1} + c_0 x_t + \varepsilon_t, \tag{3}$$

where y_t is the number of tourists visiting Spain during period t; x_t is the number of terrorist incidents in Spain during period t; and ε_t is the error term. Equation (3) simply states that the number of tourists visiting Spain during any period, y_t, is affected by its own past, y_{t-1}, as well as by the number of terrorist events in Spain, x_t. Because periods with high versus low levels of tourism tend to cluster, we expect b_1 to be positive; a large y_t would tend to follow a large y_{t-1}. The magnitude of c_0 measures the contemporaneous effect of a terrorist incident on tourism. If c_0 is negative, the number of tourists declines in response to an increase in the number of incidents. To illustrate the point, suppose that $c_0 = -2$ and that there are three terrorist incidents during a particular period (so that $x_t = 3$). The contemporaneous effect of terrorism on tourism is then -6. If the unit of measure is a thousand, then there are six thousand fewer tourists. Since there is persistence in the system (so long as b_1 is not equal to zero), the effects of terrorism could be long-lasting.

The central feature of equation (3) is that it is can be used to estimate the indirect effects of terrorism. To perform the desired counterfactual analysis, a researcher would estimate equation (3) to obtain the magnitudes of a_0, b_1, and c_0. Once these magnitudes are known, one can calculate what each value of y_t would have been if all values of x_t had been zero. The difference between this counterfactual value and the actual value of y_t is due to the effect of terrorism.

Moreover, equation (3) can be generalized to allow for the possibilities (i) that additional lagged values of the dependent variable (i.e., y_{t-2}, $y_{t-3}, \dots$) affect the current value of y_t, and (ii) that current and past values of the x_t series affect the dependent variable y_t. For example, a generalization of (3) could be

$$y_t = a_0 + b_1 y_{t-1} + b_2 y_{t-2} + c_1 x_{t-1} + \varepsilon_t, \tag{4}$$

where both the first and second lagged values of tourism affect the current value of y_t. Because the lagged value of x_{t-1} appears in the equation, it takes one period for terrorism to begin to affect tourism. We note that the transfer function analysis assumes that x_t is the independent variable and that y_t is the dependent variable. If terrorism is affected by tourism, then there is reversed causality, so that a regression equation in the form of equation (3) or (4) does not show the effects of terrorism on tourism.

THE EFFECTS OF TERRORISM ON TOURISM AND TRADE

Enders, Sandler, and Parise (1992) use transfer function analysis to analyze the economic impact of terrorism on tourism. Tourists are viewed as rational consumers allocating their resources between various goods and services, including tourist trips. An increase in terrorist activities in country *i* places tourists at risk, which is especially true when terrorists explicitly target tourists. The higher risk to tourists induces a substitution away from that country toward other countries. The overall prediction is that terrorism in a country reduces tourism in that country and increases tourism in close substitute tourist venues.

Enders, Sandler, and Parise gather total tourism receipts over the 1970:Q1–1988:Q4 period for twelve countries: Austria, Canada, Denmark, Finland, France, West Germany, Greece, Italy, the Netherlands, Norway, the United Kingdom, and the United States. The estimated transfer function for Greece is

$$y_t = -0.00165 + 0.70851 y_{t-1} - 0.00638 x_{t-3}, \tag{5}$$

where y_t is the seasonal change in Greece's share of revenues relative to those for all twelve countries, and x_t is the quarterly number of transnational terrorist incidents in Greece. Since y_t is a logarithmic change, it can be interpreted as the percentage change in Greece's share of tourism revenues. The transfer function shows a three-quarter lag (nine-month lag) before a terrorist incident in Greece will affect Greek tourism revenues. This type of lag may be expected, because it takes time for tourists to revise plans; bookings on airlines and cruise ships cannot be cancelled without sizable penalties. The implication is that existing plans are generally honored, but new bookings to Greece are curtailed. The "memory" in the system is given by the coefficients of y_{t-1} and x_{t-3}. Thus, the interpretation of the transfer function is straightforward: a terrorist incident during period *t* has a negative direct effect on the growth rate of Greece's share of tourism revenues three periods hence of −0.00638. Approximately 71% of the direct effect persists for a quarter owing to this memory.

Going from the change in the log-share of Greece's tourism revenues to the actual value of revenue losses is not so straightforward. The effect of an incident lasts for a number of quarters, and the number of incidents differs for each period. Nevertheless, using a 5% real interest rate, Enders, Sandler, and Parise calculate the cumulated sum of all tourism losses for Greece arising from terrorism to be about $575 million. This total was equal to 23.4% of the annual tourism revenues for 1988.

Similar calculations are performed for Greece, Austria, and a number of other continental European nations. The Austrian case is particularly interesting because Austria is rather small and experienced a number of brutal attacks that attracted substantial media attention. The first wave of Austria's terrorist attacks was directed against Jewish interests during 1979 and 1980. Another wave of incidents occurred during the 1985–1987 period, including the infamous Abu Nidal attack on tourists at the Vienna airport on 27 December 1985. As a result, the cumulated sum of all tourism losses for Austria was \$3.474 billion or 40.7% of the country's annual tourism revenues for 1988. By contrast, Italy lost only the equivalent of 6% of its 1988 tourism revenues. France's tourism losses from terrorism were statistically insignificant. The sum of the effects for all of continental Europe was greater than the sum of the individual countries' effects, thereby implying a strong transnational externality. Terrorism in one European nation – say, France – may not have a particularly strong effect on France, but may deter tourists from visiting Europe in general.

Drakos and Kutan (2003) extend the Enders, Sandler, and Parise (1992) methodology to explicitly allow for cross-border and regional effects. The essential insight is that terrorism in a country will lead to a decrease in tourism for that country but may increase tourism elsewhere. Drakos and Kutan, however, consider only the shares of Greece, Italy, Turkey, and Israel. They disaggregate terrorist attacks in a number of interesting ways: that is, they look at the particular geographic location (rural versus urban) where the attack occurs and the intensity of the attack (measured by the number of fatalities). In its simplest form, their transfer functions is

$$G_t = a_0 + b_1 G_{t-1} + c_0 x_{Gt} + c_1 x_{It} + c_2 x_{Tt} + \varepsilon_t, \tag{6}$$

where G_t denotes Greece's share of tourism revenues relative to those of the four-country composite; G_{t-1} indicates this share during the previous period; x_{Gt} represents terrorist attacks in Greece during period t; x_{It} indicates terrorist attacks in Israel during period t; and x_{Tt} depicts terrorist attacks in Turkey during period t.

Terrorist attacks in Turkey will not affect Greek tourism revenues when $c_2 = 0$. If $c_2 > 0$, tourism in Greece and Turkey are substitutes, so that a Turkish terrorist attack will increase Greek tourism. If, however, $c_2 < 0$, tourism in Greece and Turkey are complementary, and a Turkish terrorist attack will decrease Greek tourism. Tourists will thus avoid the region altogether. Drakos and Kutan use monthly data for the period January 1991 to December 2000. Their estimates of the memory for each country are very similar to those of Enders, Sandler, and Parise in that about 70% of the direct effect persists for three months for all countries except Greece.

Attacks of low and medium levels of severity have a significant negative effect on Greek tourism. High-intensity attacks (those with three or more deaths) have an immediate impact on tourism revenues. Overall, the own-effects of terrorism on tourism are a loss of 5.21% in Turkey's share of revenues. Drakos and Kutan also find significant spillover effects — low-intensity terrorist attacks in Israel increased Greek tourism revenues, but high-intensity terrorist attacks in Israel reduced Greek tourism revenues. The overall regional effects are negative.

Sloboda (2003) also uses transfer functions to analyze the effects of terrorism on tourism revenues for the United States. The estimated transfer function is such that a terrorist incident aimed at US interests has immediate and lagged direct effects on US tourism revenues. The anti-US terrorism initiated with the start of the Gulf War in 1991 is calculated to have caused a total decline in US tourism revenues of over $56 million.

Trade Effects

Nitsch and Schumacher (2004) estimate the effects of terrorism on trade openness. They speculate that the higher risks and enhanced security measures raise transaction costs and reduce the volume of international transactions. Increases in airline and port security act like a tariff by raising the cost of trading. Additionally, enhanced terrorist activities may keep goods from arriving on time or intact.

They formally estimate the effects of terrorism within each country on all of the nation's trading partners. The control variables include the distance between the two countries, dummy variables (for speaking the same language or sharing a common border), measured GDP, and population. The data set consists of 217 countries and territories over the 1968–1979 period. They find that terrorism strongly affects the pattern of international trade. The estimated effect of terrorism is such that a doubling of the number of terrorist incidents reduces bilateral trade by 4%; hence, high-terrorism nations have a substantially reduced trade volume. The magnitude of the terrorism effect on trade is robust to a number of alternative terrorism measures.

THE EFFECTS OF TERRORISM ON FOREIGN DIRECT INVESTMENT

If terrorists target foreign firms, the risk of subsequent attacks can induce investors to move out of the now-riskier holdings of foreign assets for several reasons. First, even in the absence of a direct terrorist attack, the acquisition of the necessary resources to protect a facility from potential attacks raises operating costs. In addition to these direct costs, a firm facing terrorism risk must maintain security clearance for its employees and is subject to additional insurance charges. Second, terrorist attacks can destroy infrastructure, causing business disruptions. An attack on a railroad line may cause substantial shipping delays. Third, recruiting costs may rise because personnel from the home office may not wish to work in a terrorism-prone region. Similarly, domestic firms in high-terrorism countries may find it cheaper to shift operations to countries relatively free of terrorism.

Enders and Sandler (1996) provide estimates of the effects of terrorism on net foreign direct investment (NFDI) in the relatively small European economies of Greece and Spain. Large countries, such as the United States and the United Kingdom, draw their foreign capital inflows from diversified sources and are better able to withstand attacks without a measurable diversion of inflows. Large countries also have adequate resources to thwart potential terrorist attacks and restore a feeling of security. Greece and Spain were selected as case studies because both have experienced a number of terrorist attacks directed against foreign commercial interests. In Spain, the ETA, Iraultza, and the Autonomous Anti-Capitalist Commandos (CAA) have directed attacks against foreign enterprise. An explicit aim of Iraultza was to discourage foreign investment in the Basque region. In Greece, the Revolutionary Organization 17 November and the Revolutionary Popular Struggle had the goals of attacking capitalist interests and ending the US and NATO presence in Greece.

The amount of NFDI curtailed by such attacks cannot be directly measured. Even if it were feasible to survey all potential firms to ask how their international investment plans had been altered by terrorism, such an approach would improperly measure the net effects of terrorism on NFDI. Insofar as firms perceive risks differently, a curtailment of an investment by one firm may leave an unexploited profit opportunity for another firm. The alternative is to conduct a counterfactual analysis using the transfer function methodology to estimate an equation in the form of (4). If the dependent variable, y_t, is net foreign direct investment and if x_t measures terrorism, the fitted equations should reveal the dynamic relationship between NFDI and terrorism. Once the coefficients of the equation are determined, we can calculate what would have happened to the time path of NFDI had all values of x_t been equal to zero.

Enders and Sandler (1996) estimate a transfer function for the effects of terrorism on Spain's NFDI. The form of the transfer function is similar to that of equation (4). One notable feature of their equation is the long lag time of eleven quarters between the advent of a terrorist incident and the response in net foreign direct investment. A typical transnational terrorist incident in Spain is estimated to cause a $23.817 million reduction in NFDI. There is a reasonable amount of memory in the system, since 59.3% of the impact remains after the first quarter.

The nature of their estimated equation is such that the effect of a one-time increase in terrorism will cause the change in NFDI to decay to zero. However, once NFDI returns to its long-run level, the cumulated values have a permanent effect on the capital stock. The relationship between NFDI and net foreign capital holdings is

$$K_t = K_{t-1} + NFDI_t - \text{depreciation}_t, \tag{7}$$

where K_t is total net foreign capital holdings in Spain during period t, and depreciation$_t$ denotes the depreciation of the capital stock between periods t and $t-1$.

Equation (7) indicates that the total net foreign capital holdings in Spain during period t are equal to the previous period's holdings (K_{t-1}) plus any augmentation due to net foreign direct investment less depreciation. To ascertain the total effects of terrorism in Spain, we calculated what each period's $NFDI_t$ would have been had all values of terrorism been equal to zero. We called these values hypothetical values $NFDI_t^*$. Next, assuming a depreciation rate of 5%, we used equation (7) and the $NFDI_t^*$ sequence to construct the hypothetical capital stock had there been no terrorism. The comparison between the actual and theoretical capital stocks is shown in Figure 9.2. Our estimates show that a bout of terrorism from late 1979 through early 1981 resulted in a gap of approximately $1.8 billion. A second terrorist campaign from mid-1985 through 1987 expanded the size of the gap by nearly $3 billion, or approximately 15% of the amount of total foreign capital in Spain.

We repeated the exercise for Greece and found similar results. The major difference is that the response of NFDI to terrorism is larger and more rapid in Greece than in Spain. We were able to detect a measurable

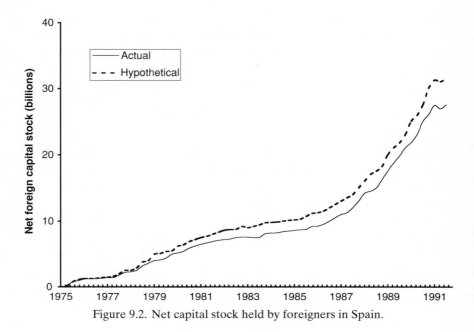

Figure 9.2. Net capital stock held by foreigners in Spain.

response within only a single quarter. Moreover, terrorism explains as much as 33% of the total variation in Greece's NFDI.

CONCLUSIONS

The International Monetary Fund (2001b) has concluded that the global costs of terrorism are small. Their report indicates that the average annual growth rate of real GDP in the industrialized nations is 2.75%. "If the impact [of terrorism] on the level of potential output were relatively sizable, say 1% of GDP, its impact on medium-term growth would be significantly smaller then current estimates of information technology in US growth since the mid-1990s..." (International Monetary Fund, 2001b, p. 15). This result is consistent with the findings of Blomberg, Hess, and Orphanides (2004) and Tavares (2004). However, the direct and indirect costs of terrorism on particular countries and on particular sectors can be sizable. The indirect costs include foregone output, increased security costs, and a high risk premium. Because growth effects are cumulative, slight changes in growth rates can have substantial effects on the long-term standard of living. There is strong evidence that these effects are proportionately larger for small economies than for large, diversified economies.

Moreover, the impact of any particular terrorist incidents tends to be lowest in democratic nations.

In viewing all of these results, one must remember that it is very difficult to precisely measure the various costs of terrorism. This is especially true for the indirect costs of terrorism. For example, the quantity of capital never formed is clearly unobservable and must be estimated using a counterfactual technique such as the transfer function methodology. The nature of the various government policy responses also needs to be considered. Had the Federal Reserve not provided additional liquidity to financial markets, the macroeconomic consequences of 9/11 might have been far greater than they actually were. Obviously, the psychological costs of stress, anxiety, and the loss of a loved one are impossible to measure.

TEN

Homeland Security

The unprecedented attacks on 9/11 underscored the importance of an overall strategy for homeland security that not only coordinates agencies' efforts to prevent terrorist attacks, but also takes decisive actions to promote recovery following an attack. The magnitude of the 9/11 incidents, with approximately 3,000 deaths and over $80 billion in property and earnings losses (Kunreuther and Michel-Kerjan, 2004a, 2004b), indicates that terrorism poses a significant risk. On 11 March 2004 (henceforth 3/11), Madrid's commuter train bombings again emphasized the vulnerability of industrial countries to terrorist events. As terrorists seek in the future to outdo the carnage of 9/11 and 3/11, they may eventually resort to the use of weapons of mass destruction (WMD) (see Chapter 11). Thus, preventive measures by the authorities must address a wide range of possible attack scenarios, including standard terrorist attacks and those involving biological and chemical agents. By the same token, plans must be in place to respond to all possible attack scenarios. The digital age and the complexity of modern-day society provide terrorists with the opportunity to cause mass disruptions in communications, energy supply lines, and transportation.

In order to have effective homeland security, component agencies must act in unison not only at the same jurisdictional level but also between jurisdictional levels. That is, the federal, state, and local agencies must cooperate. Agencies' collective action failure will lead to wasteful duplication and the inability of agents at one jurisdictional level to inform those at another level about a pending attack or threat. The creation of the Department of Homeland Security (DHS) in 2002 was, in principle, a move to eliminate waste and foster synergy among component agencies at all jurisdictional levels in the United States. Hearings following 9/11 revealed coordination errors, especially in terms of intelligence. In the wake of 9/11, the US government had to take steps to provide its people with a greater sense of security. Clearly, the ability of the 9/11 hijackers to bring weapons on board four flights demonstrated that the nation's airports were not safe. The success of the terrorists in obtaining visas and even flight training in the United States also highlighted vulnerabilities. The failure of US law enforcement and customs officials to stop the terrorists at the border, even though some were on a watch list, also reflected the system's failure to protect Americans prior to 9/11.

Along with the war on terror, DHS represented a bold initiative to make America safer from the threat of terrorism. The purpose of this chapter is to present and evaluate US post-9/11 efforts to curb the threat of terrorism through the creation of DHS and other actions. Many questions are addressed, including whether the US response has been appropriate. Can US action serve as a role model for other countries confronted with transnational and domestic terrorist threats? Clearly, only rich prime-target countries can afford such a large response, as just the new defensive actions run into the tens of billions of dollars. We are also interested in raising issues that require further analysis. For instance, what is the proper mix of defensive and proactive measures? Another concern involves the proper combination of private and public efforts and how best to finance security measures. There is also a need to explore the implications that US homeland security policies have for other countries, insofar as a more secure America may induce terrorists to seek softer targets abroad (see Chapters 5 and 8).

INITIAL REACTION TO 9/11: USA PATRIOT ACT

After the smoke had settled at the World Trade Center, the Pentagon, and in rural Pennsylvania, the Bush administration and the US Congress needed to regain the confidence of America. The first two responses were the US-led invasion of Afghanistan on 7 October 2001 and the passage of the USA Patriot Act, signed by President George W. Bush on 26 October 2001 (Congressional Research Service, 2002). The former was a proactive response after the Taliban failed to hand over Osama bin Laden, while the latter gave federal officials greater ability to monitor communications and prevent future terrorist acts. The USA Patriot Act traded off personal freedoms for collective security – a trade-off that some were willing to make in light of the threat of future terrorism (see Chapter 2).

Table 10.1. *Highlights of the USA Patriot Act (HR 3162)*

➤ *Enhanced domestic security measures against terrorism*
  • Counterterrorism fund
  • $200 million for FBI's technical support center
  • National Electronic Crime Task Force Initiative
  • Allows for antiterrorism military assistance
  • Ability to delay notice for execution of a warrant
➤ *Greater surveillance and reduced privacy protection*
  • Expanded authority to intercept wire, oral, and electronic communications for suspected terrorism or computer offenses
  • Clearance to share criminal investigative findings among foreign and domestic law enforcement agencies
  • Reduced restrictions on foreign intelligence gathering inside the United States
  • Voice-mail message seizures allowed
  • Access to Foreign Intelligence Surveillance Act records for domestic law enforcement agents
  • Trade sanctions
➤ *Expanded action against money laundering*
  • Securities brokers, dealers, and financial institutions must file Suspicious Activity Reports (SARs)
  • Greater authority of the US secretary of the treasury to control activities within US financial institutions regarding foreigners' deposits
  • Greater transparency of accounts
  • Enhanced international cooperation
➤ *Augmented border protection*
  • Fingerprinting and biometric identification of some foreign visitors
  • Foreign student monitoring program
  • Machine-readable passports
  • Other improved safeguards
➤ *Increased ability to investigate terrorism*
  • Attorney general and secretary of state authorized to pay rewards in the war on terror
  • Greater coordination among law enforcement agencies
  • Collect DNA samples from convicted criminals and terrorists
➤ *Provision for victims of terrorism, including safety officers*
➤ *Enhanced criminal laws and penalties against terrorism*
  • Improved definitions of domestic and transnational terrorism
  • Penalties extended to those who aid, abet, or harbor terrorists
  • Reduced statute of limitations on some terrorist offenses
  • Greater penalties on terrorist offenses
  • Penalties extended to include cyberterrorism

➢ *Improved intelligence*
  • Tracking of foreign terrorists' assets
  • Less congressional oversight on intelligence gathering
  • More cooperation internationally
  • More cooperation among federal, state, and local jurisdictions
➢ *Miscellaneous*
  • First-responder assistance
  • Denies entry to aliens who engage in money-laundering activities
  • Examine feasibility of domestic identifier system
  • Grant program to state and local agencies for domestic preparedness
  • Provides for critical infrastructure protection

Sources: US Congress (2001) and Congressional Research Service (2002).

The USA Patriot Act is a complicated piece of legislation that is over 340 pages long (US Congress, 2001). In Table 10.1, we list the act's nine major provisions in italics, along with select subprovisions. The act is meant to enhance domestic security by allowing for a counterterrorism fund, a Federal Bureau of Investigation (FBI) technical support center, a National Electronic Crime Task Force Initiative, and other measures. One of the act's more controversial provisions authorizes greater surveillance and curbs on privacy. The main subprovisions involve the power to intercept and seize a wider range of communications, including voice-mail messages. A second aspect encourages collaboration among foreign and domestic law enforcement agencies – for example, the FBI and the Central Intelligence Agency (CIA). A third provision augments anti-money-laundering activities by mandating greater regulation of money transfers through actions at home and in concert with counterparts abroad. The act also provides for augmented border protection – for example, biometric identification, a foreign student monitoring program, machine-readable passports, and other measures. Another freedom-limiting provision increases the investigative abilities of law enforcement agencies. Under this provision, the US attorney general and the US secretary of state have expanded powers to pay rewards to capture terrorists. A sixth set of provisions provides relief and compensation not only for the victims of terrorist attacks but also for safety officers injured or killed in the line of duty. Another provision increases criminal penalties against terrorists and greatly limits the statute of limitations on various terrorist acts. Penalties are also increased for those who aid terrorists. Penalties are extended to apply to acts of cyber terrorism. The USA Patriot Act also allows for improved intelligence to monitor terrorists and their resources. In so doing, cooperation is encouraged between international law enforcement organizations and among agencies at different juris-dictional levels within the United States. Finally, the act's miscellaneous provisions support a first-responder program at the state and local levels. Grants are mentioned as a means to bolster state and local authorities' domestic preparedness against terrorist attacks. In addition, there is a call to examine the feasibility of a citizen-identification system, not unlike the one instituted in Germany during its era of left-wing terrorists. There is also a recognition of the need to protect critical infrastructure against terrorist attacks throughout the United States.

The USA Patriot Act is a noteworthy piece of legislation for at least three reasons. First, it highlights how civil liberties may be traded away following a devastating terrorist attack. The bounds of these new surveillance, investigative, and intelligence-gathering powers will surely be tested in the courts in future years as the authorities extend their powers. Second, the USA Patriot Act demonstrates that taking action against terrorists involves a host of activities, including victim protection, interjurisdictional cooperation, increased criminal penalties, augmented authority, and international cooperation. Third, the Patriot Act is a clear forerunner of DHS, which is reflected in the first-responder program, grants for domestic preparedness, the protection of critical infrastructure, and other activities.

Some of the most controversial surveillance provisions of the act must be renewed at the end of 2005. A spirited fight is set to ensue as propo-nents of the act (for example, the Bush administration) argue that the risks of terrorism remain as great today as they were after 9/11, while opponents stress that such powers are unnecessary and can be abused by law enforcement agencies. Recent statistics on transnational terrorist attacks indicate that the level of such events is higher compared to the last decade. These statistics should be quite influential, we believe, in sup-porting the renewal of these surveillance provisions despite their costs in terms of lost privacy. The recent London bombings will reinforce public fears. As long as public opinion places terrorism as the country's primary concern, the USA Patriot Act's controversial sections will remain.

DEPARTMENT OF HOMELAND SECURITY

The origins of the DHS came in an executive order establishing the White House Office of Homeland Security and the Homeland Security Council on 8 October 2001, the day after the US-led invasion of Afghanistan (Department of Homeland Security, 2002). The office was created to work with federal, state, and local agencies to develop an integrated national strategy to counter and prevent terrorist attacks. In the event of an attack, the office would coordinate actions to respond and to help citizens recover from the attack's consequences. The Homeland Security Council served to advise and help the president in addressing all issues of homeland security.

In 2002, the Bush administration realized that a significant reorganization of the government was needed if a fully integrated approach to homeland security was to be achieved. Thus, President Bush called for the creation of the DHS, which would bring together twenty-two agencies in a cabinet-level department (White House, 2002, 2004). DHS has four primary missions: to prevent terrorist events at home, to limit US vulnerability to terrorism, to minimize damage from attacks, and to recover quickly following attacks. DHS would secure borders, the transportation sector, ports, and critical infrastructure, while mobilizing all available resources. In so doing, DHS would coordinate agencies at all jurisdictional levels. If properly constituted, DHS would eliminate duplication among agencies, coordinate activities among different authorities, centralize intelligence, address the WMD threat, and foster research and development efforts in counterterrorism.

In Table 10.2, the five major directorates and the three main mission agencies of DHS are indicated. Border and Transportation Security (BTS) includes the Transportation Security Administration (TSA) (for airport safety), customs and border protection, the Bureau of Immigration and Customs Enforcement, the Office of Domestic Preparedness, the Federal Law Enforcement Training Center, and the oversight of customs abandoned goods. The Emergency Preparedness and Response

Table 10.2. *Directorates and Mission Agencies of Homeland Security*

Five Directorates
- Border and Transportation Security (BTS)
- Emergency Preparedness and Response
- Information Analysis and Infrastructure Protection
- Science and Technology
- Departmental Management

Three Mission Agencies
- US Coast Guard
- US Citizenship and Immigration Services
- US Secret Service

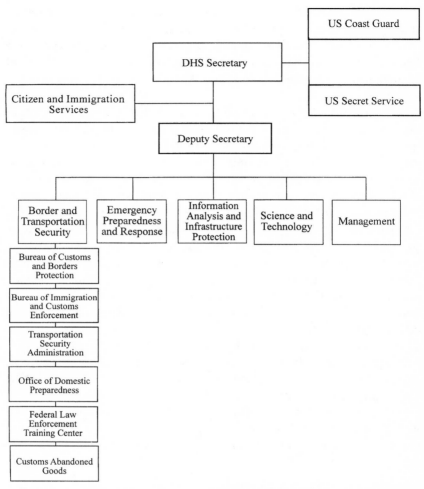

Figure 10.1. Organizational chart of the Department of Homeland Security.

directorate addresses national emergencies, including natural and terrorism-based disasters. Part of this directorate's mission is to develop pharmaceutical and vaccine stockpiles to counter bioterrorism or chemical attacks (for example, a sarin gas attack). The Information Analysis and Infrastructure Protection (IAIP) directorate has two primary functions: to coordinate intelligence and to protect the nation's infrastructure. In its intelligence role, IAIP is charged with issuing terrorist alerts and advisories for law enforcement agencies and the general public. IAIP is supposed to collaborate with the FBI, CIA, and other intelligence bodies

in fulfilling its advisory role. The Science and Technology (S&T) directorate coordinates research and development on all homeland security
issues. In particular, S&T chooses and funds the research centers, including the first center at the University of Southern California. A prime duty
of S&T is to develop countermeasures for biological, chemical, radiological, and nuclear terrorist attacks. The S&T budget has increased significantly since the establishment of DHS. The DHS directorate handles the
general management and administration of the various components of
the department.

In Table 10.2, the three mission agencies are the US Coast Guard,
the US Citizenship and Immigration Services, and the US Secret Service.
Each of these missions has both homeland and nonhomeland security
functions. In guarding US coastlines, the Coast Guard protects US claims
to territorial waters and resources within 200 miles of the shore as well
as keeping out illegal immigrants. Also, the Guard interdicts illegal drug
shipments. Such functions do not involve homeland security in regard
to terrorism. Similarly, the other two missions perform many nonhomeland security functions – for example, issuing passports, granting tourist
visas, limiting counterfeiting, and protecting the president – that are not
terrorism-related. The organizational structure of DHS is displayed in
Figure 10.1. In 2004, DHS had 183,000 employees and a discretionary budget authority, excluding fee-supported and mandated activities, of $33.8
billion (White House, 2004). Official estimates identify 61% of the DHS
budget as going to homeland security.

DHS BUDGET

In Table 10.3, we break down the DHS budget into four functional areas:
security, enforcement, and investigations; preparedness and recovery;
research, development, training, assessment, and services; and departmental management and operations. These are the categories given in the
official budget documents (DHS, 2004). Three fiscal years – 2003, 2004,
and 2005 – are displayed in Table 10.3 in millions of current-year dollars.
Under security, enforcement, and investigations, the US VISIT program
monitors and tracks visitors to the United States. The TSA is concerned
with all aspects of airport and aircraft safety. Since 9/11, TSA has done the
following: replaced cockpit doors, expanded air marshal flight protection,
modernized the passenger and baggage screening system, improved passenger and baggage prescreening, shored up aircraft access, and increased
intelligence on aircraft-related threats. TSA is currently evaluating the

Table 10.3. *Total Budget Authority by Organization as of 31 January 2004*
($ millions)

Organization	Fiscal Years[a]		
	2003	2004	2005
Security, Enforcement, and Investigations	*21,566*	*22,606*	*24,691*
BTS Under Secretary	0	8	10
US VISIT	380	328	340
Bureau of Customs and Borders Protection	5,887	5,942	6,199
Bureau of Immigration and Customs Enforcement	3,262	3,654	4,011
Transportation Security Administration	4,648	4,405	5,297
US Coast Guard	6,196	6,935	7,471
US Secret Service	1,193	1,334	1,363
Preparedness and Recovery	*5,175*	*5,493*	*7,372*
Federal Emergency Management Agency	5,175	4,608	4,844
Biodefense	0	885	2,528
Research, Development, Training, Assessments, and Services	*2,330*	*3,591*	*3,810*
Bureau of Citizenship and Immigration Services	1,422	1,653	1,711
Federal Law Enforcement Training Center	170	191	196
Information Analysis and Infrastructure Protection	185	834	864
Science and Technology	553	913	1,039
Departmental Management and Operations	*2,111*	*4,851*	*4,294*
Departmental Operations	22	211	405
Technology Investments	47	184	226
Counterterrorism Fund	10	10	20
Office of Domestic Preparedness	1,961	4,366	3,561
Inspector General	71	80	82
TOTAL	31,182	36,541	40,167

[a] Figures for 2004 are estimates, and figures for 2005 are requests.
Source: Department of Homeland Security (2004, p. 13).

need for antimissile defenses on commercial flights to protect against shoulder-fired missiles. The TSA budget has grown from $4.6 billion in 2003 to a budget request of $5.3 billion for 2005. TSA deploys federally trained professional screeners at US airports with the aim of providing an acceptable standard of vigilance nationwide. The other subcategories are self-explanatory.

Under emergency preparedness and recovery, the main agency is the Federal Emergency Management Agency (FEMA), which helps people to recover from disasters – either natural or terrorist-related. FEMA takes up approximately 12% of the DHS budget in 2005. The biodefense shield is a growing program to stockpile drugs, vaccines, antidotes, and other medical supplies needed in the event of a biological attack by terrorists. Further budget increases for this shield are anticipated. Once adequate supplies are stockpiled, a certain percentage of the stockpile will have to be replenished annually as expiration dates are reached.

The research, development, training, assessment, and services portion of DHS includes citizenship and immigration services. These latter services offer little homeland security per se. As shown in Table 10.3, this third organizational category of DHS also encompasses the Federal Law Enforcement Training Center, IAIP, and S&T. The increase in the budgets of IAIP and S&T since 2003 is clearly displayed.

The primary component of DHS management and operations is the Office of Domestic Preparedness, which distributes money to the state and local levels to bolster security nationwide. Money is given out based on areas containing high-threat urban centers, population, density, and other considerations. This redistribution scheme uses federally collected tax revenues to provide a degree of safety at all jurisdictional levels. The federal government has a greater ability than local jurisdictions to raise tax revenues to foster antiterrorism measures. Without such a redistribution scheme, less-protected local areas will draw the terrorist attack. The scheme is analogous to revenue-sharing arrangements, where the federal government raises funds that are subsequently shared with state and local governments.

In Table 10.4, the DHS budget is again displayed by functional categories for 2004 and 2005. This new table, however, distinguishes the expenditures going to homeland (HS) and nonhomeland security (NHS) for each function. As indicated, large nonhomeland security components are associated with the US Coast Guard, fee accounts (for example, passport applications), trust and public funds, and customs and border protection. Given its diverse activities, the homeland security component of the US Secret Service appears grossly exaggerated. The table also distinguishes gross discretionary funds from mandatory and fee accounts. In 2005, $33.8 billion of the DHS budget is discretionary, while $6.3 billion is nondiscretionary. From an economic efficiency standpoint, activities with distinct user benefits – for example, passports and visas – should be financed through fees paid by the beneficiaries rather than through general tax revenues. This benefiter-pay scheme promotes efficiency by directing resources to activities where effective demand is high.

Table 10.4. *Homeland versus Nonhomeland Security Funding Breakdown, Fiscal Years 2004 and 2005 ($ millions)*

	FY2004		FY2005	
	HS	Non-HS	HS	Non-HS
Gross Discretionary Funding				
Security, Enforcement, and Investigations	*15,153*	*4,808*	*16,629*	*5,084*
BTS Under Secretary	0	8	0	10
US VISIT	328	0	340	0
Bureau of Customs and Borders Protection	3,862	1,038	4,008	1,114
Bureau of Immigration and Customs Enforcement	2,928	478	3,283	503
Transportation Security Administration	4,405	0	5,042	0
US Coast Guard	2,556	3,224	2,856	3,394
US Secret Service	1,074	60	1,100	63
Preparedness and Recovery	*113*	*2,776*	*120*	*2,937*
Research, Development, Training, Assessments, and Services	*1,839*	*334*	*1,986*	*253*
Bureau of Citizenship and Immigration Services	0	235	0	140
Federal Law Enforcement Training Center	131	60	135	61
Information Analysis and Infrastructure Protection	834	0	864	0
Science and Technology	874	39	987	52
Departmental Management and Operations	*3,724*	*1,127*	*3,869*	*425*
Departmental Operations	142	69	157	248
Technology Investments	3,441	925	3,561	0
Counterterrorism Fund	131	53	131	95
Office of Domestic Preparedness	10	0	20	0
Inspector General	0	80	0	82
SUBTOTAL	20,829	9,045	22,604	8,699
Biodefense	885	0	2,528	0
Mandatory Funding and Fee Accounts				
Mandatory Appropriations	491	729	528	757
Fee Accounts	1,287	1,418	1,554	1,571
Trust and Public Enterprise Funds	0	1,857	0	1,926
SUBTOTAL	1,778	4,004	2,082	4,254
TOTAL	23,492	13,049	27,214	12,953

Source: Department of Homeland Security (2004).

DHS is financed by the federal government through income taxes, security taxes on airline tickets, fees, and other federal taxes. Following 9/11, the state and local governments covered much of the costs associated with preventing terrorism in their jurisdictions or responding to elevated terrorism-alert levels issued by DHS. For 2001, the National Governors Association estimated added antiterrorism expenses of $650 million, while the US Conference of Mayors estimated added counterterrorism costs of $525 million in 2001 (Bush, 2002, p. 5). Clearly, something needed to be done to give state and local governments some fiscal relief.

Relief came from four sources within the DHS budget. First, the Office of Domestic Preparedness instituted a first-responder program to support local efforts. Grants under this program paid for law enforcement personnel training, wages (including overtime pay during heightened alerts), equipment, and exercises. States are required to distribute 80% of the grants to local jurisdictions. Second, the Federal Law Enforcement Training Center provides basic and advanced training in countering terrorism to state and local agents. Third, some of the biodefense program is set aside to assist the state and local jurisdictions. Fourth, the IAIP division of DHS provides intelligence on terrorism to state and local jurisdictions.

EVALUATION OF DHS

DHS has many pluses and minuses. On the positive side, DHS seeks to address the weakest-link problem by achieving greater security standards countrywide. This is particularly germane to TSA's efforts to secure the nation's airports by deploying professional screeners. Prior to 9/11, airline companies hired their own screeners and faced a moral hazard problem, because airlines could pocket cost savings from security fees collected on tickets by using cheap screeners with little training (also see Hainmüller and Lemnitzer [2003] on the failure of private airline companies to provide adequate security). DHS utilizes the revenue-generating ability of the federal government to provide funding to lower-level jurisdictions, including small townships that, without federal assistance, are unable to prepare for biological or chemical terrorist attacks. Another favorable factor is the greater coordination that DHS can achieve by bringing agencies performing related and complementary chores under the same department and leadership. DHS also spearheads a crucial research and development program to investigate a wide range of issues, including identifying improved counterterrorism practices, addressing threats to US agriculture, limiting potential attacks against the nation's food supply, and understanding the root causes of terrorism. DHS has tried to recognize new exigencies and take action before the threat is realized.

Because terrorism poses a nationwide threat, action needs to be directed at the federal level, and this is precisely what DHS does. In so doing, DHS must coordinate federal, state, and local responses, which is yet another mission of the department. Independent antiterrorism action at the state or local level will merely displace the attack to a less-protected jurisdiction. Because much of the terrorism threat within the United States is coming from abroad, the inclusion of the Bureau of Customs and Borders Protection, TSA, and the US Coast Guard is sensible.

In mid-April 2005, the Associated Press reported that the US General Accounting Office (GAO) and the office of the DHS inspector general would soon release reports stating that recent tests had revealed that federal screeners today perform no better than private screeners prior to 9/11 in detecting prohibited items. This finding, if true, raises real concerns about the effectiveness of professional screeners. Apparently, the alleged screening failure is attributed to inadequate equipment and the protection of passenger privacy. In drawing this comparison to pre-9/11 screening, some things must be kept in mind. Most important, screeners must now check for many more prohibited items, including box cutters and knives. There are, thus, more items that can escape detection. Moreover, auditors' increased knowledge of the equipment gives them an edge that terrorists may not have in exploiting the equipment's blind spots. Screeners' training cannot compensate for inadequate equipment, which sets performance limits. If the equipment is the weakest link, as the news reports suggest, then upgraded equipment needs to be installed and the screeners duly trained. Federal standards are then needed to ensure that, when this is accomplished, all airports will achieve similar levels of vigilance, which is essential. Finally, attempting to compare today's screeners to those before 9/11 is fraught with difficulties – for example, yesterday screeners may have been tipped off about tests.

There are many other aspects of DHS that can be improved. In its mission to bring relevant agencies within the same department, DHS does not go far enough in terms of intelligence. There is still intelligence duplication with the FBI, the CIA, the Department of Defense (DoD), the National Security Council, and other entities collecting information on the terrorism threat. The same logic that justifies bringing twenty-two agencies within the DHS also supports including these intelligence offices *within* DHS. Currently, IAIP's interface with these other intelligence organizations is incomplete. Proper intelligence is essential to all of the DHS missions – for example, intelligence informs DHS about where to concentrate its research and development efforts and tells TSA what steps should be taken to keep commercial air travel safe. Intelligence allows S&T to know what WMD threats are the most immediate. An explicit linkage between the military and DHS is also needed. Military operations – for example, raids on al-Qaida caves in Afghanistan – can yield information crucial to homeland security. Planned military operations may create grievances that erupt in terrorist attacks, which further justifies the proposed link.

Another concern with DHS is to better address the financial burdens placed on the state and local jurisdictions in regard to counterterrorism. Heightened terrorism alerts, issued by DHS, can stress city and other jurisdictional budgets as police and other officials are paid additional wages. Clearly, DHS is aware of the problem and has instituted grant programs to bring relief, but it will take time for local jurisdictions to understand what funds are available and how to obtain them. For example, the police play an important role in responding to security alerts and incidents at the Los Angeles International Airport (LAX). These police forces represent the first line of defense. Financial relief is needed between the time that the local jurisdictions apply for the funds and when they are finally received. Politics must not play a role in determining the allocation of funds among jurisdictions. This allocation must equalize the marginal risk so that there are no weakest links to draw the attack.

To improve DHS operations, an international viewpoint is required. By improving security for Americans and foreign visitors in the United States, DHS activities will surely divert some attacks to locations abroad. This transference is apt to gravitate to two venues: poor countries with less capacity for homeland security and countries where the terrorists can obtain safe haven. The latter class of countries includes "failed states," where there is no stable government to maintain order. In other instances, the terrorists may operate in their own country and target foreigners. At home, terrorists can blend in easily and establish a support system (see Chapter 8; Enders and Sandler, 2005b). To address these venue shifts, there must be permanent ties between DHS and foreign authorities. This transfer of attacks puts Americans and their property more at risk abroad. DHS is currently focused on domestic security, thereby ignoring the fact that actions at home have far-reaching ramifications.

Terrorism Alert System

One DHS innovation merits some special evaluation. Prior to 9/11, terrorism warnings were not always shared with the public – for example, a terrorism advisory prior to the downing of Pan Am flight 103 on 21 December 1988 had not been made public. The failure of the public to know of a terrorism advisory can bring outrage once an incident occurs and the advisory is revealed. Apparently, the US government was aware of increased chatter on the internet about a pending terrorist attack before 9/11 but did not publicize the information. To stem future criticism, DHS instituted a five-tier terrorism alert system: green, low threat; blue, guarded risk; yellow, elevated or significant threat; orange, high alert; and red, severe risk. For each tier, there are certain actions required by the authorities and DHS – for example, an orange alert mandates coordinated security actions by federal, state, and local law enforcement bodies. DHS uses the alert system, in part, to make the public more vigilant and accepting of delays at airports, public events, and critical infrastructure.

Despite these benefits, the terrorism alert system has some shortfalls. Intelligence provides the authorities with information that the terrorists may not know that the authorities have. In such a situation, the authorities can use this one-sided information to lay a trap for the terrorists. By making the information public, the authorities lose a strategic advantage. The current alert system allows the terrorists to manipulate the system. That is, the terrorists can increase their chatter or level of activity, thereby creating enhanced fear in the public and greater security expenditures by the authorities. By limiting their chatter, the terrorists can reduce DHS vigilance prior to a planned attack. The current system also informs the terrorists when attacks are more difficult to execute owing to the watchfulness of the authorities. Another drawback is the proclivity of the authorities to maintain an elevated or high-alert level, because they do not want an attack to occur during a low-alert period. Not surprisingly, the alert level has never fallen below yellow since the system was instituted. This practice leads to public fatigue; the system loses its immediacy because vigilance is always heightened. Orange alerts are costly for state and local law enforcement. The current system is a nationwide alert that does not permit action to be tailored to places where the potential threat is most relevant. In 2005, DHS issued some localized warnings.

OTHER ISSUES OF HOMELAND SECURITY

DHS is primarily concerned with defensive measures that harden targets, foil terrorist attacks, and keep terrorists or their weapons from entering the country. Proactive responses that attack transnational terrorists or their assets directly are left to the military, the intelligence community, and other government agencies. The relative expenditure breakdown between defensive and proactive responses is difficult to ascertain. In fiscal year 2004, the US General Accounting Office (2004) offered the following breakdown among departments: DHS, $23.9 billion; DoD, $15.2 billion; Department of Justice, $2.3 billion; Department of State, $2.4 billion; Department of Health and Human Services, $3.8 billion; and other departments and agencies, $5.2 billion. In total, these antiterrorism expenditures were $52.8 billion, but this did not include spending on intelligence by the CIA, the FBI, and other agencies outside of the DHS. Of this total, proactive measures included $15.2 billion spent by DoD and some of the other expenditures that went for freezing terrorist assets or bringing terrorists to justice. Some researchers have put the proactive spending at over $100 billion by including spending on the Iraq war and its aftermath, even though there was no evidence of a terrorist threat in Iraq prior to the war (see, for example, Williams, 2004).

What Is the Proper Mix between Proactive and Defensive Measures?

In coming up with an overall homeland security strategy, the US government must address this issue. The proper budget for DHS can be ascertained only if the level of proactive measures is known. If, for example, a larger offensive against the terrorists were to reduce their numbers, then less defensive homeland security would be needed. When, however, proactive responses create grievances, greater terrorism may ensue and enhanced defensive measures may be needed. The proper mix poses a difficult question that requires some careful analysis. The best that we can accomplish here is to indicate some of the trade-offs that a proper study must take into account.

Proactive strategies can result in potential *long-run* savings from eliminating the terrorist threat. This means that a dynamic analysis is appropriate, one that accounts for the immediate proactive costs and the longer-run proactive benefits as the terrorists are reduced in number. By contrast, defensive measures provide primarily short-term benefits from current safeguards. Such measures involve a continual flow of spending because actions must be applied during *every* period when the threat persists. In calculating defensive benefits, a researcher must net out transference externalities as attacks are shifted to less-guarded venues. As a rough rule of thumb, the *net* additional benefits per dollar of expenditure should be equated between defensive and proactive policies. Because the unit costs of proactive and defensive responses are likely to differ, it is essential to divide *net* additional gains from each kind of activity by its respective price. If, for example, proactive policies have a higher unit price than defensive actions, then the net marginal benefits from proactive measures must exceed those of defensive actions to justify implementing as much proactive policy. Some combination of both policies is required depending on their time profile of benefits, their prices. and any offsetting negative consequences (for example, from transference or enhanced grievances).

Other Allocative Choices

Once an appropriate division between proactive and defensive measures is decided upon, resources must be allocated within each class based on payoffs and costs. For proactive responses, the military must account for the expected gain in terms of reduced terrorism from offensive actions. If two proactive choices are equally costly, then action favors the choice whose success is more assured and whose payoff is greater. A smaller likelihood of success can be compensated for by a larger payoff in terms of reduced terrorism.

When DHS is making allocations among alternative defensive measures, several factors are key: the value of the protected target, the ease of protecting the target, collateral damage, and intelligence on the terrorists' predilection for the target. A target's value is determined by the potential loss of life, the loss of property value, and its symbolic value. Collateral damage to nearby areas can augment a target's value. Knowledge of the terrorists' preferences can allow the authorities to estimate how likely a target is to be hit, thereby permitting an estimate of a target's *expected value* – its likelihood-weighted losses from an attack. Keeping other things constant, defensive measures should favor high-value targets that are *likely venues and easier to protect*. The latter consideration determines how much in resources must be assigned to achieve a given level of protection. Targets with easy-to-protect distant perimeters may require fewer defensive resources than ones where there is no safety buffer. In Los Angeles, the Staples Center has no defensive perimeter, while Dodgers Stadium does. Defensive resource budgets are usually fixed, so that more protection at one place implies less at other places. Resources should be allocated among venues so that the expected *net* marginal gain is equated across targets, where these net gains account for the target's value after deducting marginal defensive costs. Given their high values, high-profile sporting events and public gatherings should receive greater protection.

Technological breakthroughs may result in greater effective protection as associated costs are reduced.

Private versus Public Provision of Security

Private enterprises also have a role and incentives to provide defensive measures and not solely rely on DHS for protection. For example, cruise ships can gain passengers and increase their revenues if security measures appear adequate. The associated costs can, in part, be passed on in the ticket price. Adequate terrorism precautions may also save cruise ships on insurance. Cruise ships and other enterprises (for example, amusement parks and race tracks) at risk for terrorist attacks must also balance greater security costs against savings in insurance premiums. Clearly, DHS will direct most of its protection to public venues, so private corporations will have to finance their own protection. In some cases where there are public spillovers, DHS provides grants to assist some enterprises with terrorism protection – for example, grants are offered to oil companies.

INSURANCE AND TERRORISM

Another issue of homeland security following 9/11 has been the ability of firms to obtain terrorism insurance.[1] Without this insurance, a future terrorist incident could put firms in the impacted industry out of business. Commercial airline companies needed insurance to continue to provide flights to the public. Prior to 9/11, insured losses from transnational terrorist attacks had been modest: $907 million in the 24 April 1993 NatWest tower bombing in London; $725 million in the 26 February 1993 World Trade Center bombing; $671 million in the 10 April 1992 financial district bombing in London; $398 million in the 24 July 2001 aircraft bombing at the Columbo International Airport in Sri Lanka; and $259 million in the 9 February 1996 IRA South Key Docklands bombing in London (Wolgast, 2002).[2] The 9/11 attacks resulted in economic and property losses of $80 billion, of which about $40 billion was insured. These covered losses included business interruption, workers compensation, life

[1] The information in this section draws from facts provided in Kunreuther and Michel-Kerjan (2004a, 2004b) and Wolgast (2002).
[2] The Oklahoma City bombing resulted in over $650 million in losses, of which $145 million was insured (Wolgast, 2002).

insurance, liability payments, and property damage. Insured losses from the most costly natural disasters do not rival those of 9/11: $20 billion from Hurricane Andrew in 1992; $17 billion from the Northridge earthquake in 1994; $7.3 billion from Typhoon Murielle (Japan) in 1991; and $6.2 billion from Winterstorm Daria (Europe) in 1990 (Wolgast, 2002).[3] The losses from 9/11 prompted the insurance industry to exclude terrorism coverage or to charge extremely high premiums.

Terrorism presented the insurance industry with dilemmas not characteristic of other insurance liabilities (Kunreuther and Michel-Kerjan, 2004b). The experience of 9/11 demonstrated that catastrophic losses could result from a terrorist event. For example, a radiological bomb that explodes in a major city could result in losses that would dwarf those of 9/11. More important, modelers have great difficulty in computing the likelihood of future terrorist events and the potential losses. This difficulty can be appreciated by reflecting on terrorism prior to 9/11, when the highest death toll from any terrorist attack had been under 500 persons. The 10 April 1992 bombing of the London financial district represented the greatest pre-9/11 terrorist-induced loss, estimated at $2.9 billion.[4] Thus, historical data does little to help the insurance industry to calculate what types of risks are associated with terrorism insurance. With natural disasters, there is more data that permits actuarial calculations.

Other factors distinguish insurance risks for terrorist incidents from other contingencies. Unlike natural disasters, government actions can influence the likelihood of terrorist events. Proactive measures can create grievances that may result in more terrorism. After the US retaliatory raid on Libya in April 1986 for its alleged involvement in the La Belle discotheque bombing, there were numerous terrorist attacks against US and UK interests worldwide (Enders and Sandler, 1993). The same experience characterized Israeli retaliations (Brophy-Baermann and Conybeare, 1994). Another difficulty in insuring terrorist attacks is the displacement effect, where defensive actions can merely shift the attack elsewhere. This means that private or public protective measures may have no effect on the overall risk exposure of the insurance industry. In the case, say, of fire, individual actions to limit risks do not make other structures more vulnerable. Another concern of insuring terrorism is the interdependent

---

[3] Different sources will report different insured losses for these events. Somewhat lower figures are found in Navarro and Spencer (2001) and reported in Table 9.1. Figures may differ because of different price deflators, exchange rates, and estimations.

[4] Only $671 million of the $2.9 billion was insured (Wolgast, 2002).

security problem, where individual precautions may be useless unless similar steps are taken by others (Kunreuther and Heal, 2003; Kunreuther and Michel-Kerjan, 2004a, 2004b). This problem reduces individual incentives to curb risks.

If incentives to reduce risk exposure are absent, then insurance premiums may be prohibitively expensive. This became the situation in the United States after 9/11. As a temporary fix, the US government passed the Terrorism Risk Insurance Act (TRIA) on 26 November 2002. Under TRIA, the federal government paid 90% of any losses beyond the deductible from a transnational terrorist attack, while the insurance company covered the remaining 10%. For coverage, the US secretary of the treasury had to certify that the attack was transnational. TRIA allows the insurance company to place a surcharge on all property and casualty policies to recoup losses. Insured buildings and firms did not have to pay any premiums for federal coverage. TRIA was in effect until 31 December 2004 and extended by the treasury secretary until the end of 2005.

The events of 9/11 single-handedly disrupted an important aspect of the private insurance market. In so doing, terrorism created a significant market failure that required federal intervention and amelioration. Without federal action, significant portions of the transportation industry would not have had the necessary liability coverage. Currently, most US companies have not purchased terrorism insurance, which means that another 9/11-type attack could have ruinous effects on some industries. The insurance concerns show that the security of a nation with a market economy may require actions by its government that go beyond protecting against terrorist incidents.

CONCLUDING REMARKS

During fiscal years 2004 and 2005, the DHS budget increased by 17% and 9.6%, respectively. These increases illustrate how homeland security can represent an ever-expanding drain on resources. When the costs of proactive measures and intelligence are added to the expense of DHS defensive actions, one gets a better picture of the burdens imposed by modern-day terrorism on a prime-target nation. Other burdens, not reflected by government expenditures, involve private protection, insurance premiums, and lost time in security lines. The events on 9/11 have had profound economic consequences that are now part of everyday life.

Our evaluation of DHS shows that, in principle, it was a move in the right direction to improve coordination among agencies involved in homeland security and to prevent duplication. However, we conclude that DHS, by not including the intelligence community, did not fully realize its mission. Additionally, a better liaison is needed between the military and DHS if the latter is going to make the right allocations to defensive measures. DHS needs to go further to integrate all aspects in the war on terror. This integration also requires greater interface with foreign counterparts charged with homeland security.

ELEVEN

The Future of Terrorism

Despite the war on terror, the one certainty is that terrorism will continue as a tactic associated with conflicts. As long as there are grievances, there will be conflict and, thus, terrorism. Terrorism will always be present owing to its cost effectiveness and its favoring of the weak against the strong. A bomb that costs a mere few hundred dollars may cause hundreds of millions in damage – for example, the 1993 bombing of the north tower of the World Trade Center. Desperation and frustration are key motives for terrorism. Its cruelty can, at times, make it an end in itself.

Since the start of the modern era of terrorism in the late 1960s, terrorism experts have used current experiences and trends to predict the future of terrorism.[1] Predictions are based on two paradigms: (i) an induction derived from recent events, and (ii) forecasts stemming from statistical methods.[2] Both paradigms have their shortcomings. When experience is used, predictions tend to be reactive, coming from an unanticipated driver – for example, the shift from leftist-based to fundamentalist transnational terrorism. Such predictions are useful until the next major unseen upheaval. Policy ends are better served if changing grievances, players, and tactics are recognized near their onset so that countervailing actions can be proactively engineered at the outset of change. Forecasts based on statistical techniques are less accurate as they are projected into the future. As in the case of experience-based predictions, a

---

[1] For a recent example, see Hoffman (1999). Examples can be found every year in the journals *Terrorism and Political Violence* and *Studies in Conflict & Terrorism*.

[2] Hoffman (1998, 1999) falls into the first category, while Enders and Sandler (1999, 2000, 2005a) fall into the second category.

statistical-fitted trend cannot foresee shocks that throw off forecasts. Trend analysis provides an "average" description that cannot identify an unusual future pattern.

The short-run nature of forecasts may be understood by considering the recent past. Starting in the early 1990s, the sharp downturn in transnational terrorism (see Chapter 3, Figure 3.2) came as a surprise, as did the accompanying upturn in the *proportion* of terrorist incidents involving deaths and casualties (see Chapter 3, Figure 3.6). In this case, the influences of the end of the Cold War, the decline of leftist terrorism, and the rise of fundamentalist terrorism were unanticipated. Until the 20 March 1995 sarin gas attack on the Tokyo subway, most terrorist experts viewed the possibility of chemical, biological, or nuclear terrorist attacks as remote (Jenkins, 1975). The conventional view was that terrorists were constrained by their constituency from using such attacks because they would unleash a sustained retribution by the authorities. After the sarin attack, terrorist experts focused on terrorist events involving weapons of mass destruction (WMDs).[3] This concern escalated after 9/11 and the subsequent discovery of evidence in al-Qaida's hideouts in Afghanistan that the group had actively tried to acquire WMDs. The events of 9/11 and the earlier attempted implosion of the World Trade Center on 26 February 1993 demonstrated that some groups would engage in mass-casualty terrorism. Given this realization, the possible use of WMDs had to be seriously considered, along with effective countermeasures to such attacks.

This final chapter has three purposes. First, we assess the risk of terrorists acquiring and deploying WMDs. Second, we evaluate the current threat of terrorism. Third, we indicate future directions for domestic and transnational terrorism. During the course of the chapter, we argue that domestic terrorism continues to be the predominant form of terrorism, as it has been in the past. Any use of WMDs by terrorists is anticipated to be on a small scale, with a preference for chemical weapons deployed in closed places. The greatest threat of mass-casualty terrorism still comes from bombs or from turning everyday objects – for example, airplanes or tanker trucks – into formidable weapons. Terrorist attacks will remain low-tech and simple, because such attacks allow terrorists to stay clandestine. Moreover, these attacks are cost effective and can still create tremendous fear in a target audience. Suicide attacks are expected to come to North America and Europe.

---

[3] See articles by Cameron (2004), Campbell (1997), Hoffman (1997, 1998, 1999), and Parachini (2003). This interest was bolstered by the rise in fundamentalist terrorism.

MASS-CASUALTY TERRORIST ATTACKS

Officially, WMDs consist of any mine, bomb, or device that releases chemicals, biological organisms, or radiation in sufficient quantity to cause the loss of human life (Bunker, 2000). There is no official requirement that this loss of life be extensive – the mere application of chemical, biological, radiological, or nuclear (CBRN) substances is sufficient to qualify a weapon as a WMD. CBRN weapons can be small-scale, intended for discriminate targeting, or large-scale, meant for mass casualties. The use of chlorine gas by the Tamil Tigers to rout a Sri Lankan army encampment on 18 June 1990 was a small-scale attack of opportunity, whereas the dispersion of sarin by Aum Shinrikyo to murder morning commuters on 20 March 1995 was a large-scale attack with just twelve deaths (Cameron, 2004).

Nuclear terrorism can take two main forms. There can be an attack against a facility containing highly radioactive materials, such as a nuclear power plant, in hopes of causing widespread contamination. For example, a 9/11-type plane attack can be directed at the containment building of a nuclear power plant. Given the reinforced concrete used in these buildings, however, the intended goal of dispersing nuclear material may be difficult to achieve in practice in this scenario. A bomb directed at a truck transporting nuclear waste to a disposal site may be a more realistic method for dispersing radioactive material. A second type of attack involves exploding a nuclear device that is either stolen or built by the terrorists. The former scenario is more likely, since building a bomb would require considerable expertise and access to sufficient quantities of enriched uranium. Most experts do not see the nuclear scenarios as likely in the foreseeable future (see, for example, Ackerman, 2004; Cameron, 2004; Hoffman, 1999; Parachini, 2003). Even stealing a nuclear device presents formidable challenges given that all nations deploy significant safeguards to keep these weapons out of the hands of their enemies.

A radiological weapon consists of radioactive material attached to a dispersion device such as a bomb or a mine. This weapon is known as a *dirty bomb*, which is intended to have long-term economic consequences from long-lived radiation. The necessary material could be stolen from a university laboratory, a nuclear power plant, or a hospital. Highly radioactive daughter elements, such as plutonium, would pose the greatest threat owing to their lengthy half-lives. In some instances, this material could be spread without an explosive device. Dirty bombs are particularly worrisome because they are low-tech and can have significant consequences. Even a small device could disrupt economic and other activities if exploded in a busy harbor (for example, Long Beach, California) or along a city street.

Chemical weapons fall into four general categories and are best used in confined areas where victims are exposed to greater concentrations of the poison (White, 2003). Nerve agents (for example, sarin and VX) enter a person's body through food, drink, or the skin and result in muscle spasms or the rapid discharge of bodily fluids. In some cases, these substances can cause paralysis, leading to suffocation and death. Blood agents (for example, hydrogen cyanide) are typically absorbed through breathing and result in death as they interact with bodily enzymes. Choking agents (for example, chlorine) also enter through breathing and cause the victim's lungs to fill with fluids. Finally, blistering agents (for example, mustard gas) burn the victim's skin and cause disfigurement. Chemical weapons are the easiest of the CBRN for terrorists to acquire and deploy and, thus, pose the greatest terrorism threat (Ackerman, 2004). Aum Shinrikyo's action in 1995 demonstrates that proper dispersion to cause widespread casualties is not always easy to achieve.

Biological agents also fall into four categories (Institute of Medicine, 2002). First, there are highly toxic poisons, such as ricin (obtained from castor beans) and botulinum toxin. These poisons lend themselves to assassinations or small-scale poisonings. Second, there are viruses – smallpox, viral hemorrhagic fevers, and virulent influenzas – that can kill thousands or more victims if a population is exposed. Such viruses can be spread from person to person. A vaccine can protect a population from smallpox if administered in time, but the vaccine carries its own risks, and the authorities must know of the exposure in time. The Department of Homeland Security is stockpiling smallpox vaccine under its biodefense program (see Chapter 10). Third, there are bacteria such as anthrax, which is difficult to "weaponize" so that the bacteria will be inhaled in sufficient quantity by the victims. The optimum aerosol particle size is one to five microns, which is sufficiently small to remain airborne for hours and sufficiently light to be readily dispersed through air-exchange systems in buildings and other closed spaces. The anthrax letters in 2001 contained particles in this size range. Moreover, the spore concentration was 10^{12} per gram, sufficient to infect most people who entered the contaminated buildings (Institute of Medicine, 2002, p. 72). If the infection is caught in time, there are effective antibiotics that can protect infected persons – the key is to know of the exposure. Fourth, there are plagues, including the black plague and tularemia. Sufficiently fine aerosols can be used to disperse all of the biological agents. Efforts by Aum Shinrikyo, al-Qaida, and others to acquire such agents show that there is an interest in engaging in biological terrorist attacks. This then necessitates large expenditures on biodefense even if the probability of an attack is small.

As demonstrated by 9/11, mass-casualty terrorist attacks do not require a WMD. High death tolls can result from using fully fueled airplanes as bombs, the destruction of chemical plants, setting fires in crowded underground stations, or large-scale car bombings. Just the release of deadly chemicals from a plant can kill thousands. Recent statistical analysis of transnational terrorism reveals a greater reliance on deadly car bombings since 9/11 (see Chapter 8). To outdo the carnage of 9/11, terrorists would have to resort to a CBRN attack or an attack on a high-rise building. In the latter case, an attack on a low floor is apt to cause large-scale casualties by limiting the number who can escape. As terrorists escalate attacks to vie for greater media attention, a time may come when terrorists will stage a large-scale CBRN incident. The likelihood of this eventuality is investigated in the next few sections.

For ready reference, Table 11.1 indicates the five types of mass-casualty terrorist events along with their subclasses.

Table 11.1. *Potential Mass-Casualty Terrorist Attacks*

➢ *Nuclear terrorism*
  • Attack against a nuclear facility
  • Exploding a nuclear bomb
➢ *Radiological attacks*
  • Radiological device (for example, dirty bomb)
  • Spread radioactive contaminants without a bomb
➢ *Chemical attacks*
  • Nerve agents (for example, sarin, VX)
  • Blood agents (for example, hydrogen cyanide)
  • Choking agents (for example, chlorine)
  • Blistering agents (for example, mustard gas)
➢ *Biological attacks*
  • Poison (for example, ricin, botulinum toxin)
  • Viruses (for example, smallpox, viral hemorrhagic fevers, flu)
  • Bacteria (for example, anthrax)
  • Plagues (for example, black plague, tularemia)
➢ *Conventional attacks with mass casualties*
  • Airplanes used as bombs
  • Blowing up a chemical plant
  • Large-scale car bombing

Sources: Institute of Medicine (2002), White (2003), and authors' research.

PAST MASS-CASUALTY ATTACKS

To put terrorism carnage in perspective, Table 11.2 lists some of the major mass-casuality terrorist attacks, starting with the 22 July 1946 bombing by Zionist terrorists of the British military headquarters at the King David Hotel, Jerusalem. This bombing greatly contributed to the British decision that its occupation was leading to larger costs than the benefits derived. This incident was the role model for the massive bombings of the 1980s and beyond. The 1980 Bologna railway station bombing by right-wing terrorists is one of the largest European bombings in terms of casualties until the late 1990s and the Chechen bombings in Moscow. The Madrid commuter train bombings of 11 March 2004 are the deadliest nonaerial European terrorist attack so far. Throughout the modern era of terrorism, public transport stations – rail, bus, and plane – have been a favorite venue for major attacks. A landmark suicide truck bombing is the October 1983 bombing of the US Marines' barracks that killed 241 and caused the United States to withdraw its peacekeepers from Lebanon. The Tamil Tigers adopted this form of attack in its domestic terrorist campaign for independence.

A number of features of Table 11.2 are noteworthy. First, no mass-casualty incident killed over 500 persons until the hijackings on 9/11. Second, most major events either involved blowing up a plane in midair or a car or truck bomb. Third, some of these events were simultaneous attacks. Fourth, suicide attacks have been associated with a number of the deadliest attacks since 1983. Fifth, compared with the carnage of past mass-casualty incidents, the successful use of a WMD could result in casualties that dwarf past events. For example, Aum Shinrikyo's 1995 subway attack could have resulted in casualty figures in excess of those of 9/11 had the sarin been purer and had it been dispersed more effectively (Cameron, 2004). Clearly, terrorist attacks involving WMDs could surpass a casualty threshold that no previous incident has approached.

ASSESSING THE LIKELIHOOD OF CBRN ATTACKS

This assessment requires recognition of those factors that either inhibit or promote CBRN attacks. Inhibitors are many and so far have represented a formidable barrier. Most groups are inhibited from CBRN attacks by a need to maintain constituency support and funding, which may end with the indiscriminate use of a WMD. This is particularly true of separatist, ethno-nationalist, and leftist terrorists, but is not true of fundamentalists

Table 11.2. *Select Mass-Casualty Terrorist Attacks*

Date	Event	Perpetrator	Death Toll
22 July 1946	Bombing of local British military headquarters at King David Hotel, Jerusalem.	Irgun Zvai Leumi	91
2 Aug. 1980	Bombing of Bologna railway station.	Armed Revolutionary Nuclei	84
23 Oct. 1983	Suicide truck bombing of US Marines' barracks in Beirut.	Hezbollah	241
23 June 1985	Downing of Air-India Boeing 747 en route from Montreal to London.	Sikh extremists	329
15 March 1987	Car bombing of the main bus terminal in Colombo, Sri Lanka.	Tamil Tigers	105
21 Dec. 1988	Downing of Pan Am flight 103, en route from London to New York.	Libyan intelligence agent	270
19 Sept. 1989	Downing of Union des Transports (UTA) flight 772 en route from Brazzaville to Paris.	Hezbollah	171
12 March 1993	Thirteen bombings in Bombay.	Pakistani agents	317
19 April 1995	Truck bombing of the Alfred P. Murrah Federal Building in Oklahoma.	Timothy McVeigh	168
7 Aug. 1998	Simultaneous bombings of US embassies in Nairobi, Kenya, and Dar es Salaam, Tanzania.	al-Qaida	301
13 Sept. 1998	Car bombing of an eight-story Moscow apartment building. Bombs on 8 and 9 September in Dagestan and Moscow also killed 64 and 94, respectively.	Chechen rebels	118
11 Sept. 2001	Four suicide hijackings that crashed into the World Trade Center towers, the Pentagon, and a field in rural Pennsylvania.	al-Qaida	2,871[a]
11 March 2004	Bombing of commuter trains and stations during morning rush hour in Madrid	al-Qaida	190
1 Sept. 2004	Barricade hostage seizure of school children and parents in Beslan.	Chechen rebels	344

[a] Updated death toll as of 20 December 2004 at National Obituary Archive-Honor Roll (2004) [http://www.arrangeonline.com/notablePersons/honorroll.asp].
Source: Quillen (2002a, 2002b).

and some nontraditional extremists – for example, Aum Shinrikyo (Gurr, 2004; Post, 2004). There is also the retribution worry – a WMD attack might result in an all-out effort by the authorities to destroy the group, not unlike what happened to al-Qaida in the aftermath of 9/11. The latter experience, however, shows that complete eradication is not so easy.

Technical considerations also hamper the use of WMDs. First, there is a weaponization hurdle that must be overcome to mount a chemical, biological, or nuclear attack. For example, the necessary implosion required to set off a nuclear bomb is a formidable technical requirement. Second, the requisite ingredients must be acquired, which is a relevant consideration for some but not all WMDs. Third, efforts to acquire these materials put members in jeopardy from sting and counterterrorist operations. Fourth, there are handling risks to members from chemical, biological, and radiological agents that must be managed.

As they adopted loosely connected organizational structures to minimize infiltration risk, some terrorist groups compromised their ability to acquire CBRN (Merrari, 1999). This follows because reduced centralization limits the resources and personnel that can be coordinated to make the necessary technological breakthroughs. Aum Shinrikyo stayed centralized and, hence, sustained an organization-wide setback when their headquarters were raided in 1995. By contrast, al-Qaida's decentralized structure protected it during the post-9/11 attacks, but at the price of not being able to develop CBRN weapons.

A final impediment is the cost-effectiveness of conventional attacks. As long as conventional incidents can create sufficient anxiety at a lower cost than nonconventional incidents, terrorists will not find the latter attractive. The recent cost-effectiveness of suicide attacks make them a likely alternative to WMD in the near term. A suicide attack on a US shopping mall would attract much media attention. Moreover, suicide attacks are easily managed with current loosely tied terrorist structures.

Other factors promote terrorist WMD attacks. The rise of fundamentalist terrorists, who demonize a target population, increases the likelihood of such attacks, as does the presence of terrorists possessing millenarian, apocalyptic, or messianic visions (Post, 2004). These groups are not trying to win over a constituency and view the act as an end in itself; thus, they are not constrained in the carnage that they cause. Their deepseated grievances require the destruction of the "enemy." Heavy-handed proactive measures by targeted governments may heighten grievances and encourage the acquisition of more formidable weapons (Rosendorff and Sandler, 2004). Such proactive responses may also enhance recruitment, thereby attracting members with the capabilities needed to produce

Table 11.3. *Inhibiting and Promoting Factors Regarding Terrorists'*
Use of WMDs

➢ *Inhibiting factors*
- Losing constituency support and fund raising
- Absorbing retribution/reaction from target
- Acquiring required ingredients
- Handling risk to members
- Surmounting weaponization hurdle
- Succumbing to counterterrorist efforts (including sting operations)
- Organizational structure and need for clandestine operations
- Utilizing the cost effectiveness of conventional attacks

➢ *Promoting factors*
- Possessing fundamentalist beliefs that demonize a target population
- Possessing millenarian, apocalyptic, or messianic vision
- Having a deep-seated grievance that requires destruction of one's enemy
- Reacting to excessive proactive measures
- Supporting efforts by a rogue or failed state

WMDs. Another facilitator is support by rogue or failed states. This may be particularly true for chemical weapons, because twenty-six nations currently possess chemical weapons and others seek them (White, 2003, p. 251).

Table 11.3 lists the inhibiting and promoting factors regarding terrorists' use of WMDs. Most terrorist experts see *small-scale* chemical and radiological attacks as likely in the near term. Large-scale CBRN attacks and/or nuclear bombs are not likely given the overwhelming influence of the numerous impediments. Loose terrorist structures, the cost-effectiveness of conventional attacks, and the weaponization hurdle are the main inhibitors that should continue to limit the possibility of large-scale WMD terrorism in the foreseeable future, despite the presence of fundamentalists and extremists willing to cross the WMD threshold.

CBRN ATTACKS: PAST RECORD

A good way to gauge the likelihood of WMD terrorism is to examine a past record of such attacks. Table 11.4 displays some past incidents involving chemical, biological, and radiological agents. This list includes only some of the important events. For a more complete list, consult Ackerman (2004) and the Center for Nonproliferation Studies, Monterey Institute of International Studies. The Monterey WMD Terrorism Database contains over 1,200 incidents; about a third of these are hoaxes (Ackerman, 2004). Most past incidents involve chemicals. This database is intended to be as

Table 11.4. *Past Incidents of Chemical, Biological, and Radiological Terrorism*

➤ *Chemical attacks*
  - April 1984: Christian Patriots stockpiled 30 gallons of cyanide to poison reservoirs in Chicago and Washington, DC.
  - 18 June 1990: Tamil Tigers used chlorine gas to rout a Sri Lankan army encampment, injuring sixty.
  - 28 March 1992: Kurdistan Workers' Party (PKK) put cyanide in three water tanks of a Turkish air force base outside Istanbul. There were no injuries.
  - 26 February 1993: Sodium cyanide canister was placed near a fertilizer bomb at the World Trade Center. The heat of the bomb destroyed the chemical.
  - June 1994: Aum Shinrikyo members released sarin gas near the judicial building in Matsumoto, Japan. Seven people died and 150 were injured.
  - 15 March, 1995: Attaché case with vents and fans found at Tokyo subway station.
  - 20 March 1995: Aum's sarin attack on a Tokyo subway station during morning rush hour. Twelve died and over 1,000 were sickened.
  - 5 May 1995: Hydrogen cyanide device set to go off in a men's room in Shinjuku station by Aum members. Device deactivated in time.

➤ *Biological attacks*
  - October 1984: Followers of Bhagwan Shree Rajneesh poisoned twelve salad bars with salmonella in The Dalles, Oregon, in hopes of winning a local election. 751 people were sickened.
  - April 1990: Aum members dispersed botulinum toxin near the Japanese Diet. There were no injuries.
  - 11 September 2001 and 9 October 2001: The mailing of anthrax letters to US elected officials and the news media. Five dead and twenty-two people sickened.

➤ *Radiological attacks*
  - November 1995: Chechen rebels bury caesium-137 in Moscow's Izmailovsky Park. Warned authorities. No injuries were reported.
  - 1998: Chechen rebels attached radioactive materials to a mine near a railway line in Argun, Chechnya. No injuries were reported.

Sources: Ackerman (2004), Cameron (2004), Campbell (1997), especially for Aum Shinrikyo incidents, Hoffman (1998), Institute of Medicine (2002), Merrari (1999), and Parachini (2003).

inclusive as possible and, hence, includes some events that do not fit the definition of terrorism – for example, incidents with no political motive.

As indicated in Table 11.4, Aum Shinrikyo launched a sarin attack near the judicial building in Matsumoto, Japan, in June 1994, well in advance of the 20 March 1995 sarin attack on the Tokyo subway. Aum Shinrikyo tried a hydrogen cyanide attack at a train station on 5 May 1995, but the device was deactivated before anyone was injured. The chemical attack on the Sri Lankan army outpost by the Tamil Tigers was very limited and put the group's own members at risk when the chlorine gas drifted back over them. No subsequent chemical attacks were tried by the Tamil Tigers.

There have been three noteworthy biological incidents, two involving religious cults and one undertaken by an unknown perpetrator. This latter incident concerns the anthrax letters. Given its temporal proximity to 9/11, the anthrax incident created more anxiety than its consequences warranted, with just five dead and twenty-two people sickened. The most notable thing about this incident is the weapons-grade anthrax used in the attack, leading authorities to suspect someone involved with the government's biological weapons program. If these anthrax spores had been placed surreptitiously into the ventilation system of one of the targeted buildings, the number of deaths could have been quite large. This incident indicates the possibility of such attacks. Moreover, it highlights the fact that the weaponization hurdle *may* be circumvented by taking materials from a government weapons program or a research laboratory. This risk also applies to chemical, radiological, and nuclear attacks.

In Table 11.4, the two noteworthy radiological incidents both involved Chechen rebels and resulted in no casualties. The second incident is of interest because it indicates that terrorists once tried to set off a crude dirty bomb.

The past record tends to confirm the experts' assessment that a chemical attack is the most likely and that a nuclear attack is highly unlikely. Radiological and biological attacks have intermediate probabilities. In addition, the likely perpetrators of a large-scale WMD attack would be religious extremists or fundamentalist terrorists. Other terrorist types might engage in a small-scale WMD attack with little or no collateral damage. With the exception of the Tokyo subway attack, the past record does not include CBRN use that would have resulted in thousands of casualties, such as one associates with WMDs. The most likely future scenario is the continued reliance by terrorists on an occasional large-scale conventional attack like those of 9/11 and 3/11. Nevertheless, resources will still need to be allocated to biodefense and to preparing for chemical and/or radiological terrorist attacks.

SHAPE OF TERRORISM TO COME

We now come to the most difficult task – that of predicting the future of terrorism. We take a conservative approach and base our predictions on our knowledge of terrorism since 1968 and our body of past empirical work. Our intention is to come up with predictions that are likely to hold; our intention is not to be provocative.

Domestic terrorism will continue to overshadow transnational terrorism in terms of the number of incidents. With so many civil conflicts raging around the globe, this is a sure prediction. Moreover, domestic terrorist incidents typically outnumber transnational incidents by more than eight to one. Both domestic and transnational terrorism will remain cyclical in nature, so that a downturn should not necessarily be projected into the future. Terrorists will continue to respond to countermeasures by shifting tactics, venues, and targets in order to exploit opportunities. They will also be inventive in developing new ways to circumvent countermeasures. Successful innovations will be rapidly disseminated worldwide.

As long as religious-based terrorism remains the dominant influence in transnational terrorist attacks, these attacks will remain more deadly *per incident* than during the 1970s and 1980s. Suicide terrorist incidents will increase in prevalence and will occur in the United States and Europe – e.g., the London suicide bombings of 7 July 2005. On average, suicide attacks are thirteen times more deadly per incident than a typical transnational incident and have caused some targeted governments to make major concessions (Pape, 2003). Suicide missions are logistically simple and relatively inexpensive, making them attractive to some terrorist groups. Geographically, the region of concentration for transnational terrorist attacks will be the Middle East, followed by Asia and Eurasia. Most transnational terrorist incidents against US and European interests will occur in these three regions. Because of augmentation of homeland security in both the United States and Europe, the venue for transnational terrorism will remain poorer countries, less able to protect against such attacks. The regional shift to the Middle East, Asia, and Eurasia began with the rise of fundamentalist terrorism in the 1980s (Enders and Sandler, 2005b). On rare occasions, terrorists will resort to a large-scale conventional attack; only a couple of terrorist spectaculars are anticipated each year. Any use of WMDs will involve chemical weapons on a local scale.

Terrorists will increasingly rely on the internet as a way to link widely dispersed networks and to coordinate attacks. The internet has greatly facilitated the ability of terrorist groups to expand their territorial reach and to become less vulnerable by keeping links loose. For some groups, individual cells are quite autonomous. In Iraq, Abu Masab al-Zarqawi used the internet to post videos of beheadings and hostages pleading for their lives as a means to heighten anxiety and public pressure and to induce governments and firms to withdraw their personnel. In many ways, the internet is serving the same purpose as city walls in medieval times, when severed heads were displayed to warn off one's enemies. Many terrorists groups use web sites to post political statements, list grievances, claim responsibility for past attacks, and recruit new members. The internet also allows for the possibility of cyber terrorism, where a politically motivated attack is directed at disrupting some organization's computers, servers, and web postings. Terrorism can also take the form of viruses and worms when disseminated for a political purpose. To date, most terrorist groups have used the internet to facilitate their own operations rather than to disrupt the operations of a target audience.

Future terrorist attacks are likely to be directed at economic targets. For example, diseases can be introduced into American cattle herds to create significant losses. Research Centers of Excellence have been established by the Department of Homeland Security (DHS) at Texas A & M University, with links to other universities, to protect against terrorist-induced animal diseases and at the University of Minnesota to limit terrorist attacks on the US food supply. The first DHS Research Center of Excellence at the University of Southern California assesses the risks to critical infrastructure (for example, ports, communication networks, energy grids, and transportation links) from terrorist attacks, including the possibility of a dirty bomb in Long Beach. This center is also developing policy recommendations for protecting this infrastructure through hardening and redundancy (for example, "parallel" electricity transmission lines).

CONCLUDING REMARKS

As stated at the outset, terrorism is here to stay. Terrorism levels the playing field between the weak and the strong and, as such, provides the weak with a cost-effective means to engage in conflict. We do not see the nature of terrorism showing much change in the near term. Although expenditures on counters to WMDs will increase annually, we do not view a large-scale WMD attack as being very likely. The bomb will remain the terrorists' favorite mode of attack. Nevertheless, terrorists will exploit modern technology and adapt innovations to their purposes, as they have done with the internet. Such innovations mean that counterterrorism measures will become ever more costly. This increased expense is further bolstered by an increase in the variety of potential attacks.

References

Abadie, Alberto and Javier Gardeazabal (2003), "The Economic Cost of Conflict: A Case Study of the Basque Country," *American Economic Review*, 93(1), 113–32.

Ackerman, Gary (2004), "WMD Terrorism Research: Where to from Here?," unpublished manuscript, Center for Nonproliferation Studies, Monterey Institute of International Studies, Monterey, CA.

Alexander, Yonah and Dennis Pluchinsky (1992), *Europe's Red Terrorists: The Fighting Communist Organizations* (London: Frank Cass).

Anderton, Charles H. and John R. Carter (2005), "On Rational Choice Theory and the Study of Terrorism," *Defence and Peace Economics*, 16(4), 275–82.

Arce M., Daniel G. and Todd Sandler (2005), "Counterterrorism: A Game-Theoretic Analysis," *Journal of Conflict Resolution*, 49(2), 183–200.

Arquilla, John and David Ronfeldt (eds.) (2001), *Networks and Netwars* (Santa Monica, CA: RAND).

Atkinson, Scott E., Todd Sandler, and John Tschirhart (1987), "Terrorism in a Bargaining Framework," *Journal of Law and Economics*, 30(1), 1–21.

Azam, Jean-Paul (2005), "Suicide-Bombing as Inter-Generational Investment," *Public Choice*, 122(1–2), 177–98.

Basile, Mark (2004), "Going to the Source: Why Al Qaida's Financial Network Is Likely to Withstand the Current War on Terrorist Financing," *Studies in Conflicts & Terrorism*, 27(3), 169–85.

Becker, Gary S. and Kevin M. Murphy (2001), "Prosperity Will Rise out of the Ashes," *Wall Street Journal* (Eastern edition), 29 October 2001, A.22.

Berman, Eli and David D. Laitin (2005), "Hard Targets: Theory and Evidence on Suicide Attacks," unpublished manuscript, University of California at San Diego, San Diego, CA.

Blomberg, S. Brock, Gregory D. Hess, and Athanasios Orphanides (2004), "The Macroeconomic Consequences of Terrorism," *Journal of Monetary Economics*, 51(5), 1007–32.

Blomberg, S. Brock, Gregory D. Hess, and Akila Weerapana (2004), "Economic Conditions and Terrorism," *European Journal of Political Economy*, 20(2), 463–78.

Brophy-Baermann, Bryan and John A. C. Conybeare (1994), "Retaliating against Terrorism: Rational Expectations and the Optimality of Rules versus Discretion," *American Journal of Political Science*, 38(1), 196–210.

Bruce, Neil (2001), *Public Finance and the American Economy*, 2nd ed. (Boston: Addison-Wesley).

Bueno de Mesquita, Ethan (2005), "Conciliation, Commitment and Counterterrorism: A Formal Model," *International Organization*, 59(1), 145–76.

Bunker, Robert (2000), "Weapons of Mass Disruption and Terrorism," *Terrorism and Political Violence*, 12(1), 37–46.

Bureau of Economic Analysis (2001), "Business Situation," *Survey of Current Business*, 81(11), [http://www.bea.doc.gov/bea/ARTICLES/2001/11november/1101bsa.pdf], accessed 10 January 2005.

Bureau of Labor Statistics (2003), "Extended Mass Layoffs and the 9/11 Attacks," *Monthly Labor Review: The Editor's Desk*, [http://www.bls.gov/opub/ted/2003/sept/wk2/art03.htm], accessed 10 January 2005.

Bush, George W. (2002), *Securing the Homeland: Strengthening the Nation* (Washington, DC: White House).

Cameron, Gavin (2004), "Weapons of Mass Destruction Terrorism Research: Past and Future," in Andrew Silke (ed.), *Research on Terrorism: Trends, Achievements and Failures* (London: Frank Cass), 72–90.

Campbell, James K. (1997), "Excerpts from Research Study 'Weapons of Mass Destruction and Terrorism: Proliferation by Non-State Actors,'" *Terrorism and Political Violence*, 9(2), 24–50.

Chen, Andrew H. and Thomas F. Siems (2004), "The Effects of Terrorism on Global Capital Markets," *European Journal of Political Economy*, 20(2), 249–66.

Combs, Cindy C. (2003), *Terrorism in the Twenty-First Century*, 3rd ed. (Upper Saddle River, NJ: Prentice-Hall).

Congressional Budget Office (2004), *The Budget and Economic Outlook: An Update*, [http://www.cbo.gov/ftpdocs/57xx/doc5773/08-24-BudgetUpdate.pdf], accessed 12 January 2005.

Congressional Research Service (2002), "The USA Patriot Act: A Sketch," CRS Report No. RS21203, Library of Congress, Washington, DC, [http://www.fas.org/irp/RS21203.pdf], accessed 11 July 2004.

Cornes, Richard and Todd Sandler (1996), *The Theory of Externalities, Public Goods, and Club Goods*, 2nd ed. (Cambridge: Cambridge University Press).

Cross, John G. (1969), *The Economics of Bargaining* (New York: Basic Books).

Cross, John G. (1977), "Negotiations as a Learning Process," *Journal of Conflict Resolution*, 21(4), 581–606.

Davis, Darren W. and Brian D. Silver (2004), "Civil Liberties vs. Security: Public Opinion in the Context of the Terrorist Attacks on America," *American Journal of Political Science*, 48(1), 38–46.

Department of Homeland Security (DHS) (2002), "DHS Organization," [http://www.dhs.gov/dhspublic/display?theme=59&content=312&print=true], accessed 25 August 2003.

Department of Homeland Security (DHS) (2003), "Budget in Brief," [http://www.dhs.gov/interweb/assetlibrary/FY_2004_BUDGET_IN_BRIEF.pdf], accessed 5 March 2004.

Department of Homeland Security (DHS) (2004), "Budget in Brief, Fiscal Year 2005," [http://www.dhs.gov/interweb/assetlibrary/FY_2005_BIB_4.pdf], accessed 3 April 2004.

Department of Justice (2004), website on victim compensation, [http://www.usdoj.gov/final_report.pdf], accessed 14 March 2005.

Doyle, Michael W. (1997), *Ways of War and Peace* (New York: Norton).

Drakos, Konstantinos (2004), "Terrorism-Induced Structural Shifts in Financial Risk: Airline Stocks in the Aftermath of the September 11th Terror Attacks," *European Journal of Political Economy,* 20(2), 436–46.

Drakos, Konstantinos and Ali M. Kutan (2003), "Regional Effects of Terrorism on Tourism in Three Mediterranean Countries," *Journal of Conflict Resolution,* 47(5), 621–41.

Durch, William J. (1993), "Paying the Tab: Financial Crisis," in William J. Durch (ed.), *The Evolution of UN Peacekeeping: Case Studies and Comparative Analysis* (New York: St. Martin's), 39–55.

Eckstein, Zvi and Daniel Tsiddon (2004), "Macroeconomic Consequences of Terror: Theory and the Case of Israel," *Journal of Monetary Economics,* 51(5), 971–1002.

The Economist (2003), "Al-Qaeda Operations Are Rather Cheap," *The Economist,* 369(8344), 45.

The Economist (2004), "Terror's New Depths," *The Economist,* 373(8392), 23–5.

Eldor, Rafi and Rafi Melnick (2004), "Financial Markets and Terrorism," *European Journal of Political Economy,* 20(2), 367–86.

Enders, Walter (2004), *Applied Econometric Time Series,* 2nd ed. (Hoboken, NJ: Wiley).

Enders, Walter and Todd Sandler (1991), "Causality between Transnational Terrorism and Tourism: The Case of Spain," *Terrorism,* 14(1), 49–58.

Enders, Walter and Todd Sandler (1993), "The Effectiveness of Anti-Terrorism Policies: A Vector-Autoregression-Intervention Analysis," *American Political Science Review,* 87(4), 829–44.

Enders, Walter and Todd Sandler (1995), "Terrorism: Theory and Applications," in Keith Hartley and Todd Sandler (eds.), *Handbook of Defense Economics, Vol. 1* (Amsterdam: North-Holland), 213–49.

Enders, Walter and Todd Sandler (1996), "Terrorism and Foreign Direct Investment in Spain and Greece," *Kyklos,* 49(3), 331–52.

Enders, Walter and Todd Sandler (1999), "Transnational Terrorism in the Post-Cold War Era," *International Studies Quarterly,* 43(2), 145–67.

Enders, Walter and Todd Sandler (2000), "Is Transnational Terrorism Becoming More Threatening? A Time-Series Investigation," *Journal of Conflict Resolution,* 44(3), 307–32.

Enders, Walter and Todd Sandler (2004), "What Do We Know about the Substitution Effect in Transnational Terrorism?," in Andrew Silke (ed.), *Research on Terrorism: Trends, Achievements and Failures* (London: Frank Cass), 119–37.

Enders, Walter and Todd Sandler (2005a), "After 9/11: Is It All Different Now?," *Journal of Conflict Resolution*, 49(2), 259–77.

Enders, Walter and Todd Sandler (2005b), "Distribution of Transnational Terrorism among Countries by Income Classes and Geography after 9/11," unpublished manuscript, University of Southern California, Los Angeles, CA.

Enders, Walter, Todd Sandler, and Jon Cauley (1990a), "UN Conventions, Technology, and Retaliation in the Fight against Terrorism: An Econometric Evaluation," *Terrorism and Political Violence*, 2(1), 83–105.

Enders, Walter, Todd Sandler, and Jon Cauley (1990b), "Assessing the Impact of Terrorist-Thwarting Policies: An Intervention Time Series Approach," *Defence Economics*, 2(1), 1–18.

Enders, Walter, Todd Sandler, and Gerald F. Parise (1992), "An Econometric Analysis of the Impact of Terrorism on Tourism," *Kyklos*, 45(4), 531–54.

Eubank, William L. and Leonard B. Weinberg (1994), "Does Democracy Encourage Terrorism?," *Terrorism and Political Violence*, 6(4), 417–35.

Eubank, William L. and Leonard B. Weinberg (2001), "Terrorism and Democracy: Perpetrators and Victims," *Terrorism and Political Violence*, 13(1), 155–64.

Faria, João R. (2003), "Terror Cycles," *Studies in Nonlinear Dynamics and Econometrics*, 7(1), 1–11.

Faria, João R. and Daniel G. Arce M. (2005), "Terror Support and Recruitment," *Defence and Peace Economics*, 16(4), 263–73.

Feichtinger, G., R. F. Hartl, P. M. Kort, and A. J. Novak (2001), "Terrorism Control in the Tourism Industry," *Journal of Optimization Theory and Applications*, 108(2), 283–96.

Frey, Bruno S. (2004), *Dealing with Terrorism – Stick or Carrot?* (Cheltenham, UK: Edward Elgar).

Frey, Bruno S. and Simon Luechinger (2003), "How to Fight Terrorism: Alternatives to Deterrence," *Defence and Peace Economics*, 14(4), 237–49.

Gallagher, Robert P. (2003). "The Psychological Impact of 9-11 on College Students and Suggestions for How Counseling Centers Can Prepare for War and/or Future Terroristic Attacks," *Commission for Counseling and Psychological Services Newsletter*, [http://www.acpa.nche.edu/comms/comm07/feature3-03.htm], accessed 18 February 2005.

Gerges, Fawaz A. and Christopher Isham (2003), "Sign of Weakness? Do Overseas Terror Strikes Suggest Al Qaeda Inability to Hit US?," *ABC News*, November 22.

Graham, Sarah (2001), "9-11: The Psychological Aftermath," *Scientific American*, [http://www.sciam.com/article.cfm?articleID=00092E93-AAAB-1C75–9B81809EC588EF21], accessed 18 February 2005.

Gurr, Ted Robert (2004), "Which Minorities Might Use Weapons of Mass Destruction?," unpublished manuscript, Minorities at Risk Project, University of Maryland, College Park, MD.

Hainmüller, Jens and Jan Martin Lemnitzer (2003), "Why Do Europeans Fly Safer? The Politics of Airport Security in Europe and the US," *Terrorism and Political Violence*, 15(4), 1–36.

Heal, Geoffrey and Howard Kunreuther (2003), "You Only Die Once: Managing Discrete Interdependent Risks," unpublished manuscript, Columbia University, New York, NY.

Heal, Geoffrey and Howard Kunreuther (2005), "IDS Models of Airline Security," *Journal of Conflict Resolution*, 49(2), 201–17.

Hirshleifer, Jack (1983), "From the Weakest-Link to Best-Shot: The Voluntary Provision of Public Goods," *Public Choice*, 41(3), 371–86.

Hoffman, Bruce (1997), "The Confluence of International and Domestic Trends in Terrorism," *Terrorism and Political Violence*, 9(1), 1–15.

Hoffman, Bruce (1998), *Inside Terrorism* (New York: Columbia University Press).

Hoffman, Bruce (1999), "Terrorism Trends and Prospects," in Ian O. Lesser, Bruce Hoffman, John Arquilla David Ronfeldt, and Michele Zanini (eds.), *Countering the New Terrorism* (Santa Monica, CA: RAND), 7–38.

Im, Eric I., Jon Cauley, and Todd Sandler (1987), "Cycles and Substitutions in Terrorist Activities: A Spectral Approach," *Kyklos*, 40(2), 238–55.

Institute of Medicine (2002), *Biological Threats and Terrorism: Assessing the Science and Response Capabilities* (Washington, DC: National Academy Press).

International Monteary Fund (IMF) (2001a), *Intensified Fund Involvement in Anti-Money Laundering Work and Combating the Financing of Terrorism* (Washington, DC: IMF).

International Monetary Fund (IMF) (2001b), "How Has September 11 Influenced the Global Economy?," *World Economic Outlook*, 18 December 2001, 14–33.

Islam, Muhammad Q. and Wassim N. Shahin (1989), "Economic Methodology Applied to Political Hostage-Taking in Light of the Iran-Contra Affair," *Southern Economic Journal*, 55(4), 1019–24.

Ito, Harumi and Darin Lee (2004), "Assessing the Impact of the September 11 Terrorist Attacks on U.S. Airline Demand," unpublished manuscript, Brown University, Providence, RI.

Jain, Sanjay and Sarun Mukand (2004), "The Economics of High-Visibility Terrorism," *European Journal of Political Economy*, 20(2), 479–94.

Jenkins, Brian (1975), "Will Terrorists Go Nuclear?," Report No. P-5541, RAND Corp., Santa Monica, CA.

Krueger, Alan B. and Jitka Maleckova (2003), "Education, Poverty, and Terrorism: Is There a Causal Connection?," *Journal of Economic Perspectives*, 17(4), 119–44.

Kunreuther, Howard and Geoffrey Heal (2003), "Interdependent Security," *Journal of Risk and Uncertainty*, 26(2–3), 231–49.

Kunreuther, Howard and Erwann Michel-Kerjan (2004a), "Policy Watch: Challenge for Terrorism Risk Insurance in the United States," *Journal of Economic Perspectives*, 18(4), 201–14.

Kunreuther, Howard and Erwann Michel-Kerjan (2004b), "Dealing with Extreme Events: New Challenges for Terrorist Risk Coverage," unpublished manuscript, Wharton School of Economics, University of Pennsylvania, Philadelphia, PA.

Kunreuther, Howard, Erwann Michel-Kerjan, and Beverly Porter (2003), "Assessing, Managing and Financing Extreme Events: Dealing with Terrorism," Working Paper 10179, National Bureau of Economic Research, Cambridge, MA.

Landes, William M. (1978), "An Economic Study of US Aircraft Hijackings, 1961–1976," *Journal of Law and Economics,* 21(1), 1–31.

Lapan, Harvey E. and Todd Sandler (1988), "To Bargain or Not to Bargain: That Is the Question," *American Economic Review,* 78(2), 16–20.

Lapan, Harvey E. and Todd Sandler (1993), "Terrorism and Signalling," *European Journal of Political Economy,* 9(3), 383–97.

Laqueur, Walter (ed.) (1976), *The Israel-Arab Reader: A Documentary History of the Middle East Conflict* (New York: Bantam).

Laqueur, Walter (ed.) (1978), *The Terrorism Reader: A Historical Anthology* (New York: New American Library).

Lee, Dwight R. (1988), "Free Riding and Paid Riding in the Fight against Terrorism," *American Economic Review,* 78(2), 22–6.

Lee, Dwight R. and Todd Sandler (1989), "On the Optimal Retaliation against Terrorists: The Paid-Rider Option," *Public Choice,* 62(2), 141–52.

Levitt, Matthew (2003), "Stemming the Flow of Terrorist Financing: Practical and Conceptual Challenges," *Fletcher Forum of World Affairs,* 27(1), 59–70.

Lexis Nexis (2004), "Academic Search Engine," [http://web.lexis-nexis.com/universe], accessed throughout September and October 2004.

Li, Quan (2005), "Does Democracy Promote Transnational Terrorist Incidents?," *Journal of Conflict Resolution,* 49(2), 278–97.

Li, Quan and Drew Schaub (2004), "Economic Globalization and Transnational Terrorism," *Journal of Conflict Resolution,* 48(2), 230–58.

Lichbach, Mark I. (1987), "Deterrence or Escalation? The Puzzle of Aggregate Studies of Repression and Dissent," *Journal of Conflict Resolution,* 31(2), 266–97.

Merrari, Ariel (1999), "Terrorism as a Strategy of Struggle: Past and Future," *Terrorism and Political Violence,* 11(4), 52–65.

Mickolus, Edward F. (1980), *Transnational Terrorism: A Chronology of Events 1968–1979* (Westport, CT: Greenwood Press).

Mickolus, Edward F. (1982), *International Terrorism: Attributes of Terrorist Events, 1968–1977* (ITERATE 2), Inter-University Consortium for Political and Social Research, Ann Arbor, MI.

Mickolus, Edward F., Todd Sandler, and Jean M. Murdock (1989), *International Terrorism in the 1980s: A Chronology of Events,* 2 vols. (Ames: Iowa State University Press).

Mickolus, Edward F., Todd Sandler, Jean M. Murdock, and Peter Flemming (2004), *International Terrorism: Attributes of Terrorist Events, 1968–2003* (ITERATE) (Dunn Loring, VA: Vinyard Software).

Mills, Susan R. (1990), "The Financing of UN Peacekeeping Operations: The Need for a Sound Financial Basis," in Indar Jit Rikhye and Kjell Skjelsback (eds.), *The United Nations and Peacekeeping: Results, Limitations and Prospects: The Lessons of 40 Years of Experience* (Houndmills, UK: Macmillan), 91–110.

Nasr, Kameel (1997), *Arab and Israeli Terrorism: The Causes and Effects of Political Violence, 1936–1993* (Jefferson, NC: McFarland and Co.).

National Commission on Terrorist Attacks upon the United States (2004), *The 9/11 Commission Report* (New York: Norton).

National Obituary Archive-Honor Roll (2004), "Death Toll from 9/11," [http//:www.arrangeonline.com/notablePersons/honorroll.asp], accessed 24 December 2004.

Navarro, Peter and Aron Spencer (2001), "September 11, 2001: Assessing the Costs of Terrorism," *Milken Institute Review*, Fourth Quarter 2001, 16–31.

Nelson, Paul S. and John L. Scott (1992), "Terrorism and the Media: An Empirical Analysis," *Defense Economics*, 3(4), 329–39.

Nitsch, Volker and Dieter Schumacher (2004), "Terrorism and International Trade: An Empirical Investigation," *European Journal of Political Economy*, 20(2) 423–33.

Organization of Economic Cooperation and Development (OECD) (2003), "Financial Action Task Force on Money Laundering," [http://www1.oecd.org/fatf], accessed 16 September 2003.

Overgaard, Per B. (1994), "The Scale of Terrorist Attacks as a Signal of Resources," *Journal of Conflict Resolution*, 38(3), 452–78.

Pape, Robert A. (2003), "The Strategic Logic of Suicide Terrorism," *American Political Science Review*, 97(3), 343–61.

Parachini, John (2003), "Putting WMD Terrorism into Perspective," *The Washington Quarterly*, 26(4), 37–50.

Pearl, Marc A. (1987), "Terrorism – Historical Perspective on U.S. Congressional Action," *Terrorism*, 10(2), 139–43.

Post, Jerrold M. (2004), "Differentiating the Threat of Chemical/Biological Terrorism: Motivations and Constraints," unpublished manuscript, George Washington University, Washington, DC.

Post, Jerrold M., Keven G. Ruby, and Eric D. Shaw (2000), "From Car Bombs to Logic Bombs: The Growing Threat from Information Terrorism," *Terrorism and Political Violence*, 12(2), 97–122.

Post, Jerrold M., Keven G. Ruby, and Eric D. Shaw (2002), "The Radical Group in Context 1: An Integrated Framework for the Analysis of Group Risk for Terrorism," *Studies in Conflict & Terrorism*, 25(2), 73–100.

Quillen, Chris (2002a), "A Historical Analysis of Mass Casualty Bombers," *Studies in Conflict & Terrorism*, 25(5), 279–92.

Quillen, Chris (2002b), "Mass Casualty Bombings Chronology," *Studies in Conflict & Terrorism*, 25(2), 293–302.

Rapoport, David C. (1984), "Fear and Trembling: Terrorism in Three Religious Traditions," *American Political Science Review*, 78(3), 658–77.

Rapoport, David C. (2004), "Modern Terror: The Four Waves," in Audrey K. Cronin and James M. Ludes (eds.), *Attacking Terrorism: Elements of a Grand Strategy* (Washington, DC: Georgetown University Press), 46–73.

Rosendorff, B. Peter and Todd Sandler (2004), "Too Much of a Good Thing? The Proactive Response Dilemma," *Journal of Conflict Resolution*, 48(5), 657–71.

Sandler, Todd (1992), *Collective Action: Theory and Applications* (Ann Arbor: University of Michigan Press).

Sandler, Todd (1995), "On the Relationship between Democracy and Terrorism," *Terrorism and Political Violence*, 7(4), 1–9.

Sandler, Todd (1997), *Global Challenges: An Approach to Environmental, Political, and Economic Problems* (Cambridge: Cambridge University Press).

Sandler, Todd (2003), "Collective Action and Transnational Terrorism," *World Economy*, 26(6), 779–802.

Sandler, Todd (2004), *Global Collective Action* (Cambridge: Cambridge University Press).

Sandler, Todd (2005), "Collective versus Unilateral Responses to Terrorism," *Public Choice*, forthcoming.

Sandler, Todd and Daniel G. Arce M. (2003), "Terrorism and Game Theory," *Simulation & Gaming*, 34(3), 319–37.

Sandler, Todd and Walter Enders (2004), "An Economic Perspective on Transnational Terrorism," *European Journal of Political Economy*, 20(2), 301–16.

Sandler, Todd and Walter Enders (2005), "Transnational Terrorism: An Economic Analysis," in Harry W. Richardson, Peter Gordon, and James E. Moore II (eds.), *The Economic Impact of Terrorist Attacks* (Cheltenham, UK: Edward Elgar), forthcoming.

Sandler, Todd and Harvey E. Lapan (1988), "The Calculus of Dissent: An Analysis of Terrorists' Choice of Targets," *Synthèse*, 76(2), 245–61.

Sandler, Todd and Keith Sargent (1995), "Management of Transnational Commons: Coordination, Publicness, and Treaty Formation," *Land Economics*, 71(2), 145–62.

Sandler, Todd and John Scott (1987), "Terrorist Success in Hostage-Taking Incidents: An Empirical Study," *Journal of Conflict Resolution*, 31(1), 35–53.

Sandler, Todd and Kevin Siqueira (2005), "Global Terrorism: Deterrence versus Preemption," unpublished manuscript, University of Southern California, Los Angeles, CA.

Sandler, Todd, John Tschirhart, and Jon Cauley (1983), "A Theoretical Analysis of Transnational Terrorism," *American Political Science Review*, 77(1), 36–54.

Schmid, Alex P. (1992), "Terrorism and Democracy," *Terrorism and Political Violence*, 4(4), 14–25.

Schulze, Richard H. and Andreas Vogt (2003), "It's War! Fighting Post-11 September Global Terrorism through a Doctrine of Preemption," *Terrorism and Political Violence*, 15(1), 1–30.

Seale, Patrick (1992), *Abu Nidal: Gun for Hire* (New York: Random House).

Selten, Reinhard (1988), "A Simple Game Model of Kidnappings," in Reinhard Selten (ed.), *Models of Strategic Rationality* (Boston: Kluwer Academic), 77–93.

Shahin, Wassim N. and Muhammad Q. Islam (1992), "Combating Political Hostage-Taking: An Alternative Approach," *Defence Economics*, 3(4), 321–7.

Shapiro, Robert (2004), "Al-Qaida and the GDP: How Much Would Terrorism Damage the U.S. Economy? Less than You'd Expect." *Slate*, [http://slate.msn.com/id/2079298/], accessed 28 October 2004.

Silke, Andrew (2001), "When Sums Go Bad: Mathematical Models and Hostage Situations," *Terrorism and Political Violence*, 13(2), 49–66.

Siqueria, Kevin (2005), "Political and Militant Wings within Dissident Movements and Organizations," *Journal of Conflict Resolution*, 49(2), 218–36.

Sloboda, Brian W. (2003), "Assessing the Effects of Terrorism on Tourism by the Use of Time Series Methods," *Tourism Economics*, 9(2), 179–90.

Tanzi, Vincent (1972), "A Note on Exclusion, Pure Public Goods and Pareto Optimality," *Public Finance*, 27(1), 75–8.

Tavares, Jose (2004), "The Open Society Assesses Its Enemies: Shocks, Disasters and Terrorist Attacks," *Journal of Monetary Economics*, 51(5), 1039–70.

Technical Support Working Group (2003), "Infrastructure Protection," [http://www.tswg.gov/tswg/ip/ip_ma.htm], accessed 12 April 2004.

United Nations (2002a), "Measures to Eliminate International Terrorism," A/57/273, S/2002/875, United Nations, New York.

United Nations (2002b), "Report of the Policy Working Group on the United Nations and Terrorism," A/57/273-S/2002/875, United Nations, New York.

United Nations (2003), "United Nations: Treaty Collection: Conventions on Terrorism," [http://untreaty.un.org/English/Terrorism.asp], accessed 28 August 2003.

United Nations Security Council (2001), "Resolution 1373 (2001)," S/Res/1373 (2001), United Nations, New York.

United States Congress (2001), "HR 3162, USA Patriot Act," *Congressional Record* 146, S10969, 24 October, US Congress, Washington, DC, [http://www.epic.org/privacy/terrorism/hr3162.html], accessed 11 July 2004.

United States Department of State (various years), *Patterns of Global Terrorism* (Washington, DC: US Department of State).

United States Department of State Fact Sheet (2002), "Yemen: The Economic Cost of Terrorism," [http://www.state.gov/s/ct/rls/fs/2002/15028.htm], accessed 12 December 2004.

United States General Accounting Office (2004), "Combating Terrorism: Evaluation of Selected Characteristics in National Strategies Related to Terrorism," GAO-04-408T, US General Accounting Office, Washington, DC.

USA Today (2004), "Second Uzbek Explosion Rips Bomb-Making Factory," [http://www.usatoday.com/news/world/2004-03-29-uzbek-blast_x.htm?POE=NEWI], accessed 12 April 2004.

Vicary, Simon (1990), "Transfers and the Weakest-Link: An Extension of Hirshleifer's Analysis," *Journal of Public Economic*, 43(3), 375–94.

Vicary, Simon and Todd Sandler (2002), "Weakest-Link Public Goods: Giving In-Kind or Transferring Money," *European Economic Review*, 46(8), 1501–20.

Victoroff, Jeff (2005), "The Mind of the Terrorist: A Review and Critique of Psychological Approaches," *Journal of Conflict Resolution*, 49(1), 3–42.

Viscusi, W. Kip and Richard J. Zeckhauser (2003), "Sacrificing Civil Liberties to Reduce Terrorism Risks," *Journal of Risk and Uncertainty*, 26(2–3), 99–120.

Weinberg, Leonard B. and William L. Eubank (1998), "Terrorism and Democracy: What Recent Events Disclose," *Terrorism and Political Violence*, 10(1), 108–18.

White, Jonathan R. (2003), *Terrorism: 2002 Update*, 4th ed. (Belmont, CA: Wadsworth/Thomson Learning).

White House (2002), "Press Release," [http://www.whitehouse.gov/news/releases/2002/06/print/20020618-5.html], accessed 25 August 2003.

White House (2003), "Progress Report on the Global War on Terrorism," [http://www.state.gov/s/ct/rls/rpt/24087.htm], accessed 5 February 2004.

White House (2004), "Department of Homeland Security," [http://www.whitehouse.gov/omb/budget/fy2005/pdf/budget/homeland.pdf], accessed 15 June 2004.

Wilkinson, Paul (1986), *Terrorism and the Liberal State,* revised ed. (London: Macmillan).

Wilkinson, Paul (1997), "The Media and Terrorism: A Reassessment," *Terrorism and Political Violence,* 9(2), 51–64.

Wilkinson, Paul (2001), *Terrorism versus Democracy: The Liberal State Response* (London: Frank Cass).

Williams, Cindy (2004), "Paying for the War on Terrorism," [http://www.ecaar.org/Newsletter/March04/Williams.htm], accessed 11 July 2004.

Wintrobe, Ronald (2002), "Can Suicide Bombers Be Rational?," unpublished manuscript, Department of Economics, University of Western Ontario, London, Ontario.

Wolgast, Michael (2002), "Global Terrorism and the Insurance Industry: New Challenges and Policy Responses." Paper presented at Deutsches Institut für Wirtschaftsforschung workshop, "The Economic Consequences of Global Terrorism," Berlin, 14–15 June 2002.

Wolinsky, Frederick D., Kathleen W. Wyrwich, Kurt Kroenke, Ajit Babu, and William Tierney (2003), "9-11, Personal Stress, Mental Health, and Sense of Control among Older Adults," *The Journal of Gerontology,* 58B(3), S146–50.

World Bank (various years), *World Development Report* (New York: Oxford University Press).

Author Index

Subject Index